DYNAMICS IN MARRIAGE AND COHABITATION

AN INTER-TEMPORAL, LIFE COURSE ANALYSIS OF FIRST UNION FORMATION AND DISSOLUTION

This book has been published in the PDOD publications series A (doctoral dissertations). This series has been established through cooperation between Thesis Publishers and the Netherlands Graduate School of Research in Demography (PDOD).

DYNAMICS IN MARRIAGE AND COHABITATION

AN INTER-TEMPORAL, LIFE COURSE ANALYSIS OF FIRST UNION FORMATION AND DISSOLUTION

Dorien Manting

THESIS PUBLISHERS
AMSTERDAM 1994

CIP-DATA KONINKLIJKE BIBLIOTHEEK, DEN HAAG

Manting, Dorien

Dynamics in marriage and cohabitation:
an inter-temporal, life course analysis of first union formation
and dissolution / Dorien Manting. - Amsterdam: Thesis Publishers
Also publ. as thesis Universiteit van Amsterdam, 1994.
With ref. - With summary in Dutch.
ISBN 90-5170-295-7
NUGI 651/662
Subject headings: the Netherlands; cohabitation / marriage / demography.

© Dorien Manting, 1994

All rights reserved. Save exceptions stated by the law no part of this publication may be reproduced, stored in a retrieval system of any nature, or transmitted in any form or by any means, electronic, mechanical, photocopying, recording or otherwise, included a complete or partial transcription, without the prior written permission of the publisher, application for which should be addressed to the publisher. Thesis Publishers, P.O. Box 14791, 1001 LG Amsterdam, the Netherlands.

In so far as it is permitted to make copies from this publication under the provisions of article 16B and 17 of the Auteurswet 1912 (Copywright Act), you are obliged to make the payments required by law to the Stichting Reprorecht (Repro Law Foundation) P.O. Box 882, 1180 AW Amstelveen, the Netherlands. To use any part or parts of this publication in anthologies, readers and other compilations (article 16 Auteurswet 1912) you are obliged to contact the publisher.

ISBN 90-5170-295-7
NUGI 651/662

PREFACE

This dissertation marks the end of a research project started five years ago. As many research projects, this study is embedded in a broad social and institutional setting. Many people have helped me throughout the different stages of the research project, and I would like to express my gratitude to them.

First of all, I owe a particularly large debt to my three supervisors who have assisted me throughout the years. Prof. P. Hooimeijer never failed to inspire and encourage me by showing the 'good' and 'bad' points of my earlier drafts. Prof. D.J. Van de Kaa always had valuable and worthwhile suggestions and comments. Dr A.K. Kuijsten commented on earlier drafts with care and precision.

Most of the research activities were funded by the Netherlands Graduate School of Research in Demography and were conducted in the Department of Planning and Demography in the University of Amsterdam. I am indebted to all my colleagues in the Department's demographic research group who commented on earlier outputs of this dissertation. I have enjoyed working with them, especially with my room-mate Claartje Mulder, who shared with me both the 'ups' and the 'downs' of this research project.

There are other colleagues who have helped me, too. My special thanks go to drs. J. Vermunt for helping me learn to cope with his complex computer programs used for the log linear analyses during my stay at Statistics Netherlands (previously Netherlands Central Bureau of Statistics) from June 1991 to February 1992. I am also grateful to two other colleagues at Statistics Netherlands; Drs. J. De Beer and drs. W. van Hoorn, for their valuable suggestions. I would like to thank Statistics Netherlands for offering me an opportunity to analyse their data set. Finally, I have learned a lot from Dr. N.W. Keilman of the Central Bureau of Statistics in Norway who commented thoroughly on chapter 3.

I thank Ms. M. Schouten for her excellent job of the lay-out of this manuscript and Ms. A. Hawkins for looking after my English.

Finally, my husband, Hoite Detmar, deserves a special mention for his substantial support during the writing of this dissertation.

Although this dissertation marks the end of a five-years study on union formation and dissolution, I will continue the study of union formation and dissolution at Statistics Netherlands. I hope that this will also mean that cooperation with all those that have supported, guided, and advised me throughout the years will go on in the near future.

Dorien Manting, may 1994

CONTENTS

		Page
1	**Introduction**	9
1.1	Background of the research project	9
1.2	Problem definition	13
1.3	Relevance for society	14
1.4	Scientific relevance	15
1.5	The lay-out of the study	16
2	**Theoretical background**	19
2.1	Introduction	19
2.2	Theories of marriage and divorce	20
2.3	Cohabitation: from deviant option to gradual moving-in	25
2.4	A cohort perspective	31
2.5	A life course perspective	35
2.6	Conceptual scheme	40
3	**Method and data**	45
3.1	Introduction	45
3.2	Multivariate event history analysis	46
3.3	Data	52
3.4	Summary	55
4	**Cohort experiences of women in the Netherlands: union formation, union dissolution and emancipation**	57
4.1	Introduction	57
4.2	Cohort patterns in union formation and dissolution	57
4.3	Cohort trends in fertility, education and work	63
4.4	Summary	68
5	**Moving into a first union**	69
5.1	Introduction	69
5.2	Theoretical background	72
5.2.1	Past life course experiences influencing moving into a first union	72
5.2.2	Current life course experiences influencing moving into a first union	78
5.3	Empirical findings of the process of first union formation	82
5.3.1	Methodological procedure	83
5.3.2	Empirical findings: past life course determinants influencing moving into a first union	86
5.3.3	Empirical findings: Current life course experiences influencing moving into a first union	96
5.4	Summary	102
5.5	Evaluation	105

			Page
6	**Moving into marriage during the period of cohabitation**		109
	6.1	Introduction	109
	6.2	Time and moving into subsequent marriage	111
	6.3	Past life course experiences influencing the moving into subsequent marriage	112
	6.4	Current life course experiences influencing the moving into subsequent marriage	114
	6.5	Selection procedure	117
	6.6	Past and current life course experiences and the moving into subsequent marriage	121
	6.7	Summary and conclusion	125
7	**The break up of first unions**		129
	7.1	Introduction	129
	7.2	Theoretical background	131
	7.2.1	The close link between movement into and out of a union	131
	7.2.2	The time dimension and movement out of a first union	132
	7.2.3	Past life course experiences influencing movement out of a first union	137
	7.2.4	Current life course experiences influencing movement out of a first union	140
	7.3	Empirical findings: selecting relevant past and current life course experiences	143
	7.4	Empirical findings: past and current life course experiences influencing movement out of a first union	157
	7.5	Summary	161
	7.6	Conclusion	163
8	**Summary and conclusion**		167
	8.1	Introduction	167
	8.2	Theoretical background	167
	8.3	Empirical findings	171
	8.4	Conclusions	177

Nederlandse samenvatting en conclusies   181

Literature   195

Appendix Chapter 3 (A and B)   205
Appendix Chapter 5   207
Appendix Chapter 6   216
Appendix Chapter 7   217

1 INTRODUCTION

1.1 Background of the research project

The start of a relationship is an important event in an individual's life. The decision to live with someone else has serious repercussions on the organization of daily life activities. At least one partner must move into a new residence; there has to be a new division of household labour; the network of friends changes through incorporation of the partner's network; there are financial consequences.

Marriage
In the past, the decision to live with someone of the opposite sex, other than a member of the family, on a long term basis was linked with the decision to marry. Most women born in the thirties and forties, about 95 percent, married as a 'matter of course'. Marrying is part of a life span called the period of transition from youth to adulthood. In a relatively short span of the life course, many events occur which have great impact on the later life course (Marini, 1985; Willekens, 1991). This period is structured by events generating the movement from economic dependence and participation in the family of origin, to economic independence and establishment of a family of procreation (Marini, 1985). It is a period in which individuals become less committed to the family of origin and its values and start making their own commitments. Marriage used to be a very important transition in the lives of women; their daily lives altered significantly after the wedding day. Marriage used to mark the beginning of regular sexual relationships, the onset of family formation and the moment of starting to live with someone with whom one has a close intimate relationship (Roussel & Festy, 1979). Furthermore, marriage was also a route to independence because for many women it coincided with the moment they left the parental home. Finally, for women, marriage often marked the end of the occupational career.

Nowadays, a decision to have an intimate sexual relationship, to quit the labour market, to become pregnant and rear children, to live with a partner, or to leave the labour market is no longer closely connected with the decision to marry. Table 1 shows the weakening linkage between marriage and sexual experience, childbirth and work. A rise in pre-marital experience, in children born out of wedlock and in numbers of women working after marriage has been accompanied by a decline in the attractiveness of marriage. The number of women marrying for the first time decreased steeply from 116,000 in 1970 to about 68,000 in 1983. A recovery in the years 1983-1992, albeit at a much lower level than that of the 1970s, led in 1992 to about 79,000 first marriages among women.

Table 1   The link between marriage, sexual experience, childbirth and work

Percentage of pre-marital first coitus before age 19 (women)

Period of birth:	1917-31	1932-46	1947-56	1957-60
	13	28	39	76

Children, born out of wedlock (per 100 births)

	1965	1970	1980	1985	1988	1992
	1,8	2,1	4,1	8,3	10,2	12,4

Labour force participation rates of married women (in per cent of population belonging to the labour force)

	1960	1971	1979	1985	1991
	7	16	28	36	49

Sources: Kooy (1983); Prins (1990); Hooghiemstra and Niphuis-Nell (1993); Statistics Netherlands (SN) (1990a); SN (1990b); SN (1992)

Cohabitation

Part of the decline in marriage has been offset, however, by a rise in cohabitation. Beets (1990) estimated that, for the year 1988, 85,000 couples began to cohabit in that year without getting married. Living together with someone of the opposite sex (not being a member of the family) without being married is one of the important demographic changes in the past few decades.

The emergence of cohabitation implies that a decline in marriage does not necessarily mean that more and more women live alone. The number of cohabiting couples increased from about 47,000 in the beginning of the eighties to 300,000 or 350,000 at the end of the eighties and to somewhat less than half a million in the beginning of the nineties (Van der Avort, 1987; Beets, 1990; Manting, 1994b). It also means that the increase in numbers of children born out of wedlock does not necessarily imply that these mothers live alone. On the contrary, half of the women whose children were born out of wedlock were living together with their partner at the moment of childbirth (Beets, 1989a).

Along with the rise in cohabitation, there has been a trend towards greater equality between married and nonmarried couples' rights and obligations. This does not necessarily mean that cohabiting and married couples are also alike in their behaviour, attitudes and values. There is considerable debate about what cohabitation stands for: is it similar to marriage but lacking the formal status of the union, or does cohabitation stands for an alternative way of living together? Does cohabitation signal nothing more than a shift from married to nonmarried living together, nothing more than a temporary delay of first marriage, or does cohabitation stands for another way primary relationships are perceived in current times? Until now, there has been no consensus about where cohabitation stands. Some argue that marriage and cohabitation are more or less the same (Höpflinger, 1990), while others are convinced that cohabitation is something completely different (Lesthaeghe et al., 1992, Rindfuss and VandenHeuvel, 1990).

Those who think of cohabitation as a new, permanent option, assume that a rise in cohabitation caused a *decline* in marriage. Those who view cohabitation as a temporary phase before marriage, assume that the emergence of cohabitation has led to a *delay* of marriage. The interpretation of changing patterns of nuptiality, or more broadly, the formation of unions, is thus influenced by the way cohabitation is perceived. There is surely a need to consider what cohabitation really stands for. In this study, explicit attention is given to the role cohabitation plays in the process of marriage, or in more general terms, in the process of union formation.

Divorce
The decline in marriage rates has been accompanied by a rise in marital instability. The number of divorces increased rapidly at the end of the sixties, followed by a more moderate rise after 1978. In 1960, about 56 hundred divorces were registered. In 1971, the year the divorce law in the Netherlands was revised, this figure nearly doubled to 10,000 divorces. A maximum was reached in 1984, with 34,000 divorces. After that, the level stabilized at 28,000 to 30,000 divorces per year.

Cohabitation is also an important factor in the study of divorce. Again, the difference in opinions concerning the nature of cohabitation affects the interpretation of the role of cohabitation in divorce. Those perceiving cohabitation as a temporary phase before marriage assume that cohabitation serves as a period of trial, leading to a more stable marriage. The belief is that the most unstable couples will not marry. Many couples break up before embarking on marriage. Manting (1994a) estimated that, for the year 1992, besides 30,000 marital divorces, almost 40,000 'non-marital' dissolutions of cohabiting couples occurred. Other theories which assume that cohabitation attracts people with a lower commitment to maintaining a union postulate that cohabitation leads to a higher level of marital instability. Again, the theoretical conceptualization of cohabitation affects the interpretation of its role for the breaking-up of couples. For the process of breaking-up one should also pay attention to the question of what cohabitation stands for. In this study, the role of cohabitation in the process of divorce and, more broadly, in the process of union dissolution is examined and discussed.

The individual life course
As noted above, a decreasing linkage between fertility, marriage, co-residence and work has been accompanied by a decline in marriage. Recently, researchers have seriously questioned overall abstinence from marriage (Blossfeld & Huinink, 1991; Oppenheimer, 1988). They assume that the declining number of marriages has merely been caused by a postponement of marriage until later in the life course. Developments within the female educational and occupational career are seen as major forces behind a delay of marriage. Prolonged education, increasing educational level and increasing labour force participation have been viewed as major triggers of postponement of marriage, fertility and the emergence of cohabitation. More and more studies,

in the Netherlands as well as abroad, show that there is indeed a close link between these different life domains (Blossfeld and Huinink, 1991; Hoem, 1986, Klaus & Hooimeijer, 1993; Liefbroer, 1991a; Vermunt, 1991). As a consequence, cross-sectional studies on the comparison of behaviour of married and cohabiting couples have become less informative. Even longitudinal studies, concentrating on one life domain, will yield unsatisfactory results. A life-course approach offers an integrated frame of reference in which these various life domains are taken simultaneously into account.

Individuals may readjust certain life goals in response to changes not only in their own lives but also in their environment. Societal developments may alter the preferences, opportunities or constraints that may stimulate or hamper an individual's entry into or exit from a union. Because society and the individuals living in it are continuously changing, studies failing to take these dynamics into account ignore the dynamic framework in which individual behaviour evolves. Studying social change (and, in this specific case, the formation and dissolution of unions) from a life course perspective 'helps social scientists to see patterns in variation over time - to detect order in apparent disorder. It also helps in disentangling forces occurring on different levels of aggregation (e.g., the individual, family, local neighbourhood, class, ethnic group, birth cohort) and also in distinguishing between different time dimensions (e.g., age, duration in a given social status, exposure to a particular social situation, historical eras, and point-in-time events)' (Mayer and Tuma, 1990: 8-9). This study examines the process of union formation and dissolution from a life course perspective.

Cohort membership
One of the ways of studying life course patterns is to follow the life trajectories of individuals born in the same period. Such birth cohorts share certain similar conditions that may have had impact on the formation and dissolution of their unions. They share a similar economic, social and cultural environment, a similar educational system, the same labour market opportunities and similar mate, marriage and housing markets. Facing its own historical conditions while growing up, each birth cohort shows its own life course regarding union formation and dissolution. In addition to sharing similar conditions, changes within society such as increasing educational enrolment or labour force participation among women have led to more women with higher levels of education and higher proportions of working women among later compared with earlier birth cohorts. Compositional differences between birth cohorts in the determinants influencing union formation or union dissolution might afford an explanation for inter-cohort changes in union formation or dissolution. Of course, being born in a certain period is not the only determinant influencing life course patterns. There are many other factors leading to intra-cohort differences in the life course; different family background, religious affiliation, labour and educational experiences lead to differentials between members of a birth cohort. In this study, attention is given to both *inter- and intra-cohort differences* in life course patterns regarding union formation and dissolution.

1.2   Problem definition

Most of what is known about primary relationships derives from cross-sectional studies comparing cohabiting couples with married couples at one point in time (De Feijter, 1991; Langeveld, 1985; Latten, 1992; Manting, 1994b; Lesthaeghe et al., 1992; Van der Avort, 1987; Van den Akker & Mandemaker, 1991; Moors & Van Nimwegen, 1990; Wiersma, 1983). These studies show important differences between cohabiting and married couples. However, they cannot make clear whether differentials such as work and fertility result from changes arising after, or before, entering a union. Liefbroer (1991a) showed, from a longitudinal point of view, that the 'quality' of the parental home as well as other life domains (work and education) influence the selection process into cohabitation or marriage to a large extent. However, his study was confined to people born in the beginning of the sixties, uncovering intra-cohort differentials only. It could not reveal inter-cohort developments in the process of selection. In addition, little attention has yet been paid either to the role of cohabitation or to its consequences for further life course patterns, such as entry into marriage, once one cohabits as a couple. Neither has much life course analysis been undertaken yet on the divorce or separation of cohabiting couples. Klijzing's study (1992) of union disruption in the Netherlands is an exception. His concern was, however, more with the influence of cohabitation on marital stability than with union stability, which led him to study the incidence of disruption among those cohabiting prior to marriage from the moment of marriage rather than co-residence. This study focuses on the role of cohabitation in the process of union formation and dissolution from a life course perspective.

This research project attempts to widen the scope of demographic studies on marriage and divorce to the formation and dissolution by women of both married and non-married unions. A *union* is defined as a sexual and intimate relationship between a man and a woman in which the permanence of the relationship is assumed and a common residence is shared. The definition implies that entry into a union is marked by the start of shared living. The exit from a union is marked by the moment of separation or divorce. A distinction is made between married and non-married unions to facilitate the assessment of differences between married and nonmarried unions in their formation and dissolution. Only those formations in which a woman starts to share a residence are considered. The focus on co-residence implies that all intimate relationships of individuals not living together are excluded from the analysis.
All entries into and exits from a union, as well as their timing, structure the individual union career. The focus in this study is on the first steps in the union career: the formation and dissolution of *first* unions only.

The formation and dissolution of first (un)married unions of women living in the Netherlands is examined from a *life course perspective*. This means, firstly, that attention is given to dynamics in the formation and dissolution of first unions. Explicit attention is paid to the linkage of other life domains that vary over the life course with union formation and dissolution. The role of education, work and children is thought to be of primary importance in the development of the union career. Secondly, it means that attention is paid to the varying relationships between several determinants and union formation and dissolution during the unfolding of the life course.

To account for historical developments influencing the process of union formation and dissolution, explicit attention is given to the historical time during which individual life courses unfold. Cross-sectional studies have shown a general decrease in differentials between cohabiting couples and married couples while the married couples who have never previoulsy cohabited are becoming increasingly exceptional (De Feijter, 1991, Latten, 1992). The study of *birth cohorts* provides an indication of (changing) linkages between determinants and the union career over time.

The *goal* of this study is to gain insight into the process of union formation and dissolution of women: into the selection into marriage and cohabitation at the start of co-residence, into subsequent marriage following the entry into cohabitation and into the stability of unions. Society and women's life situations are continuously changing, so the extent to which time-varying individual circumstances affect the process of union formation and dissolution differently across historical time and across the life course is examined.

1.3   Relevance for society

Insight into the dynamics of union formation and dissolution is of primary societal interest because the formation and dissolution of unions have many implications for housing, health and social (security) services.

The housing sector is particularly affected since formation and dissolution of unions are closely related to dynamics in housing and migration career (Crommentuijn, 1993; Mulder, 1993). At younger ages, entry into marriage or cohabitation is the most important reason for migration. But, even at older ages, formation of a union is the second most important reason for migration. Marriage and migration are closely linked (Mulder, 1993; Mulder and Wagner, 1993). Divorce related migrations show up at later ages (Mulder, 1993). Housing demand is greatly affected by trends in divorce, especially in the public rental sector, (Dieleman and Schouw, 1989). Changes in the timing and incidence of union formation and union dissolution lead to changes in the demands in numbers and types of dwellings. Young people leaving the parental home to live alone start less often as home-owners than do people leaving home to cohabit, although it is young people leaving home to marry who most frequently start off as home-owners. In addition, there are considerable differences in the years following the leaving of the parental home between those leaving home as singles, nonmarried or married couples (Mulder and Manting, 1993a, 1993b). Insight into the dynamics in formation and dissolution of both nonmarried and married couples is thus a prerequisite for forecasting future housing needs.

The demand for health services, legal and psycho-social assistance, social security and child care is closely linked with the number of divorces, since one-parent families appeal to these

Introduction

services to a relatively high extent (Van Delft & Niphuis-Nell, 1988). The incidence of divorce is related to increased economic inequality between men and women. Divorce often leads to severe financial setbacks and for women, particularly mothers, the transition from the married to the divorced state is often followed by a need for social (security) services. Another consequence of divorce is a setback in the housing situation with a long-lasting effect (Dieleman and Schouw, 1989).

Since cohabitation has emerged, there has been a trend towards equal rights and obligations for married and nonmarried couples. Important differences remain, however. Until now, nonmarried couples have been confronted with the situation that they are sometimes treated as equal to married couples and sometimes not. This phenomenon leads to both advantages and disadvantages. Married couples have the obligation to support each other financially, whereas nonmarried couples do not. Married couples have long-lasting obligations to each other after they divorce, while nonmarried couples do not. Cohabiting couples may decide more freely whether to be treated as a couple or not. Recently, the associated phenomenon of 'rule-shopping' has undergone critical review. Since there is no registration of whether people live together as singles, or as a nonmarried couple, people have the opportunity to pose as a couple in situations where this might be more profitable, while in other situations they might present themselves as single. Concern with this phenomenon of 'rule-shopping' was one of the motivations for studying the effects of registration of cohabitation. The "Commissie voor de Toetsing van Wetgevingsprojecten" (Commission testing projects concerning legislation) suggested voluntary registration to simplify the way nonmarried couples are treated and to develop a situation in which the financial advantages and disadvantages of such registration are in balance. In the meantime, the government has opposed such voluntary registration for nonmarried couples. Only those living together unmarried and who cannot marry (homo-sexual couples, or family related couples) are allowed to register themselves as a couple. As a consequence, inequality between married and nonmarried couples will remain for some time. Recent legal changes have further exacerbated this inequality. For instance, since 1992, municipalities have been obliged to demand financial recuperation from an ex-spouse whose ex-partner depends on social services. Ex-spouses must support each other for a period of twelve years following divorce. This rule does not apply to ex-partners who have never been married to each other. This has increased the inequality between married and nonmarried couples. Since the formation and dissolution of unions have such important repercussions on many public services, insight into the developments of union formation and dissolution is of the utmost importance.

1.4 Scientific relevance

This study has been carried out at the Institute of Planning and Demography of the University of Amsterdam as part of the larger research programme "Life course patterns of Dutch birth cohorts". The programme aims to gain insight in the way birth cohorts differ from each other regarding household formation and fertility, educational and occupational behaviour, and internal migration: at documenting inter-cohort changes in demographic transition behaviour in the Netherlands; and at identifying clusters of birth cohorts that demonstrate the same behaviour or have the same characteristics.

This study focuses on the inter-cohort differentials regarding the link between educational, occupational and union-specific behaviour. It is a socio-demographic study of union formation and dissolution. It does not examine, for instance, marital happiness, or the process of 'give and take' in primary relationships. This study does, however, concentrate on how a woman's (changing) individual characteristics and life history influence her union formation and dissolution. It does not examine male influence on the process on union formation and dissolution. As such, the approach followed in this study reflects the one-sex approach that is very common in demography. It concentrates on entry into and exit from first unions. The aim of this project is to gain insight into empirical as well as theoretical questions concerning the linkage between contextual and individual influences on the individual union career of women. How do microlevel circumstances affect the individual life course over time, given that pluriformity, freedom of choice and personal quest for self-expression have increased? A basic element of life course analysis is concern for the linkage of developments in several life domains (work, education, children, marriage) within a time-specific setting (individual age, years lived in a union and/or year of birth). A basic assumption of this study is that the union career cannot be studied in isolation from other important life domains such as education, work and children.

The linkage between these different life careers is examined with the help of multivariate event history analysis. This relatively new method offers a formal testable model for a simultaneous integration of a large number of (time-varying) determinants in the process of union formation and dissolution. It is a flexible method that overcomes several problems of cross-sectional analyses. Cross-sectional analysis is hampered by the problem that data are censored: events such as the entries into a union or the exit from a union may not *yet* have occurred, although they might occur soon. Event history analysis can deal with censoring, however, because this method utilizes both information about people who have experienced an event as well as about people who as yet have not. Furthermore, in contrast with cross-sectional analysis, event history analysis can deal with time-varying circumstances. At one point, a woman may work, while at another point she may not. Event history analysis is very well suited to dealing with the estimation of the influence of time-varying determinants on the process of union formation and dissolution. This study should further enhance insights into the importance of event history analysis for demographic studies.

1.5   The lay-out of the study

Chapter 2 reports general theories on marriage, divorce and cohabitation. Most older theories are directed to explaining the decline of marriage and divorce. More recent theories feature the timing of marriage rather than its decline. Both the older and the more recent theories are discussed. A review of the literature indicates the varying ways in which cohabitation can be considered. The role of cohabitation and its consequences for the process of first union formation and dissolution are discussed. The way in which the study of primary relationships can be enriched by the life course perspective is examined. Finally, four research questions are formulated. Chapter 3 introduces data and methods, discusses the advantage of methods of event history analysis for life course analysis and the reasons for choosing the discrete loglinear analysis of rates (one of several techniques for event history analysis). Chapter 4 examines developments in marriage, divorce and relevant determinants of marriage and divorce at the aggregate level for the case of the Netherlands. The empirical analyses of inter- and intra-cohort analysis on first union formation are divided into analyses of entry into a (first) married or a (first) nonmarried union (chapter 5) and into analyses of marriage of cohabiting couples (chapter 6). Chapter 7 shows empirical analyses of dissolution of first unions. In these chapters, the relationships between several individual determinants and union formation and dissolution are examined. Explicit attention is given to whether and how these individual circumstances affect the process of union formation and dissolution differently across historical time and across the life course. Chapter 8 contains a summary and a discussion of the results presented before. A summary in Dutch concludes the book[1].

---

[1] Parts of this book contain material from papers and articles published by the author during the execution of this project:
Manting, D. (1991). First Union Formation in the Netherlands, paper presented at the European Population Conference 1991, EAPS/IUSSP/INED, Paris, October 21-25 1991, PDOD-paper no. 5, Amsterdam, 1991;
Manting, D. (1991). The timing of marriage of cohabiting women in the Netherlands. PDOP-Paper No. 7, Department of Physical Planning and Demography, University of Amsterdam also published in: Dynamics of Cohort and Generations Research. Proceedings of a Symposium held on 12, 13 and 14 December 1991 at the University of Utrecht, Becker (eds), 1992;
Manting, D. (1992) The Break-up of Unions: The Role of Cohabitation. Paper presented at the EAPS/BIB "Seminar on Demographic Implications of Marital Status", Bonn, 27-31 October 1992;
Manting, D. & J. Helleman & A.C. Kuijsten (1992). From Youth to Adulthood; Transitions of Female Birth Cohorts in The Netherlands, in: Bevolking en Gezin, 1992, 1, 55-76 also published in: Population and Family in the Low Countries 1992: Family and Labour, G.C.N. Beets, R.L. Cliquet, G. Dooghe & J. de Jong Gierveld (eds), Swets and Zeitlinger, Amsterdam/Lisse, 1993;
Manting, D. (1993). Cohabiting Women in the Netherlands and their Timing of Marriage, in: W.F. Sleegers & Goethals A.L.J. (eds). Quantitative Geographical Methods, Applied in Demographic and Urban Planning Research, Amsterdam: SISWO, 85-92.
Manting D. and Kuijsten, A.C. (1993) Dynamics in the individual fertility career: Country-specific differentials of the impact on the fertility career of the educational, occupational, partner and housing careers in Western Europe, NWO-research proposal, June 1993.

2   THEORETICAL BACKGROUND

2.1   Introduction

Over the past decades, several of the features of entering a marriage - co-residence, sexual intimacy, independence, having and rearing children, life-long commitment and security - have lost their special quality (chapter 1). Decline in the material and immaterial advantages of marriage plays an important role in several macro- and micro level theoretical explanations of the decline in marriage, the increase in divorce and the rise of cohabitation. Long-term underlying economic and socio-cultural trends have altered individual preferences, constraints and opportunities. These long term developments go hand in hand with a changing meaning of marriage, or more broadly with a changing meaning of primary relationships over time. Section 2.2 discusses the long-term societal developments that are assumed to be of importance for the declining attractiveness of marriage and the rise in divorce. Recently, there is much discussion on whether there is indeed a decline, or merely a postponement of marriage, until later in the life course. There are several reasons why marriage has become delayed. These are further described in section 2.2.

The conceptualization of cohabitation plays an important role in the perception of past patterns in nuptiality and divorce. In the beginning of the seventies, cohabitation used to be considered a deviant way of living (Lesthaeghe et al., 1992). Today, cohabitation is most often assumed to be a short period prior to marriage and therefore a major factor in the delay of marriage. This short period of cohabitation is interpreted as a trial period before concluding a marriage. Since the trial period prior to marriage ought to lead to greater stability in marital unions, cohabitation ought to be a major factor in the development of divorce. Others believe that the emergence of cohabitation is more an indication of a change in the nature of primary relationships. This signals a shift from material to immaterial advantages of primary relationships and results in a declining attractiveness of marriage and a higher instability of both married and nonmarried unions. The way in which cohabitation is perceived is thus important for the interpretation of changes in marriage and divorce. A rethinking of cohabitation's place in the study of marriage and divorce is called for. Section 2.3 discusses this role of cohabitation both for marriage and for divorce. An evaluation of the consequences of these opposing theories for this study, is also presented in this section.

Union-specific behaviour varies between individual women as a result of the historical setting in which a woman lives and her past and current experiences. The study of inter-cohort differentials affords insight into the ways in which historical changes touch upon individual behaviour. Each cohort is unique because of the particular historical conditions of the period in which its members grow up (Ryder, 1965). But, in spite of common cohort membership, each cohort member responds differently to the historical circumstances through a complex set of individual past and current experiences, characteristics and traits. The study of intra-cohort differentials in union-specific behaviour is needed to understand how and why cohort members differ from each other in union-specific behaviour, according to past and current individual experiences and characteristics (section 2.4).

Other female life domains besides developments in the union career have changed as well. Changes in the union career cannot be studied without considering other important careers such as the educational, occupational and fertility career. The importance of individual life course changes in the study of union formation and dissolution is stressed in life course theory (section 2.5). Finally, the elements featured above are presented in a conceptual framework (section 2.6) used for a more concrete formulation of the research questions.

2.2 Theories of marriage and divorce

Most western countries show a universal trend towards decline and postponement of marriage, increasing marital instability and the emergence of cohabitation. Lesthaeghe and Van de Kaa (1986) argue that these demographic developments are closely related to each other. Since Western demographic trends are rather similar, many macro level theories have been formulated to explain these universal trends in Western Europe. These theories can also be readily applied to the Netherlands.

A complex structure of underlying long term social, economic and cultural trends has been put forward as an explanation of the decreasing attractiveness of marriage reflected in a decline in the number of marriage and an increase in the number of divorces. Urbanization, industrialization, the rise of the welfare state, emancipation, individualization and secularization are viewed as underlying causes of a broad range of demographic changes of which developments in marriage and divorce form a part. Although it remains difficult to pinpoint the most relevant underlying forces, it seems that a mixture of economic and socio-cultural factors can account for the rapid changes in fertility, marriage, cohabitation and divorce (Hoffmann-Nowotny, 1988; Lesthaeghe & Surkyn, 1983; Lesthaeghe and Van de Kaa, 1986; Lesthaeghe & Moors, 1992; Van de Kaa, 1987, 1988). They form a complex structure of different social, economic and cultural forces that have created a (continuously evolving) shift in individual preferences (towards individuality, freedom and independence), in constraints (towards less normative constraints and less affirmation to institutional regulations of the state, the church or the family) and in opportunities (women's economic independence through labour market participation and through the individualization of social security).

The decline in marriage and rise in divorce

According to Van de Kaa (1988) three basic interrelated societal dimensions - structure, culture and technology - are most relevant for explaining demographic changes in the past decades (scheme 1).

An explanatory framework for the second demographic transition

SOCIETAL DIMENSIONS/ PROCESSES	SOCIETAL UNITS			
	SECONDARY GROUPS	PRIMARY GROUPS		INDIVIDUALS
		FAMILY	PAIR	
Modernisation, development of post-industrial society and welfare state S T Increased: R - standard of living U - social security C - functional T differentiation U - structural complexity R - mobility E - education - female participation	- Development of broad middle stratum - reduction of their protective role - increased interdependence - functional loss of political and religious groupings - action groups emerge	- increased opportunity costs of marriage and childbearing - greater independence of partners, freedom of choice - increased problems of combining societal roles of partner and parent		- individual quality, ambitions and training determine position and income - exposed to many demands, which are difficult to combine - necessity to remain flexible - partial integration - early independence - individualized security
"Silent Revolution" C U Increased: L - democracy T - equality U - personal freedom R - value pluralism E - universalism - individualism - secularisation - higher needs orientation	- reduction in dominance of normative groups - reduction in degree of cohesion and normative control of these groups - increase in cross-cutting affiliations - increased contest between the sexes - increased contest between age groups etc.	- changes in balance of power between sexes - absence of strong guiding principles - need to establish own set of norms - parental role less clear and certain - children/partner reduce freedom of choice - difficult to reconcile different life courses		- reluctance to enter into long term relationships/ commitments - increased emphasis on self-realization - difficulty of establishing personal identity - search for personal life style - female life course more independent - conflict of roles in different spheres of life
"Second contraceptive revolution" T and spread of televised E information C H Improved: N - transport O - communication L - health care O - medical technology G - contraceptive Y techniques and means	- rapid spread of information and means - reduction in costs - right to services through medical insurance - equal access for all groups	- information on job opportunities, wages levels, etc. - rapid spread of knowledge - possibility to contracept "perfectly" - not to contracept conscious decision - childlessness acceptable and possible option		- contraception can be an individual decision - increased sexual freedom - "mistakes" can be corrected through abortion, etc. - greater individual responsibility

Source: Van de Kaa (1988).

Secularization and individualization (Lesthaeghe, 1983, 1991; Van de Kaa, 1987, 1988) are long-term *cultural changes* that have changed individual preferences. Secularization has led individuals to feel themselves less attached to normative guidelines from organized or institutional religion (Lesthaeghe and Surkyn, 1988: 10). Together with a quest for greater individual freedom and tolerance, personal self-expression and self-fulfilment are accentuated at the expense of institutional affirmation (Lesthaeghe and Surkyn, 1988: 13). Individualization is also linked with a move away from the acceptance of institutional regulation upon the individual life, not only by the church, but also by other institutions such as the state, the family and political organizations (Lesthaeghe and Surkyn, 1988).

Developments in both marriage and divorce are influenced by these long term processes. Marriage is one of the institutions that has come under question. In the seventies, perception of the conventional marriage as 'bourgeois' lead to a decline in the numbers of marriages. Also, a growing importance of individual's self-fulfilment relative to the demands of others (a partner, children, parents, a family) at the expense of institutional affirmation; the weakening of normative guidelines; and the increased tolerance for life situations other than marriage, may have led to the rise in divorce rates (Bumpass, 1990; Schumacher & Vollmer, 1981). Both the decline in marriage and the rise in divorce are thus manifestations of a long-term shift in individual preferences, caused by individualization and secularization.

A shift in individual preferences has accompanied an increase in individual opportunities for free choice. According to Van de Kaa, *structural changes* leading to a substantial decline of marriage as well as a rise in divorce include: modernization; increase in the standard of living and social security benefits; functional differentiation; and women's increasing earning power. The rise in women's earning capacity is seen as one of the most important underlying forces of changes in marriage and divorce. Economic theories postulate that the rising earning power of women cause 'gains of marriage' to decline (Becker, 1974; 1981). According to Becker, people marry when the expected gain of marriage is higher - for both the partners involved - than the expected gain of remaining single. Historically, through marriage, women gained economic support from the husband whereas men gained support regarding domestic services from the wife. The rise in the earning power of women, resulting from increasing education and labour force participation, has disturbed this traditional gender based division of labour. The increasing earning power of women has not only changed the division of labour within the household, but has also increased the 'opportunity costs' of children, because childbirth often coincides with a woman's exit from paid employment. The having and rearing children is one of the most important motivations for marriage, so the rise in women's earning power has led to a declining attractiveness of this institution not only because of a disturbance in the division of labour but also through raising the costs of having children. Becker stipulates that, as a result, the gains of marriage have diminished over time, as observed in a decline in marriage. Rising female economic power not only reduced the gains of marriage but also the financial barriers to divorce (Becker, et al., 1977). Women can now afford to divorce, since their work or social security provides them with an income of their own.

Macro-sociological theories emphasize not so much the decline in economic gains of marriage, but more the loss of the societal functions of marriage (Espenshade, 1985). The functions of marriage such as procreation, education and socialization of children, economic and social security of the individual household members, protection and recreation have increasingly been taken over by state support systems and by such institutions as school, day care facilities and homes for the elderly. As a consequence, both men and women have become less dependent on marriage and the family for fulfilling a variety of needs (Espenshade, 1985).

According to Roussel (1989), a shift from material to immaterial advantages of marriage has accompanied these developments. In his opinion this shift is an underlying cause for rising divorce trends. Roussel argues that historically the goal of marriage was 'to survive, to maintain the property within the family, to ensure security in old age through the procreation of children' (Roussel, 1989: 25). Marriage was meant to last forever; divorce was not considered. He assumes that, over the years, a second model of marriage has emerged, based on solidarity through affection. High expectations of primary relationships with respect to this solidarity make marriage very fragile. Marriages break down when affection and romantic love between the partners have gone. A third model based on reason has appeared since the mid-seventies. Each partner draws up a balance sheet and, explicitly or implicitly, the possibility of divorce is part of this contractual type of marriage (Roussel, 1989: 26-27). The fact that marriages were decreasingly characterized by the first and increasingly by the other two 'models of marriage' is put forward as the main force underlying increasing divorce rates in the seventies (Roussel, 1989). The change in meaning from material to immaterial aspirations of what couples want from marriage influences the process of divorce. The fact that, nowadays, people cite the material aspects of a satisfying relationship such as housing and income situation much less than immaterial aspects such as common respect, loyalty and understanding is indicative of this shift (Halman, 1991).

Besides cultural and structural changes in society, *technological* changes have also facilitated the move away from marriage (Van de Kaa, 1988). He shows that availability of good contraception initially stimulated a further decline in the age at first marriage, because it enabled couples to have marital sexual relationships without the fear of pregnancy. After the early 1970s, it allowed persons to have sexual relationships without the fear of pre-marital pregnancy, stimulating the emergence of cohabitation and the postponement of marriage. Besides good contraception, television is another important technological innovation that allowed persons to acquire information outside their own cultural environment. Mass media led to a reducing dominance of normative guidance by institutions, such as the church and the family.

Marriage - a decline or a delay?
Theoretical ideas addressing the declining attractiveness of marriage derived from the declining number of marriages and rising number of divorces, have been discussed so far. Recently, researchers have begun to question this notion of widespread abstinence from marriage (Blossfeld & Huinink, 1991; Oppenheimer, 1988). They ascertain that the yearly number of marriages has declined because young women tend to delay marriage until later in the life course. They

believe that younger women postpone marriage, but that they catch up later in life. There are several theoretical ideas explaining why marriage is delayed.

Oppenheimer (1988) challenges the idea that the desire to marry has declined as the result of increased female labour force participation. On the contrary, she is convinced that the greater economic independence of women leads to a temporary delay in marriage rather than an overall reduction in the numbers of people marrying. She assumes that, since marriage no longer plays such a major part for women in acquiring financial stability, quality demands for a 'suitable' marriage partner have risen. The result is a more careful and critical search period, which is likely to be longer, so that marriage is concluded at older ages than hitherto. Although she does not overlook the possibility that a side effect of a longer search period may be that some women may be more likely to abstain from marriage, the basic assumption of her search theory is that women will progressively delay rather than abstain from marriage.

Another explanation of the delay of marriage refers to the widening of the choice set as a side effect of the processes of individualization and secularization. Confronted with so many options, women postpone decisions involving a high degree of irreversibility: 'The biographic theory interprets the decline in marriage and fertility rates as the consequence of the attempt to avoid or to delay the risk involved in long-term commitments within biographically relevant choices' (Birg et al., 1990;147). People thus increasingly opt for flexibility in the life course in order to avoid (temporarily) crucial life events involving a high level of commitment and severe emotional, social and financial costs associated with undoing such commitments (Mulder and Manting, 1993). Marriage is postponed until later in the life course since, because of the legal barriers to divorce, marriage involves a higher level of commitment than such living arrangements as cohabitation.

An explanation of a different order derives from the fact that engagement in other life domains may have hampered entry into marriage. Marriage is a highly age-specific event, concentrated in the short period in life generally referred to as the transition from youth to adulthood (Blossfeld & Nuthmann, 1990; Manting et al., 1993; Marini, 1985; Willekens, 1991). Many crucial life events are concentrated in the period of life between the ages of approximately 15 and 30. Besides marriage, exit from school and the parental home, entry into the labour market or entry into parenthood are concentrated in this period of life. These events are closely intertwined. Since marriage mostly occurs after one has left the educational system, increasing educational enrolment has been identified as one of the main underlying forces leading to the postponement of marriage. The longer one stays in school, the longer is marriage delayed (Blossfeld & Huinink, 1991; Lesthaeghe & Moors, 1992).

Evaluation
The many long-term processes put forward to explain declining marriage, marriage delay and rising divorce form a complex structure of social, economic and cultural forces operating simultaneously. Long-term macro-level developments have created a (continuously evolving)

shift in individual preferences (towards individuality, freedom and independence), in constraints (towards less normative constraints and less affirmation to institutional regulations of the state, the church or the family) and in opportunities (women's economic independence through labour market participation and through the individualization of social security).

Marriage and divorce are closely linked: the determinants considered to be factors underlying the declining attractiveness of marriage are also often thought to be determinants in the rise in marital instability. Increasing female economic autonomy, for instance, is seen as a major force behind the decline in marriage and the rise in divorce.

The earlier theories, such as Becker's (1981), predict an overall decline in marriage, while the more recent theories, such as Oppenheimer's (1988), expect a delay in marriage. Women's rising education levels and labour force participation play a role in theories of marriage decline as well as of marriage postponement. In theories featuring its declining popularity, rising educational levels and higher rates of labour participation are assumed to lead to an overall decline in the gains of marriage. In theories about the timing of marriage, longer enrolment in education and longer periods at work are thought to lead to a delay of marriage. In simple terms, the longer the period at school, the longer the period at work, the longer the period of childlessness: the later the marriage is entered.

Very recently, longitudinal cohort studies have shown that it is only relative to women born in the 1940s, that the recent decline in marriage appears to be so dramatic (Blossfeld & Huinink, 1991; Blossfeld et al., 1993a). An important part of the decline in marriage seems to be more the result of changes in *timing* of marriage than in overall *decline* of marriage. This implies that a study of marriage should account for the aspect of timing in the process of marriage. On the other hand, changes in timing of marriage are closely intertwined with the emergence of cohabitation. Cohabitation is a very important factor in the delay of marriage. The role of cohabitation is important not only for understanding developments in marriage but also for understanding chances in divorce. The role of cohabitation therefore requires detailed discussion.

2.3 Cohabitation: from deviant option to gradual moving-in

The different conceptualizations of cohabitation (Trost, 1988) affect the interpretation of past developments in marriage and divorce. Cohabitation interpreted as a temporary phase before marriage is seen as a major reason for the delay, but not for an overall decline of marriage (Höpflinger, 1990). But cohabitation viewed as a more or less permanent alternative to marriage is seen as a major factor for its decline. Cohabitation is interpreted as being a new option allowing for more individual self-expression and freedom than marriage, as a reaction to high divorce rates and, more recently, as a way of entering a union gradually, one step at a time. Since the interpretation of its role for marriage and divorce depends on the way cohabitation is regarded, the need to consider what cohabitation really stands for is evident. That is the reason why in the next section the role of cohabitation is discussed in more detail.

Cohabitation as a temporary phase before marriage

The large number of options from which a person may nowadays choose has been hypothesised as causing a postponement of decisions with a high degree of irreversibility. Cohabitation might be seen as an institution creating fewer 'irreversible' barriers to disruption than marriage. The emergence of cohabitation is merely another outcome of a shift towards retaining flexibility. In comparison with marriage, cohabitation offers a higher level of individual freedom. The economic interpretation of cohabitation is that it facilitates the reduction of costs during the search process for a marital partner: 'Cohabitation gets young people out of high-cost search activities during a period of social immaturity but without incurring what are, for many, the penalties of either heterosexual isolation or promiscuity, and it often offers many of the benefits of marriage, including the pooling of resources and the economies of scale that living together provide... It can therefore serve as an important prelude to marriage itself - as an extension of the courtship process' (Oppenheimer, 1988: 583-584). Cohabitation is assumed to be a temporary phase before marriage: marriage remains, however, the ultimate life goal: "Handelte es sich bei der Partnerwahl früher um einen Prozeß, der sich Vergleichsweise schnell durch den Akt der Verlobnung, mithin auf Eheschließung vorprogrammiert, zu legitimieren hatte, ist es in der Zwischenzeit zur allgemeinen und auch weithin akzeptierten Regel geworden, daß zwischen einer erfolgten Partnerwahl und der Eheschließung längere Zeiträume vergehen, in der sozusagen als "Ehe auf Probe" die Tragfähigkeit einer Partnerschaft sich erst erweisen muß" (Schumacher und Vollmer, 1981: 509). From this point of view, marriage is postponed as a consequence of the emergence of cohabitation. It is likely that, in the longer term, fewer marriages occur since the relatively unsuccesful matches do not reach the stage of marriage.

The notion that cohabitation is only a temporary phase is most vivid in explanatory frameworks of divorce. Many researchers have recently studied the role of cohabitation in the process of divorce. Conceptualizing cohabitation as a temporary phase before marriage implies that cohabitation is a trial period before marriage. By living together as nonmarried, cohabiting couples people take time getting to know each other in daily life situations. Cohabitation serves as a trial period. If the trial is experienced as being successful, the couple marry; if not, they break up. This 'weeding-process' assumes that only the most stable cohabiting couples enter marriage and consequently they will subsequently have a high level of marital stability (Bennett et al., 1988; Hoem and Hoem, 1988, Klijzing, 1992). In the longer term, fewer legal divorces would occur since relatively unsuccessful matches would not reach the stage of marriage and legal divorce. This interpretation has not yet been confirmed, however. On the contrary, many empirical studies on the role of cohabitation in the divorce process show that people who have cohabited before marriage have a much lower marital stability than persons who did not cohabit before marriage (for different countries: e.g. Axinn & Thornton, 1992; Balakrishnan et al., 1987; Bennett et al., 1988; Bumpass and Sweet, 1989; Hoem and Hoem, 1988; DeMaris and

Rao, 1992; Schoen, 1992; Teachman et al., 1991; for the Netherlands: Klijzing, 1992; Manting, 1993a).

Cohabitation as an alternative to marriage
An alternative reasoning seems to fit the empirical findings better. Differences in disruption between couples who cohabited before marriage and those who did not might also be caused by the fact that it is a certain *type* of person that is attracted to cohabitation (Newcomb, 1987). People with a lower commitment to a permanently shared life are, at the start of it, attracted to cohabitation. Eventually they marry, but probably still keeping a lower attachment to marriage as a permanent institution than those who did not cohabit. Couples holding more traditional values and attitudes towards marriage and divorce will marry without having previously cohabited. They are strongly committed to the institution of marriage and attach high value to it. Their acceptance of divorce is much lower than that of people who are less traditional in their values and attitudes. From this point of view, cohabitation offers individuals a way of formulating rules and obligations according to each other's personal wishes.

In several research projects in the Netherlands in which a distinction was made between married and cohabiting couples, evidence could be found for the idea that cohabiting couples differed from married couples. Most of what is known about cohabitation has been obtained from cross-sectional studies comparing cohabiting couples with married couples at one point in time (De Feijter, 1991; Langeveld, 1985; Latten, 1992; Manting, 1994b; Lesthaeghe et al., 1992; Van der Avort, 1987; Van den Akker & Mandemaker, 1991; Moors & Van Nimwegen, 1990; Wiersma, 1983). In contrast with married couples, cohabiting couples have a greater urge for independence in their relationship (e.g., in their financial arrangements), are more critical towards the quality of their relationship (Van der Avort, 1987, Wiersma, 1983) and are less convinced that their relationship will succeed to be a permanent, life-long commitment. Planning of children is less frequently anticipated among cohabiting couples (Wiersma, 1983). Cohabiting couples have lower levels of commitment towards maintaining their relationship than married couples do. Young adults in the Netherlands, Belgium, France and Germany differ according to their living arrangements in a number of family oriented, religious and political attitudes: Cohabiting couples attach greater value to symmetrical relations, oppose less to unfaithfulness, have a greater orientation to the adult dyad, are far less oriented towards having children, attach less importance to material conditions, or social and religious backgrounds and favour female economic autonomy and non-domestic roles more than married couples (Lesthaeghe et al., 1992). Moreover, cohabiting couples view marriage more often as a contract and less as a crown to their relationship (Manting, 1994b). De Jong Gierveld & Liefbroer (1993) showed that young people leaving home to marry have much less individualistic attitudes than people leaving home to cohabit before marriage. People who want to minimize risks and maximize flexibility, independence and freedom tend to opt for cohabitation whereas the others tend to choose marriage (De Jong Gierveld & Liefbroer, 1993). Couples that (intend to) cohabit have lower levels of commitment towards maintaining their relationship than married couples have. These findings suggest that cohabitation is an alternative to marriage.

If cohabitation is viewed as an alternative to marriage, the emergence of cohabitation can, then, be interpreted as being one of the results of the process of individualization. In this case, an increasing need for flexibility, for individual freedom and for independence make people prefer cohabitation to marriage. Cohabitation offers individuals an opportunity to formulate their own rights, obligations and/or functions: it is the outcome of a tension between quests for independence as well as relatedness (Newcomb, 1987). Cohabitation, as an alternative to marriage, is an institution without the legal sanctions of marriage; an institution with individual-specific rights, obligations and/or functions. In contrast with cohabitation, marriage offers a set of standard rights and obligations described by (Dutch) law. Cohabitation may also be seen as an institution with a lower level of commitment, since cohabitation creates fewer barriers in the case of a break-up than does marriage. Lesthaeghe and colleagues (1992: 15) argue that 'a lower familial commitment at the onset lies at the core of the selection into cohabitation and subsequent union dissolution'. If cohabitation is indeed different from marriage, the emergence of cohabitation is not so much a major reason for the delay of marriage. It is rather, besides a decline in marriage, another consequence of the long term process of individualization.

Cohabitation as an alternative to singlehood
A final conceptualization of cohabitation is the definition of cohabitation as an alternative to singlehood. According to Rindfuss and VandenHeuvel (1990), cohabitation is neither similar to marriage, nor is it an alternative to marriage. On the contrary, it is an alternative to singlehood, because the inherent goal of stability and permanence is not always evident at the start of union formation: 'cohabitation does not assume a commitment to permanency at the beginning of the relationship. The necessity of a long-term commitment does not exist...' (Rindfuss and VandenHeuvel, 1990: 707). They view cohabitation as a long term and gradual moving-in process; '.. a common reason for deciding to cohabit is that, in view of the amount of time the couple already spend together, it would simplify their lives to share a dwelling unit' (Rindfuss and VandenHeuvel, 1990: 706). This does not necessarily mean that both partners no longer maintain their own separate units at the moment of moving-in. In fact, it is possible to distinguish different stages with increasing commitment, beginning with sharing one or more nights, living together more or less permanently, followed by giving up one's own separate unit, and sharing and buying expensive and permanent goods such as a house. At the beginning of the process, marriage is not even considered; the decision to cohabit is only a consequence of the time shared with each other. Rindfuss and VandenHeuvel point to the gradual nature of the process of cohabitation. From this point of view, both the delay of marriage as well as the emergence of a gradual moving-in process are, again, outcomes of an underlying process of individualization: the fact that normative pressure has weakened (Bumpass and Sweet, 1989; De Feijter, 1991) has left room for the emergence of cohabitation in such a way.

Cohabitation: varying meaning across time
All these conceptualizations of cohabitation can be grouped in chronological order through historical time. Cohabitation started as a deviant and alternative way of living, as a 'manifestation of a refusal of the conventional "bourgeois marriage" which was accused of being hypocritical

in the sense that conformism was more important than the quality of the relationship' (Lesthaeghe et al., 1992: 2). As such, in the beginning, cohabitation attracted a selective subgroup of the population and more or less automatically, differences between cohabiting and married couples were indeed important (De Feijter, 1991).

The 'revolutionary' meaning of cohabitation diminished rapidly, however. Instead of being an alternative to marriage, cohabitation became a strategy to 'test' one's relationship prior to marriage. In the Netherlands, social disapproval of cohabitation as a temporary phase before marriage disappeared very soon (De Feijter, 1991). The proportion of people approving of people who cohabit as a period of trial before marriage rose from 60 (1980) to 85 percent (1991). It took the majority of the Dutch population somewhat more time to accept cohabitation without any intention to marry. The proportion of the Dutch population approving of cohabiting couples with no intention of marrying increased from 41 to 71 percent between 1980 and 1991 (SCP, 1992). Because normative pressure to marry soon after cohabitation diminished, cohabitation, as a gradual way to move into a union, could occur. Cohabitation has become a strategy for moving into a union without any considerations regarding a future marriage.

Evaluation
It has become apparent that the way in which cohabitation is regarded highly influences interpretations of past developments in marriage and divorce. In turn, the way in which cohabitation is regarded is highly influenced by the past, or the historical moment in which a definition of cohabitation was formulated. Cohabitation used to be a revolutionary act against society. It developed into being an intermediate stage prior to marriage to test the relationship in daily life situation. Finally, it became a way of moving into a union gradually, without making any explicit decisions regarding the permanence of the relationship or to a future intention to marry.

Until today, these different historic-specific conceptualizations of cohabitation are visible in, for instance, an individual's perceptions of cohabitation. Of the people born in 1961, some characterize their entry into cohabitation as a process of gradual moving-in, others consider the marriage issue of little importance and yet another group has no intention of marrying their cohabiting partner at all (Liefbroer, 1991a). A major proportion of younger women in the Netherlands, however, anticipate cohabitation as a temporary phase before marriage - or they have already married after a period of cohabitation (Statistics Netherlands, 1994). In this variation, support is found for the idea that developments in the meaning of cohabitation have led to a diversity among young persons today. A minority may still see cohabitation as an act against marriage, whereas another relatively small section sees cohabitation as a gradual moving-in process. The large majority still perceives cohabitation as a temporary phase before marriage.

All in all, it is evident that cohabitation and marriage have different meanings both across time and across individuals. This assumption, that cohabitation and marriage have different meanings for different people and in different periods is completely in line with the assumption that a continuous shift in preferences, constraints and opportunities is also associated with increasing pluriformity. Implications for the way processes of union formation and dissolution should be studied are far reaching. These implications are now discussed.

Implications for the process of union formation
The assumption that both marriage and cohabitation have changed in meaning over historical time has important consequences for the way the process of union formation can best be studied. To understand the (changing) underlying causes leading people to enter a union, one has to study the (historic-specific) selection process into a union. For some, cohabitation is a marker of the moment one starts living together with a partner, whereas for others marriage is that marker. Liefbroer (1991a, 1991b) has shown that in order to gain insight into the process of union formation, one has to study the process of entry from the moment a couple lives together instead of from the moment of marriage, as has generally been done in more conventional studies. Given that cohabitation was an act against marriage, and has gradually become a strategy to enter a union, it seems very unlikely that, firstly, causal structures leading to marriage will be similar to those affecting entry into cohabitation and, secondly, that these causal relationships will be similar across time. Better understanding about the process of first union formation requires explicit attention to the legal status of the union at entry.

This does not mean, however, that one should ignore the time-varying element of legal status *during* the union. For some women, entry into a union is characterized by two transitions; entry into cohabitation, and entry into marriage. For some cohabiting couples, marriage may either be a matter of convenience, motivated by practical reasons, or the wish to have children, or it may be a passage of confirmation (Trost, 1979a). Cohabiting couples may or may not have any intention to marry; they may eventually marry, or they may not. To understand more about the circumstances that may lead cohabiting couples to enter marriage, one has to study the process of (subsequent) marriage from the moment a couple cohabits, thereby giving explicit attention to individual changes in different life domains that may affect a legal change from cohabitation to marriage.

This study seeks to gain insight into the changing circumstances that may stimulate women to move into a union, thereby drawing attention to the fact that some women move into cohabitation, sometimes to be followed by marriage, whereas others move directly into marriage.

Implications for the process of union dissolution
The assumption that there are different meanings of cohabitation across historical time influences not only the way the processes of first union formation is examined, but also the definition of the process of breaking up. In 'conventional' studies, the phase of cohabitation is interpreted as a period of weeding out the unstable couples or as a life style that attracts a selective - more divorce prone - part of the population. In these divorce studies, unions that have not (yet) entered marriage are neglected. This focus on marriage and divorce rather than the entry into and exit from shared life surely reflects that: '...information concerning nonmarital cohabitation is tied

to prevailing theoretical notions about the centrality of marriage as a socially constructed arrangement for economic and emotional exchanges between adult men and women' (Teachman et al., 1991: 572). If cohabitation is a way of entering a union gradually, studying the dissolution process of cohabiting couples and the circumstances that may lead to a dissolution becomes interesting. Comparatively little research has yet, however, been undertaken on the disruption of cohabiting couples.

If entry into marriage at the start of a union is a proxy for a higher level of commitment, then this would suggest that the incidence of a dissolution would be higher among cohabiting than among married women. If the transition to marry after a period of cohabitation is an indicator for feeling more confident about each other or having survived the trial period, then union stability should be higher once marriage is entered. This does not, however, imply that the primary issue of cohabitation is its 'weeding' effect on marital stability. 'Weeding' starts the moment people meet each other and continues during the union, irrespective of its legal status. The high divorce rates support the idea that weeding continues to take place after entering marriage. Co-residence is a moment when the daily life contents of the relationship change significantly. Sharing a residence with a partner means that one has to incorporate the daily life needs and wishes of the partner within one's own. Both for married and nonmarried unions, weeding in the sense of 'trying the relationship out in daily life situations' starts with higher intensity at the start of co-residence. It is certainly not limited exclusively to the start of cohabitation. Hence, it is far more interesting to analyse the stability of unions from the moment they are entered, and not from the moment of marriage. For the process of breaking up, this implies that one should not study the divorce process from the time couples are married, but the dissolution process from the time couples live together. That is not to say the time-varying element of status during the union should be ignored (Teachman et al., 1991). The process of dissolution from the moment a couple lives together requires study, thereby giving explicit attention to the fact that some couples may enter marriage during the union: the time-varying element of union status must thus be included to facilitate understanding of whether the stability of a union alters after marriage is entered. This study seeks to gain insight into the process of union dissolution, giving attention to individual changes in several life domains, including union status.

2.4   A cohort perspective

It was argued above that a mixture of societal changes has influenced the process of union formation and dissolution. Support for such a general notion that increasing educational and labour force participation of women go together with changes in union formation and dissolution is found - at the aggregate level - in many internationally comparative studies. There is evidence for the idea that cultural shifts such as secularization were also correlated with demographic trends (Lesthaeghe & Verleye, 1992).

Inter-birth cohort patterns
One of the ways of analysing the impact of (varying) contextual circumstances on individual behaviour is to follow a series of birth cohorts as they grow up. Ryder (1965: 12) introduced the cohort concept in the study of social change. He defined a cohort as 'the aggregate of individuals (within some population definition) who experienced the same event within the same time interval'. A birth cohort is a group of individuals born in the same calender period.

People born in different periods face different historical conditions, alternatives or possibilities and norms regarding primary relationships while growing up. 'Each new cohort makes fresh contact with the contemporary social heritage and carries the impress of the encounter through life' (Ryder, 1965, 11). Many studies, from different disciplines, show a close linkage between social differentiation and cohort membership (Becker, 1990, 1992). To start with, they are exposed to different norms and beliefs in the different periods in which they grow up. Cultural and ideational shifts reflect themselves in the personal preferences of birth cohorts (Lesthaeghe and Surkyn, 1988; Lesthaeghe and Moors, 1992). They found that new cohorts manifest a higher degree of individual autonomy, a lower degree of conventional morality, a lower degree of institutional affirmation than earlier birth cohorts. Also, family formation values tend to differ across the cohorts. Evaluations of factors thought to be important for a good marriage, such as mutual respect and trust, a happy sexual relationship and independence from in-laws vary between cohorts.

In addition, members of the same birth cohort are confronted with an approximately similar set of macro-level constraints and opportunities, sharing the same economic, social and cultural environment, the same educational system, equal opportunities on the labour market and equal mate, marriage or housing markets. According to Becker (1990), the year of birth determines one's future life course patterns to a great extent. Year of birth is important, because it determines the historical period in which one grows up and the conditions, favourable or unfavourable, which confront all members of a cohort. Facing equal historical conditions during the socialization period, members of a birth cohort have, to a certain extent, similar life course behaviour: Increasing female educational enrolment, educational level, labour force participation, incidence of illegitimate birth and secularization might have led to higher proportions of non-religious, pregnant, highly educated or working women or of mothers among later birth cohorts compared with earlier birth cohorts. If education, work, children and religion are indeed important determinants of the processes of union formation and dissolution, then compositional differentials across birth cohorts will be a cause of differences in union formation and dissolution across birth cohorts.

Furthermore, the continuous shift in meaning of marriage, cohabitation and divorce indicates that women born earlier were confronted with other options regarding union formation and/or dissolution than women born more recently. Women born at the beginning of the fifties grew up during the 'golden age of marriage' (Van de Kaa, 1987). For women born in this period, cohabitation was not an option to be taken for granted. Women born at the beginning of the sixties grew up in a period of high marital instability. At the time when they were thinking about shared life, the negative consequences of divorce were common knowledge. This may have made them more aware of the consequences of marriage. As a result, they might have preferred to enter cohabitation first (Lesthaeghe and Moors, 1992). Women born at the end of the sixties, however, grew up in a period in which cohabitation was highly tolerated. For them, it was almost 'a-matter-of-course' that they should cohabit (Liefbroer, 1991c).

As a result, *inter-cohort* differentials will occur in the process of union formation and dissolution: in the timing, the type and the stability of a union. This study seeks to gain insight into inter-cohort differentials in union formation and dissolution.

Intra-birth cohort patterns
Of course, within cohorts, members differ from each other because of their past and current individual experiences. Members of cohorts have different family backgrounds and religious denominations. They are exposed to different individual circumstances in their past and current life course. Younger birth cohorts, for instance, have more often experienced a parental divorce. Parental divorce has long-lasting influences on children's life course (Kiernan & Chase-Lansdale, 1993). Influence of family background on children's behaviour has been well documented (Kiernan & Chase-Lansdale, 1993; Liefbroer, 1991a; McLanahan & Bumpass, 1988; Thornton, 1991). Young people build a complex of social norms, values and attitudes internalized through institutions such as the family, the school or the church. De Feijter (1991) showed convincingly that new developments in values or demographic behaviour are transmitted by subgroups within the population. This means that the life course position people find themselves in affects their response to historical conditions. The declining attractiveness of marriage, for instance, has a different meaning for the nonmarried as opposed to the married. It may lead the nonmarried to postpone entry into marriage, whereas it may lower the barriers to a divorce for the married. Over and above inter-cohort differentials there will therefore be *intra-cohort* differentials in union formation and dissolution resulting from individual past and current experiences.

Varying relationships of underlying determinants and the process of union formation and dissolution across birth cohorts
If the meaning of marriage and cohabitation varies with historical time, the meaning of the determinants underlying the processes of union formation and dissolution has to change across birth cohorts, too.

Chapter 1 documented the weakening linkage of marriage with fertility, sexual intimacy and work. In earlier times, a woman accidentally becoming pregnant would marry as soon as possible, because it was highly unacceptable to have and rear children without being married. Today, more and more women do not marry when pregnant or after childbirth. To a certain extent, the strong pressure to marry when children are born has diminished. This implies that the incidence of pregnancy or childbirth would have a diminishing impact on entry into marriage, although the relationship is still very close. This is just one example of how a linkage of determinants underlying the process of union formation might have changed across time. In addition, the presence of children used to be a factor hampering the decision to divorce. Today, increasingly more people believe that divorce might sometimes be a better solution for the children (Van den Akker, 1988). Again, this is an example of the assumption that a relationship between underlying determinants and union dissolution does not necessarily remain static through time.

Recently, De Feijter (1991) has found that factors such as religion and level of education have had a diminishing differential impact on the incidence of cohabitation across the years. He suggested that the processes of individualization and secularization are accompanied by a decline in the impact of such factors on individual behaviour. In the early days of the rise in cohabitation in the mid seventies, a subgroup with a particularly high level of education and no religious denomination cohabited. In the mid eighties, a larger part of the population cohabited at a certain point in their life course. As a result, it became much more difficult to detect a select subgroup (De Feijter, 1991). De Feijter made it clear that factors such as educational attainment and religion have become less important for behaviour that has become 'mainstream' behaviour. The observation that individual background characteristics have a diminishing differential impact on demographic behaviour was made for forms of behaviour that have become more common across time. These observations were not very often made for behaviour that has become exceptional behaviour. Yet, a by-effect of processes such as individualization and secularization is that people make different choices: pluriformity suggests that, besides standard options, less standard options will remain present in society. That social differentiation decreases when cohabiting couples are compared with married couples may result from the fact that the majority of the people cohabit and marry. What would happen if not only mainstream behaviour, but also less standard options were studied? Here, it is assumed that pluriformity in society means that certain determinants will diminish in impact for behaviour becoming increasingly standard through time, but will increase in impact for options becoming decreasingly standard through time, or for 'new' options. Direct marriage (that is, entry into marriage without a prior period of cohabitation) is an example of behaviour that has become increasingly exceptional over time (for the case of Sweden: Hoem & Hoem, 1992; for the case of the Netherlands: Latten, 1992). Latten (1992) showed, from a cross-sectional point of view, that married couples who had never cohabited differ increasingly from those married couples who did cohabit before marriage. De Jong Gierveld and Liefbroer (1992) showed the declining impact of educational attainment on the entry into cohabitation. As such, it is quite possible that a mechanism of diminishing impact of religion, educational level, educational and occupational career as well as fertility is apparent for elements of the union career that have become - more or less - standard behaviour among the later birth cohorts together with a mechanism of increasing impact of these determinants for new options or for options that have become decreasingly standard.

The question whether differentiation will decrease or increase can be studied through the comparison of inter-birth cohort behaviour. If background characteristics have a decreasing impact on parts of union formation or dissolution, more recent birth cohorts will show less differentiation than earlier birth cohorts. If determinants have an increasing impact on parts of union formation and dissolution, then more recent birth cohorts will show more differentiation in these determinants. This study gives explicit attention to the question whether linkages are non-static across birth cohorts. In short, between-cohort comparisons reveal the importance of growing up in different historical eras, while within-cohort comparisons reveal the importance of individual characteristics for the process of union formation and dissolution. The combination of both reveals any changes in the linkage of determinants with union formation and dissolution.

2.5 A life course perspective

Recently, many researchers have studied social behaviour from a life course perspective. The core of life course research is the study of interrelated individual processes extending over the individual life span and emerging within a particular historical setting (Mayer & Tuma, 1988). 'The life course may be defined as the sequence of events and experiences in a life from birth until death and the chain of personal states and encountered situations which influence and are influenced by this sequence of events.' (Runyan, 1984: 82).

This means, firstly, that the sequence and timing of early life course events may influence later life course behaviour. Secondly, experiences early in life or experiences within the family in which they were brought up may set people on a certain track in life. With the unfolding of the life course, however, the accumulation of later life course experiences might mediate those encountered earlier. One of the main advantages of life course research is its implicit attention to time: to the passage of individual time and the individual changes occurring with the passage of time, and to the historical time-setting in which individual life courses emerge.

Since the inclination to form or break up a union is highly time-dependent, the life course perspective provides a theoretical framework for moving into and out of a union with reference to the role of different life domains and changes within them in the course of time.

The process of union formation
It became clear above that entry into a union has become more gradual. Through longer investment in other life domains, and fuelled by processes of secularization and individualization, decisions with a long-lasting impact are postponed until later in the life course. Instead of searching for explanations of why marriage has declined, one should therefore search for explanatory guidelines why union formation has been increasingly characterized as a gradual moving-in process for many people. As such, entry into a union is a process, unfolding over the life course. When women grow up, they experience continuously changing personal and contextual circumstances that may continuously alter their inclination to cohabit or to marry. Explanations for the postponement of marriage cited above referred to the role of competitive activities, such as education and work, that may hamper entry into marriage, or in more general terms, entry into a union. Motivations underlying entry into a union vary highly with the life course position people find themselves in. A young woman with a boy-friend tends to weigh practical arguments (such as study, finance, residence) much more in her cohabitation plans

than a woman with no close intimate relationship (Liefbroer, 1991a). This difference is an example of how an individual's position at a certain moment in life tends to be associated with the aspirations, values and plans that person has and so with the inclination to form a union at certain moments in life. In this study, explicit attention is given to how time-varying individual situations may or may not result in entry into a union.

The process of union dissolution
Not only is the formation of a union gradual; exit from a union also takes time. During a primary relationship, many individual and couple-related changes occur which may eventually stimulate or hamper a break-up. The stability of a union varies also with the years lived in a union. There are a few theories that address the question why marital stability varies with duration. Becker's (1981) economic interpretation is that, during the marital years, accumulation of assets not easily transferable from one marriage partner to another hamper a divorce increasingly as the marriage endures. Marriage-specific assets are material assets such as a house or a car, but also children. Trost formulated a more sociological interpretation to explain the variation in separation for both married and nonmarried unions. He assumed that the longer a relationship endures, the greater the extent to which emotional bonds are replaced by social and economic bonds. Co-residence is triggered by emotional motivations; love, mutual attraction and the need to share life with the other person are the most important motivations. But during the period of co-residence, investments are made in household goods, the social networks of the other, and having and rearing children (Trost, 1986). These substantive ideas lead to the expectation that marital stability increases the longer a union lasts. However, this has been challenged by others, including Diekmann and Mitter (1984), who assert that marital instability increases in the first years of marriage, because people make mistakes in their mutual matching (Diekmann and Mitter, 1984; Diekmann and Klein, 1991). In the first years of the process of learning to cope with each other's wishes and habits, the 'stock of sins' grows rapidly. The divorce risk decreases to a lower rate in later years of the marriage, because partners make increasingly fewer mistakes having got used to each other's habits and wishes, and through forgetting and forgiving former 'sins'. "At least for a certain phase one could therefore expect that the risk of divorce increases because unsatisfying experiences are accumulated without being compensated by satisfying ones" (Diekman and Mitter, 1984, page 129). On the other hand, '.. year by year a certain percentage of sins is forgotten or forgiven and does not strain the marriage any more'. (Diekmann and Mitter, 1984, page 129). Trussell, Rodriquez and Vaughan (1992) formulate a theory which they call "the theory of accumulated irritations". It is offered as an explanation of dissolution risks increasing with the duration of the union: '...partners become increasingly frustrated with each other's shortcomings and behaviours (until the straw finally breaks the camel's back)' (page 58). In addition, the chances of growing apart are assumed to increase with the duration of marriage. On the other hand, Trussell and colleagues also formulated 'the theory of growing acceptance', putting forward the opposite relationship between the duration of the union and the risk of a dissolution. Because 'persons come to accept their partner's faults, realizing that .... there is no Mr Right or Ms Right' (page 58), the dissolution risk decreases linearly with union duration.

These notions refer to variation in the emotional content of a relationship during a union. But other individual changes, such as exit from the labour market, might affect the process of union dissolution, too. Economic dependence on the husband implies a higher barrier to divorce. The inclination to break-up is thus also highly affected by the (varying) life position a person has. All in all, it implies that to understand more about union stability, one should study the process of separation from the moment of formation onwards, taking into account time-varying circumstances.

The influence of past life course experiences

Taking time into account implies that, to gain insight into the union formation and dissolution, one must follow people as they grow up and experience different life situations. Firstly, an individual's past may determine current and future behaviour (Elchardus, 1984; Elder, 1981; Mayer and Tuma, 1990). Despite secularization and individualization, individual norms and values reflect the norms and values of the subgroups to which the individual is exposed, as De Feijter has shown (1991). The family, the educational system and the church are institutions that socialize children early in life. There is support for the idea that the family in which an individual is brought up is important for the later life course. It affects, for instance, the choice between cohabitation and marriage (Liefbroer, 1991a) and the age at which one marries (Kobrin & Waite, 1984; Michael & Tuma, 1985; Waite & Spitze, 1981). The religious denomination in which an individual is brought up still influences demographic behaviour. Lesthaeghe and Surkyn (1988: 13) explain this as follows: "... Why then is religion so important for family formation and procreation in the West? The answer is that churches systematically engage in the institutional regulation of individuals' lives through the collective assertion of norms that restrict individualism and the externalities that individualism may produce, and through the psychological internalization of sanctions ranging in format from guilt to damnation." An assumption in this study is, therefore, that a woman's past life course experiences influences her future inclination to enter a union: past life course experiences sets a woman on a certain track of life.

In addition to an individual's family background, other past life course experiences influence current behaviour as well. The timing and order of early life course transitions are important for the later life course. Much research has made apparent that the age at which a union is formed is important for its further stability (Bracher et al., 1993; Diekmann & Klein, 1991; Klijzing, 1992; Manting, 1993; Morgan & Rindfuss, 1985; Teachman et al., 1991; Trussell et al., 1992). In addition, many studies have shown that having a child before marriage, or marrying while pregnant, are closely related to higher instability of the later marriage (Bracher e.a., 1993; Diekmann and Klein, 1991; Klijzing, 1992; Morgan and Rindfuss, 1985).

The influence of current life course experiences

Besides the assumption that past life course experiences influence the later life course, it must not be forgotten that later experiences modify past experiences and, linked with this, their impact on current behaviour (Liefbroer, 1991a). Individual preferences change during the life course because people continuously face new personal and/or societal developments. Empirical studies have shown that living alone for a certain period in life, the experience of cohabitation or divorce alter people's values of marriage, divorce and other living arrangements (Axinn and Thornton, 1992). The inclination to form a union or break it up might also be altered. The influence of an individual's past on the processes of union formation and dissolution might thus be mediated through more current experiences such as education, work and fertility (Booth et al., 1987; Liefbroer, 1991a).

The above implies that the time-varying elements in the study of union formation and dissolution require attention. Formation and dissolution of first (un) married unions of women, living in the Netherlands, are examined from a *life course perspective*. Attention is given to dynamics in the formation and dissolution of first unions. This theoretical approach draws attention to the passage of time in the lives of individuals. This passage of time takes place at the individual level: in the course of their lives, women grow up and experience several important life events, such as exit from parental home, entry into parenthood, entry into and exit from the educational system or the labour market, and entry into and possibly exit from shared life with a partner.

Historical context and individual behaviour
Often motivations to marry are emotional attachment, security, desire for children, social approval, prestige and as a 'matter-of-course'(Buunk & Van Driel, 1989). Marriage and cohabitation are instrumental goals varying between individuals. Marriage and cohabitation are individual goals for striving at optimization of basic universal needs. According to Lindenberg (1993), human beings share two universal needs: physical well-being and social approval. People try to optimize both universal needs by means of instrumental goals: comfort and stimulation are instrumental goals for attaining physical well-being; status, affirmation and affect are instrumental goals for social approval. The instrumental goals to obtain these two universal needs differ between people. For instance, men and women use different instrumental goals to obtain material well-being. While for men, marriage used to be an instrument for domestic care, for women, marriage used to be an instrument for economic security. (Lindenberg, 1993). Today, however, marriage no longer serves such an economic purpose for women. Marriage, albeit a very personal decision, is thus influenced by *(changing) opportunities at the macro level* as well. Instrumental goals not only vary between persons, but also with time. Societal developments over time contribute importantly to the understanding of the formation and dissolution of first unions. Individual norms and values are influenced by the society in which a person grows up. For instance, the fact that young people today do not feel that there are so many differences between marriage and cohabitation reflects the fact that, currently, cohabitation is highly tolerated. A larger proportion of young adults today do not really see any specific consequences of cohabitation for the educational or labour force career, the rearing of children, security, daily contact with friends, companionship or freedom (Liefbroer, 1991a). Those who perceive differences between marriage and cohabitation either view marriage as a better suited arrangement for the rearing of children and for security, or argue that cohabitation gives more independence, more time for the educational and occupational career or contacts with friends (Liefbroer, 1991a).

That many young people today do not consider the consequences a choice between cohabitation and marriage might have for education or work is another reflection of the fact that young women today are no longer assumed to leave the labour market after marriage. Older women point to the fact that, when they were young, the general feeling was that women only worked until marriage (Peters and Du Bois-Reymond, 1990).

Point-in-time events at the aggregate level, such as law changes (divorce law, social security regulations) may have an additional impact on the process of union formation and dissolution. Long-term societal developments, such as secularization, individualization, emancipation, the emergence of the welfare state, increasing labour force participation and education of women, continuously alter females' preferences, constraints and opportunities. A continuous change in preferences (towards independence), opportunities (own income) and constraints (combination of different life careers) at the macro level, affects women at every moment in life.

Women who considered entering a union in the fifties were confronted with other pros and cons than women who consider entering a union today. Women thinking about divorce today are also confronted with different advantages and disadvantages than women considering it in the fifties. Divorce, too, is a very individual decision. Reasons for breaking up are linked with the unsatisfactory relationship with the partner. Provocations frequently cited are lack of attention, love and understanding, partners having grown apart, the partner's infidelity, aggressive situations, conflicts, and so forth (Weeda, 1991). Again, the historical context in which divorce is considered influences the decision process, just as a person's personal life phase does. The presence of children used to be a factor countering divorce, but divorce in the presence of children has recently become more common (Van den Akker, 1988).

Studying processes of union formation and dissolution from a life course perspective
It is then evident that a personal decision to marry, or to cohabit, is made in a given historical period, given current and past individual experiences (see also Morgan and Rindfuss, 1985). In order to understand more about such personal decisions to enter a union or break one up, one has to study the processes, taking into account past and current micro and macro level circumstances. As such, it must be studied from an integrated framework stressing the temporal organization of the individual life course: the life course framework. The individual life course should be studied as a sequence of changing personal experiences in the past and in the present which have become closely intertwined. The assumption that the individual life course is embedded in a historical setting stems also from life course theory (Mayer and Tuma, 1990).

Life course theory offers an integrated framework for the study of union formation and dissolution. In short, life course theory draws attention to both the time, individual and contextual aspects that play a role in the individual life course. Individual determinants (such as religion, educational or occupational status) are assumed to influence union formation and dissolution by women. A union career is structured by individual time dimensions (age, or duration of the union) and by the order of events (pregnancy, or childbirth before marriage). Furthermore, the process of union formation and/or dissolution is embedded in a historical context: the period in which one is born, or the period in which a union was entered. Finally, point-in-time events (such as age at entry into a union) play a role too.

2.6 Conceptual scheme

Scheme 2 summarizes how all the relevant elements, mentioned in the former sections, relate to each other.

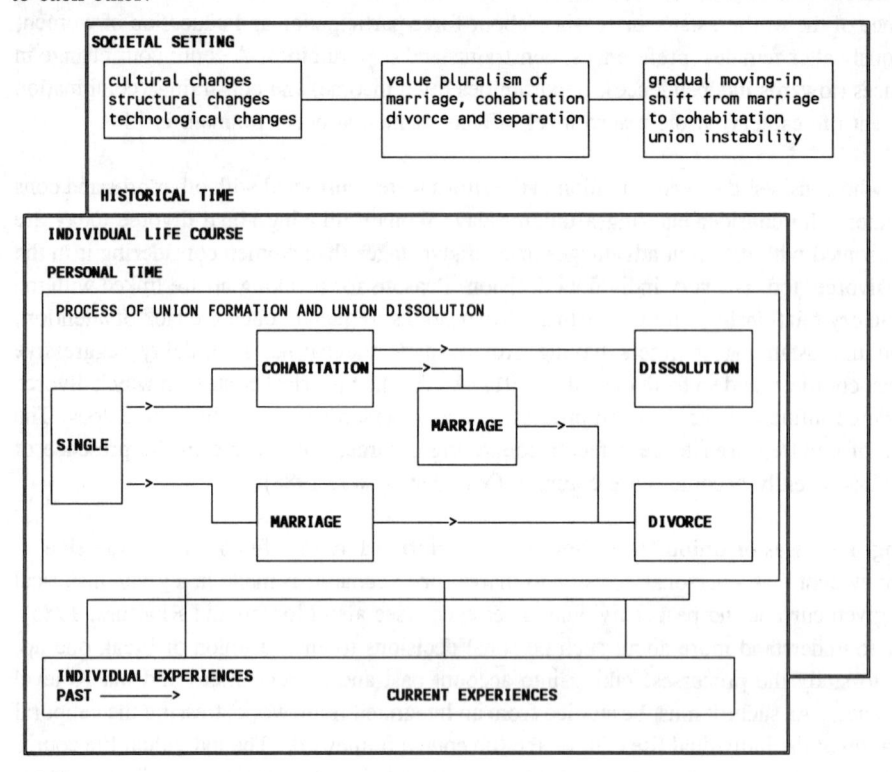

```
SOCIETAL SETTING
  cultural changes          value pluralism of          gradual moving-in
  structural changes        marriage, cohabitation      shift from marriage
  technological changes     divorce and separation      to cohabitation
                                                        union instability

HISTORICAL TIME

INDIVIDUAL LIFE COURSE
PERSONAL TIME

  PROCESS OF UNION FORMATION AND UNION DISSOLUTION

                    COHABITATION                        DISSOLUTION

  SINGLE                          MARRIAGE

                    MARRIAGE                            DIVORCE


INDIVIDUAL EXPERIENCES
PAST ———>                 CURRENT EXPERIENCES
```

Two distinct layers are shown. The first layer refers to personal experiences. The *upper* part of the first layer shows the phenomena studied: the formation and dissolution of first unions. The onset of a union starts with co-residence, either through marriage or through cohabitation. Cohabiting couples may, or may not, undergo marriage later. People may experience a disruption from the moment they live together. Those who enter marriage directly may experience divorce, while those who cohabit may experience a disruption. Some cohabiting couples not experiencing a disruption may marry and after that divorce may occur. Only entry into and exit from *first* unions are examined here.

The *lower* part of first layer contains personal phenomena thought to influence the process of union formation and dissolution. These include past and current individual life course experiences. First, early life experiences may have a direct or indirect impact through the later life course experiences on the processes of union formation and dissolution. Elements of the later life course that might influence the timing of union formation and dissolution include the educational, occupational and fertility careers. These elements are expected to have an impact varying with the unfolding of the life course. Some elements may delay entry into a union at early ages, while others may stimulate entry into a union at early ages.

The *lower layer* indicates that the relationships put down in the first layer need not be static in time. On the contrary, it is assumed that the determinants underlying union formation and dissolution may vary with historical time. Long-term macro-level developments such as secularization, individualization, increased standard of living have created a continuously evolving shift in individual preferences (towards individuality, freedom and independence), in constraints (towards less normative constraints and less affirmation to institutional regulations of the state, the church or the family) and in opportunities (women's economic independence through labour market participation and through the individualization of social security).

The meanings of marriage, cohabitation and the break up of a union vary through historical time. The attractiveness of marriage has declined, while the attractiveness of cohabitation has increased. This tendency has been accompanied by a weakening linkage of marriage and co-residence, sexual intimacy and fertility, by a delay in marriage, a rise in cohabitation, a rise in the instability of unions as a whole and by a gradual moving-in process and a varying legal status during the union. If cohabitation and marriage have increasingly become similar ways of living together, then it must be the case that the underlying forces leading to cohabitation or marriage have a decreasing impact on the choice. If this is not so, then the need to distinguish between types of union remains. Determinants influencing the choice of a union have been studied for the Netherlands (Liefbroer, 1991a), but only for one birth cohort, so this study cannot reveal historical changes through time. Another Dutch study (De Feijter, 1991) showed that cohabiting and married couples have become increasingly alike over time. This may result from the fact that increasing numbers of people are likely to cohabit for some time. However, the study of De Feijter gives no insight into moving into a union over time, nor into circumstances that may lead to a marriage after a period of cohabitation. Through studying moving into a union over time, more insight can be acquired not only into the impact of the determinants leading to it, but also their varying impact over time.

For the case of the Netherlands, the determinants that may lead to union dissolution from the moment of co-residence have been studied by Klijzing (1992). However, his study was not directed to reveal possible historical changes in the meaning of determinants through historical time.

One of the ways of analysing the impact of historic-specific circumstances on individual behaviour is following a series of birth cohorts as they grow up. The question to what extent past and current determinants affect union formation or dissolution can be studied through the comparison of inter-birth cohort behaviour. If these determinants have a decreasing impact on parts of union formation or dissolution, the union careers of more recent birth cohorts will be less influenced by these factors than will the union careers of earlier birth cohorts. An increasing tendency would bring about more differentiation among more recent birth cohorts. In addition, linking historical developments with personal developments implies an intersection of personal and historical time. Members of birth cohorts have the same age in the same historical period: as such, the intersection of individual time (ageing) and historical time (calender year) can be studied by comparing birth cohorts at different moment in the life course (Demographic Change 1990).

Formulation of research questions
In this study, an attempt is made to unravel the different aspects laid down in the conceptual scheme. It is assumed that the life course patterns of women emerge in specific historical and personal settings. The study of inter-cohort differences is a way of gaining insight into how the an individual life course is embedded in a historic-specific setting.

The influences of these circumstances are however conditioned by an individual's opportunities and constraints: intra-cohort differences emerge. These intra-cohort differences are highly age-dependent. People make decisions about cohabitation, marriage, separation or divorce in a given historical period, at a given age, and with a given set of past and current individual characteristics and experiences. This implies a search for intra-cohort differentials from a life course perspective.

These considerations lead to the following research questions:

1. How have the life course patterns in formation and dissolution of first unions changed across birth cohorts?

2. How have past and current individual life course experiences influenced first union formation?
    - How have they influenced the (timing and type of) entry into a first union?
    - Are there signs of a change in the impact of these determinants over personal and historical time, and if so, how does the impact change?

3. How have past and current individual life course experiences influenced the entry into marriage of cohabiting women?
    - How have they influenced the (timing of) entry into marriage?
    - Are there signs of a change in the impact of these determinants over personal and historical time, and if so, how does the impact change?

4. How have past and current individual life course experiences influenced first union dissolution over time?
    - How have they influenced the (timing of a) union dissolution?
    - Are there signs of a change in the impact of these determinants over personal and historical time, and if so, how does the impact change?

To provide insight into how life course patterns have changed over time (research question 1), chapter 4 documents inter-cohort patterns in first marriage, first union formation, divorce and union dissolution. In addition, cohort developments in determinants stressed above (labour force, education and fertility) are presented in order to gain insight - at the aggregate level - into the degree to which changes in the union career have coincided with changes in these life domains. This analysis is descriptive, so it cannot reveal causality, but it shows whether or not one macro-level trend occurs simultaneously with another. Causality can only be examined at the individual level, since it is the individual level through which causal inference runs, irrespective of whether one is interested in phenomena at the macro or at the micro level (De Bruijn, 1993: 10). Furthermore, the analysis presented in chapter 4 does not permit to study the simultaneous influence of several individual determinants. This is the goal of research questions 2, 3 and 4. A review of the literature on union formation and dissolution leads to the choice of the relevant past and current life course determinants, and generates the concrete expectations about (varying) relationships of these determinants and the processes of union formation or dissolution. The study of individual determinants, in the presence of each other, for union formation and dissolution is presented in chapters 5 to 7.

3 METHOD AND DATA

3.1 Introduction

The study of life course patterns has always been an essential part of demographic analysis. Ordinary life tables are fruitful tools with which to describe life course patterns. Traditionally, the life table was used to present in summary form the mortality patterns of a population. In more recent times, however, life table analysis has been applied to other events, like marriage and divorce. A mortality life table traditionally follows a group of people from birth to death. In other words, it is a tool with which to follow birth cohorts as they age. The life table method is thus very well suited to the comparison of life course patterns, in the quantitative sense, between different birth cohorts. A general, demographic, approach is the examination of a series of life tables, distinguished by a unique combination of characteristics. There are at present no available sets of Dutch data for a life table analysis large enough to permit the study of a set of individual determinants simultaneously. (see also Menken et al., 1981). Another, multivariate, technique was needed for this study. According to Hoem (1993:2), 'Event-history analysis is an extension of the cluster of methods connected with the life table..... With their regression-type features, these methods allow us to study the interaction between the various dimensions of demographic behavior as well as the mutual influence between demographic and other life arenas (such as labor-force participation and education) with a forcefulness that is shared with no other method at our disposal'.

Multivariate event history techniques are very well suited to the study of life course patterns (Allison, 1984; Blossfeld et al., 1989; Namboodiri & Suchindran, 1987). The life course theory formulates an integrated theoretical framework incorporating elements at different levels and between different time dimensions (Mayer and Tuma, 1990). Both individual determinants (such as religion, educational or occupational status) as well as couple-specific determinants (such as the presence of children) play a role in individual behaviour. Life course theory explicitly assumes that individual circumstances change with age and that behavioural patterns unfold in different ways across birth cohorts (see chapter 2). Event history analysis is a method allowing for a simultaneous integration of all these elements into a formal, testable model (Mayer and Tuma, 1990). This chapter discusses the multivariate event history technique, together with the required data organization used to analyse life course patterns of female birth cohorts, or, more specifically, to analyse the simultaneous impact of determinants on the timing and occurrence of first union and dissolution.

3.2 Multivariate event history analysis

Event history offers several advantages for the study of life course patterns of birth cohorts. First, event history methods can very easily deal with censoring. The problem of the handling of censored individuals (that is, those who have not yet experienced an event) is of special significance (see also Manting et al., 1993) when life course patterns across birth cohorts are studied and when the life histories are still in full swing. For example, women who were born in 1960-64 have not had as much opportunity to marry as women born in 1945-49. Not only have they had reduced opportunity to marry, but they have also had less time to pass through other relevant transitions of interest, such as entry into parenthood. The straightforward explanation is that the later birth cohort has not lived as long as the earlier birth cohort. This phenomenon, that some women have not *yet* experienced the event of interest, is called 'right-censoring'. The length of the observation period (in this example the duration from birth till moment of interview) influences the number of censored individuals. The longer the period of observation, the less likely is it that an event will not have occurred. Right-censoring is not only a problem when a population has not lived long enough for all to experience the event: a problem arises in cases where the event will not be experienced by every member of a birth cohort. In the case of marriage, a small - but increasing - number of women will not marry. But only a small percentage of all married couples will ever divorce. In other words, even if it were possible to observe all women till death, many women would not have made the transition from the married to divorced state. Another type of censoring is left-censoring. Data are left-censored whenever information on the entry into a certain status is lacking. For instance, if divorce is studied and the timing of marriage is unknown, data are left-censored. Since the problem of left-censored data does not arise in this study, there is no need to discuss its implications.
A second advantage of event history is that this method allows for a simultaneous examination of interdependent life domains in their impact on the occurrence and the timing of events. Since the mid 1980s, *multivariate* event history analysis has become widely practised in demography (Keilman, 1993). Since this study rests on a life course perspective for the study of life course patterns, and since life course theory addresses the question of various individual, time-specific and/or couple-related determinants for individual behaviour, event history analysis is appropriate.
A third and closely related advantage of this method is its suitability for the handling of time-varying individual characteristics, such as the number of children, or employment status.

In this study, the dependent variable in multivariate event history analysis is the hazard rate: that is, the rate at which an event occurs within an infinitesimally short time interval, given that it has not occurred previously. For instance, the hazard rate of first union formation is the rate at which a union will be entered into in an infinitesimally small age interval, given that it has not yet occurred before the start of the age interval (Liefbroer, 1991b).

There are different techniques of hazard analysis. In this study, the *log rate* model is used. This is a log-linear model, formulated for (discrete-time) rates (see Laird and Olivier, 1981, for an extensive description of the use of ordinary log-linear models for hazard analysis). For several reasons, the log rate model is preferred to other techniques of hazard analysis.

First, it requires no *a priori* assumptions of how the hazard rate varies with time. For the demographic events studied in the following chapters, the variation of the hazard rate with time is not always known. In the case of divorce, theoretical notions of the variation of the hazard rate with duration of marriage differ from each other (see chapter 2). Some authors postulate a theory in which the hazard rate increases with duration (Becker, 1981); others predict that hazard rates will increase during the first years of marriage and decrease later (Diekmann and Klein, 1991). Because theoretical notions contradict each other, it is difficult to impose *a priori* a parametric definition. Furthermore, the variation of the hazard rate with time is not known for other events, either empirically or theoretically. For example, not much is known about how the marriage rate of cohabiting couples changes with the duration of unmarried cohabitation. Nor is much known of the variation of dissolution rates with duration in the case of cohabiting couples.

Second, the log rate model relaxes the assumption of proportionality. The model assumes piecewise constancy of the hazard: rates which are assumed to be constant within certain, predefined, time intervals (or within categories of other variables), but differ from one time interval to another (or between categories of other variables). In graph 1, an example is given of hazard rates of two subgroups proportional to each other (a,b) and of two subgroups for which the proportionality assumption does not hold (c,d).

1. Example of (non) proportional hazards

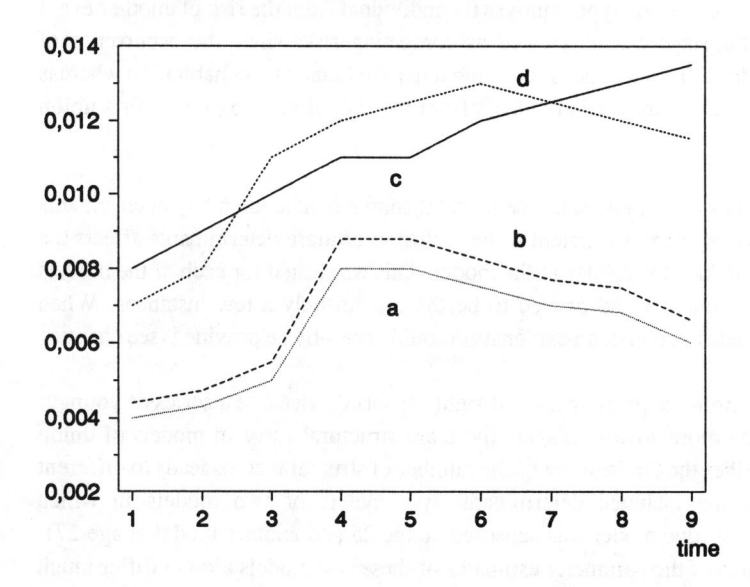

There are two reasons why a model relaxing the assumption of proportionality is preferred. First, more and more studies reveal that the assumption of proportionality is often violated (Morgan and Rindfuss, 1985, Singer and Willett, 1991). Second, and more importantly, theoretical notions from the life course perspective explicitly presuppose the presence of non-proportionality. Theories discussed in chapter 2 pointed to the fact that underlying forces were more likely to delay entry into marriage than lead to an overall decline. For example, one idea is that education may hamper marriage at younger ages but stimulates marriage at later ages (Blossfeld & Huinink, 1991). If this were the case for the Netherlands, rates would be non-proportional. For example, subgroup d in graph 1 would represent women with a high educational level who have a low rate of marriage at younger ages but a higher rate of marriage at older ages. Subgroup c would represent women with a low educational level. The log rate model can handle and test non-proportionality easily; interaction effects of age (or another) variable with other covariates can very easily be included and tested.

Third, the log rate model is preferred here because its handling of time-varying covariates does not increase computing costs as much as in some other techniques of hazard analysis. This feature is particularly important in this study because work, education, pregnancy and number of children are important determinants in the processes of interest and change over time.

A fourth advantage is that the log rate model permits the consideration of competing risks in one analysis (Larson, 1984). Liefbroer (1991a, 1991b) showed that this facility is particularly important in the study of union formation. Events compete (Hachen, 1988) when the underlying causes differ from each other: one structure defines the occurrence of one type, and another defines the occurrence of a different type. As Allison (1984) points out, competing risks are present if the occurrence of one event type removes the individual from the risk of another event type. Cohabitation and marriage can be viewed as competing risks since the occurrence of marriage removes individuals from the risk of entering into a first union by cohabitation whereas the occurrence of cohabitation removes individuals from the risk of entering into a first union by marriage.

The log rate model has a few disadvantages. One is that it cannot handle too many determinants simultaneously. This only becomes a problem if the inclusion of more determinants affects the effects of the previously included variables in the model. This was tested for each of the models presented in the following chapter and proved to be the case in only a few instances. When the impact of the determinants changed, an explanation could generally be provided (see chapters 5 to 7).
Empty cells may emerge from the phenomenon of right censoring. Because a series of younger birth cohorts do not reach more advanced ages, there are structural zeros in models of union formation. To check whether the diminishing of the number of structural zeros leads to different parameters estimates of the included determinants, parameters of two models in which observations were censored (one model was censored at age 25 and another model at age 27), were estimated. The results of the parameter estimates of these two models did not differ much

Method and data

from the model without this censoring (see Appendix A chapter 3). The model without censoring is preferred because this model uses all the information available, whereas the other two models ignore all information for events occurring after age 25 or 27.

Data organization

The dependent variable in the log rate model is a discrete time version of the *hazard rate*. The discrete hazard rate is estimated by dividing the number of events (*the occurrences*) by the numbers of duration intervals (*the exposures*) in which individuals have been exposed to the risk of the event. For each (monthly) interval, the hazard rate is calculated using data for those individuals who are still at risk. The values of constant and time varying covariates are also assessed for each monthly interval. Monthly hazard rates, in particular, are better suited to the study of cohabitation, because marriage follows cohabitation very quickly. Many cohabiting women marry within one to three years after the start of cohabitation.

Two matrices were composed for each model, one with occurrences and the other with exposures (the number of person-months women are exposed to the event). Those matrices have been used to estimate the discrete hazard rate; that is, the ratio between the number of occurrences and the number of exposures.

In table 1 and 2, an example is given of how the data need to be organized and how an occurrence and exposure matrix can be constructed with these data.

Table 1   Data organisation

months elapsed since event of origin	women, identification number:									
	a		b		c		d		e	
	p=	r=	p=	r=	p=	r=	p=	r=	p=	r=
0	0	0	0	1	0	0	1	1	0	1
1	0	0	0	1	0	0	1	1	0	1
2	0	0	0	1	0	0	1	1	0	1
3	0	0	0	1	0	0	1	1	0	1
4	0	0	0	1	0	0	1	1	0	1
5	0	0	0	1	0	0			0	1
6	0	0			0	0				
7	0	0			0	0				
8	0	0			0	0				
9	1	0								
10	1	0								
11	1	0								
12	1	0								
13	1	0								
14										
Married ?	yes		yes		yes		yes		no	
p= 0: not pregnant, p= 1: pregnant			r= 0: not religious, r= 1: religious								

Table 2 Example of an occurrence and exposure matrix

occurrence matrix			exposure matrix		
	p = 0	p = 1		p = 0	p = 1
r = 0	1	1		18	5
r = 1	1	1		12	5

p = 0: not pregnant, p = 1: pregnant   r = 0: not religious, r = 1: religious

Suppose five women cohabit. They run the risk of marriage. Four of them marry within the period of observation, but one does not (e). The determinants distinguished are whether or not a woman is religious (a constant variable with scores 0 and 1) and whether or not a woman is pregnant (a time varying variable with scores 0 and 1). For every month, the scores of the determinants are checked. Woman 'a' is not religious and not pregnant when she enters cohabitation. At the first duration, one unit (equal to one month) is added to the exposure matrix in cell p=0, r=0 (table 2). No event occurred during this month, thus no event is added to the occurrence matrix. At the next duration, the scores on the variables are again checked and another month is added to the exposure matrix, cell p=0, r=0. At duration 9, no event happens but the woman becomes pregnant. Because of that, the next exposure month is added to another cell of the exposure matrix, namely p=1, r=0. For the next five duration intervals, each time a month is added to the exposure matrix in cell p=1, r=0. At duration 14, she marries. Thus, one event is added at the occurrence matrix in the cell with r=0, p=1. This woman contributed 9 months of exposure to the exposure matrix in the cell with r=0, p=0 and five months of exposure to the cell with r=0 and p=1. This procedure is followed for all the women involved (in this case five). By the end of the observation period, there are four events (one is censored) and 40 months of exposure. Woman 'e' is an example of a woman who did not experience the event during the period of observation. This is an example of how event history treats the information of a censored event. Nothing is added to the occurrence matrix, but the information is added to the exposure matrix. In this case, six months are added to cell p=0, r=1.

The overall monthly hazard rate in this example, in which 4 events were counted and there were 40 (18+12+5+5) exposures, is 0.10 (4 occurrences divided by 40 exposures). The hazard rate for non-religious women, for example, is 0.08 (in the cell r=0, 2 occurrences are counted and there are 23 exposures) and for religious women the hazard rate is 0.12 (2/17). This example was given for a few women only. In the empirical analyses presented in chapters 5 to 7, the number of women was much larger.

Definition of the log rate model
The occurrence and exposure matrices are the input for the log rate model. Above, only two covariates were distinguished (pregnancy and religion). Hereafter, the example will relate to the situation in which duration is distinguished as a third covariate. The unsaturated log rate

model of three variables (religion -j-, pregnancy -k-, and a time variable -i-) plus the interaction effects between religion and pregnancy and duration and pregnancy, can be defined as follows:

$$\ln(m_{ijk}/N_{ijk}) = u + u_1(i) + u_2(j) + u_3(k) + u_{23}(j,k) + u_{13}(i,k)$$

where
m_{ijk}/N_{ijk}	hazard rate
m_{ijk}	expected number of events of women in duration interval i, with category j of religion and category k of pregnancy
N_{ijk}	number of exposures of women in interval i, with category j of religion and category k of pregnancy
u	main effect
$u_1(i), u_2(j), u_3(k)$	main effects of i, j, and k
$u_{23}(j,k), u_{13}(i,k)$	interaction effects of j and k, i and k

Selection procedure

If one wants to know whether or not the proportionality assumption is violated, one can test whether or not an interaction effect is indeed significant. This can be tested by studying the significance of the improvement of the fit of the model by comparing the model with and the model without this interaction effect. Several tests can be used to examine the significant improvement of the fit of the model after controlling for a number of effects (see Hagenaars, 1990). In this study, the conditional L^2 (log likelihoodratio chi-square) test has been used to test the significant improvement of the fit of the model for a number of effects. The object of this testing is to find a model that is on the one hand as parsimonious as possible, but on the other, fits the observation well. The (log) likelihoodratio chi-square is defined as follows:

$$L^2 \quad 2*\Sigma\Sigma\Sigma n_{ijk}*\ln(n_{ijk}/m_{ijk})$$
$$\text{ijk}$$

n   the number of occurrences
m   the number of expected occurrences

If one model contains a subset of parameters from another model, the two are called nested models. Nested models can be compared by subtracting the total L^2 of the first model from the total L^2 of the second model, and by subtracting the degrees of freedom (df) of the first model from those of the second model. The effects to be included are decided on the basis of an improvement in the fit of the model with a significance level of .01 or lower ($p < =0.01$). Thus, by comparing a model with an interaction effect of duration and pregnancy with a model without this effect, it is possible to estimate whether or not this effect gives a significant improvement of the model.

The models were fitted with a computer program using an Iterative Proportional Fitting (IPF) procedure and written by Vermunt. Standard errors of the parameters of the selected models were estimated with another program also written by Vermunt, using a Newton Raphson (NR) algorithm (see Hagenaars, 1990, for a comparison of IPF and NR).

3.3 Data

Event history techniques require data on the timing of events, not only of the dependent, but also of the independent, variables. For this research project, data have been taken from Statistics Netherlands' *the Netherlands Fertility and Family Survey 1988*[1], a sample of nearly six thousand women between the ages 18 to 37 (Statistics Netherlands, 1990d) which is representative of 2,39 million women born in 1950-69, irrespective of their civil status, country of birth, or nationality. It has a stratified sample design in which firstly municipalities, and secondly women (with a minimum of 12 women per municipality) within these municipalities were selected. The sample was weighted for civil status, number of children, and size of municipality (Statistics Netherlands, 1990d). The non-response rate was about 30%. The Netherlands Fertility and Family Survey 1988 contains individual life course data and a large number of individual characteristics. It was particularly important that information on entry into and exit from cohabitation and marriage was included. The questionnaire has several modules, containing questions about the formation and dissolution of households, fertility, birth control, education and employment, and some background characteristics.

The Netherlands Fertility and Family Survey 1988 is an example of a single all-round retrospective survey. Individual event history data gathered in a retrospective manner are subject to memory error (see Keilman, 1993, for a discussion of advantages and disadvantages of different data designs suited for event history analysis). Unpleasant events, such as divorce, or transitions that occur more or less gradually, such as entry into cohabitation as a gradual moving-in process, might be problematic. Another disadvantage of retrospective data is the possibility of the unrepresentative nature of the life courses of the sample studied by comparison with the population as a whole (Keilman, 1993). It is possible that at the time of the interview, individuals who have already experienced the event of interest before the interview were excluded. For example, a woman may have married and migrated to another country, or she may have died. In those cases, these women were excluded from the sample and it is possible that the life courses presented for the remaining women are no longer representative of the life courses of the whole population in the years before the interview. Because the women in the sample of the Netherlands Fertility and Family Survey 1988 are in general very young, the chances that many women were excluded at the time of the interview because of death or

---

[1]This data set could only be analysed at the Bureau itself. From June 1991 to February 1992 Statistics Netherlands offered me the opportunity to examine the data.

migration will not be very high. In addition, it would only affect the representativeness in the case of selective withdrawal.

Despite the disadvantages, a retrospective method of gathering information is the 'best' solution if one wishes to gain insight into the processes of the formation and dissolution of first unions. First of all, entry into and exit from cohabitation can only be studied in surveys, and not in population register data. Of course, it would also be possible to set up a panel. It is, however, practically impossible to follow individuals until they have (possibly) entered into a first union and until the moment of their (possible) break-up. It would mean that a group of individuals would have to be studied over a period of some twenty to thirty years or so. Furthermore, panel data have an additional disadvantage; with every round of interviews, a selective withdrawal of individuals occurs. This disadvantage can, of course, be accounted for by weighting, but this is not always as easy as it might seem (Keilman, 1993).

In the analyses presented here, unweighted data are used. This means that the sample contains somewhat fewer women who have never married (about 5%) compared with the entire population, and somewhat more married women (again, 5%). The younger women, especially those aged 18-22, are also under-represented (3%). Multivariate analyses are generally carried out on unweighted data. To examine the impact of using unweighted rather than weighted data, similar analyses have been applied to both weighted and unweighted data. The results are broadly similar (see Appendix A chapter 3).

For this research project, secondary analyses were undertaken on the data set described above. An advantage of secondary analysis is that no energy or costs have to be put into the preparation of the construction of a data set: a disadvantage is that the data set has not been specifically constructed to answer the research questions directly derived from the researcher's interest. the Netherlands Fertility and Family Survey 1988 only covers, for instance, part of the entire life course of women for specific careers such as education and occupation. Some of the individual characteristics were measured only at the time of interview, but not at earlier moments during the individual life course. Nevertheless, it can be used to study life course patterns if certain assumptions are made. These assumptions will now be discussed.

Coding of the variables
In chapter 2, it was argued that past and current life experiences, in addition to cohort membership, are expected to influence the individual life course. In the analyses presented in chapters 5 to 7, indicators of early life experiences thought to be of importance (see chapters 5 to 7 for an accountability of the choice of these determinants) are: home town, mother's age at childbearing, family size, parental divorce, living in the parental home and religion. Indicators of current life course experiences are educational enrolment, educational achievement, occupational status and pregnancy, first childbirth, number of children, age at which a union was formed, calendar period in which a union was formed, individual age, duration of the union, legal type of the union and number of children.

Parental divorce, living in the parental home, educational enrolment, occupational status, pregnancy, childbirth, number of children, duration of the union, individual age and the type of the union are time-varying covariates. This implies that information about the status of these characteristics must be known at all stages of the life course. The times at which one experiences a transition, or an event, in these statuses (for instance, events such as entry and exit into the labour market) must have been measured. Most events were registered according to the calendar year and month of their occurrence: entry into marriage, entry into cohabitation, divorce, separation of cohabitation, childbirth, parental divorce, birth date of the respondent and the mother of the respondent. However, for events such as leaving school, leaving parental home, entry into a labour market for the first time in life, only the year of occurrence was registered.

In order to estimate age in months at which one left school/got a job/left parental home, it was assumed that on average respondents experience these events in the middle of the year. In addition, because only one school-leaving date is known, the assumption is made that, from that date onwards, women did not re-enter the educational system. Thus, once a woman has left school, she can never enter the status of 'being at school' again. A similar assumption has been made for leaving the parental home, since only one leaving date is known. Women who entered a union within six months of leaving home were recoded to 'living in the parental home' at the time a union was entered. This was done to control for the fact that the assumption of experiencing an event in the middle of the year would lead to over-representation of women living singly at moment of entry. To calculate the age(s) at which women stopped working, some assumptions had to be made. For example, it is not known whether childless women who did not work for the whole period experienced periods of unemployment. It is assumed that they did not, and that when they did leave employment, they never worked again. It is assumed that those women who left employment before the birth of a child did so on the date of birth of the first child and never re-entered employed status. Furthermore, when an individual entered the labour market while still in full-time education, that individual was relabelled as 'being at work' instead of 'being at school'.

Both educational level and religious affiliation were measured only at the time of interview. Both these characteristics, however, vary for individuals during the life course. Educational level will thus be more accurate for women who have left the educational system than for women who are still at school. The empirical chapters take into account the interpretation of the influence of educational level, especially for the youngest cohort (aged 18 to 22 years). Educational attainment (measured at time of interview) has been coded into three categories (see Appendix B chapter 3).

There is evidence that church attendance varies with the legal status of the union. It is, for instance, lower while one cohabits and higher after entry into marriage (Thornton, et al., 1992). Religious denomination will, however, vary less than church attendance. That is the reason for the choice of religious denomination rather than church attendance.

3.4 Summary

Life course patterns are studied with the help of a multivariate event history technique. This technique offers several advantages to the study of life course patterns. First, it can deal with censoring, of the utmost importance to this study. Second, it allows for studying many explanatory variables simultaneously in their influence on union formation and dissolution. Third, the technique can easily deal with time-varying individual characteristics. Multivariate analyses with a loglinear hazard model (denoted as log rate model) are carried out to examine the impact of determinants simultaneously on the hazard rate. For several reasons, the log rate model is preferred to other techniques of hazard analysis. First, because the model does not require an *a priori* assumption of how the hazard varies with time. Second, this model relaxes the assumption of proportionality. Third, it can handle time-varying covariates in a simple manner. Fourth, competing risks (in this case, cohabitation and marriage) can be considered in one analysis. Multivariate analyses have been undertaken with individual data from the Netherlands Fertility and Family Survey 1988 of Statistics Netherlands. This data set contains information on union formation and dissolution and on several past and current life course experiences of nearly six thousand women born between 1950 and 1969.

4 COHORT EXPERIENCES OF WOMEN IN THE NETHERLANDS: UNION FORMATION, UNION DISSOLUTION AND EMANCIPATION

4.1 Introduction

The practice of studying demographic change through the analyses of cross-sectional and aggregate trends in demographic indicators is a long standing demographic tradition. This chapter also describes a number of demographic and related non-demographic trends at the aggregate level, but from a longitudinal point of view. Developments in marriage, union formation, divorce and union dissolution are examined for a series of female birth cohorts for the case of the Netherlands in answer to the first research question.

Research question 1: How have life course patterns in formation and dissolution of first unions changed across birth cohorts?

Long-term social developments were stated earlier to be major forces underlying developments in marriage and divorce (chapter 2). Women's changing position in society, due to their changing earning capacity and bargaining power resulting from their increasing educational and occupational participation, was noted. In addition, developments in fertility are closely linked with changes in marriage and divorce. This chapter also provides a description of female birth cohort patterns in work, education and fertility.

This chapter therefore studies inter-cohort patterns of women's union formation and dissolution as well as inter-cohort trends in women's work, education and fertility to provide a short overview of long-term trends in the Netherlands.

4.2 Cohort patterns in union formation and dissolution

Marriage
Graph 1 shows, from a cross-sectional point of view, the rise in first marriage until the mid-seventies, the decline in first marriages until the beginning of the eighties and a recovery in the eighties, albeit at a much lower level than that of the 1970s.

1. Number of first marriages per thousand unmarried women, per calender year

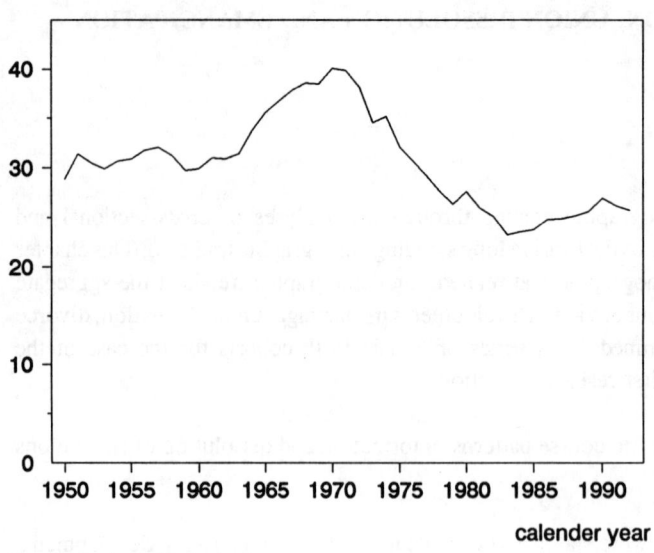

Source: Statistics Netherlands

Graph 2 shows that the rise in the sixties and early seventies is the result of an earlier timing of marriage among women born in the forties and early fifties compared with women born in the thirties.

2. Cumulative proportion of (first) married women at selected ages, by birth cohort, in percentages

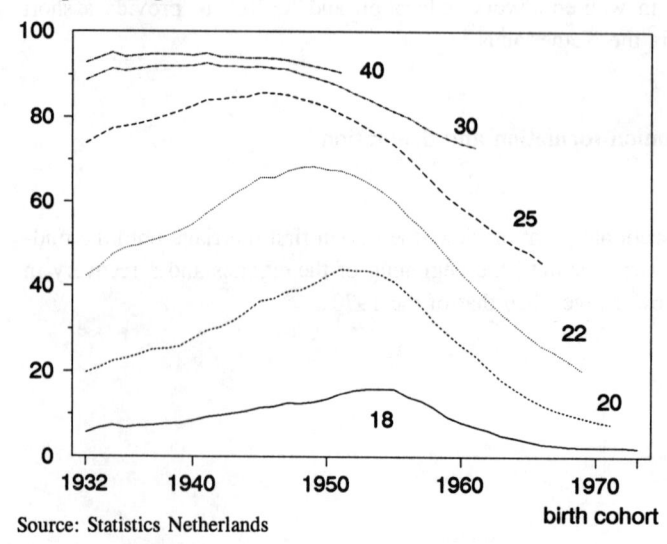

Source: Statistics Netherlands

Slightly more than 20 percent of women born in 1935 had been married by age 20, whereas more than 40 percent of women born in 1950 had been married by that age. The rapid decline in marriage in the seventies and early eighties from a cross-sectional point of view, is the result of a lower inclination of women born in the fifties and the sixties to marry. The proportion of women having married is lower the more recent their birth dates. Approximately one in seven women born in 1965 had been married by age 20. By age 25, at least three quarter of the women born in the late thirties and early forties had been married, whereas approximately half of the women born in the early sixties had been married at that age. All in all, a long-term trend towards early marriage among women born in the thirties and forties was reversed towards later marriage among women born in the late fifties and sixties.

It was previously hypothesised that the decline in marriage would have been offset by an increase in non-married cohabitation. Inter-cohort developments in union formation can be studied by using the Netherlands Fertility and Family Survey 1993 of Statistics Netherlands. This data set contains too few women to present age-specific figures for each year of birth separately. Figures are presented for women in five-year groups instead[1]. To show the degree to which cohabitation has offset marriage, graph 3 shows the proportion of women having married and graph 4 shows the proportion of women who have ever entered a union either by marriage or by cohabitation.

3. **Cumulative proportion of ever married women, by age and birth cohort, in percentages**

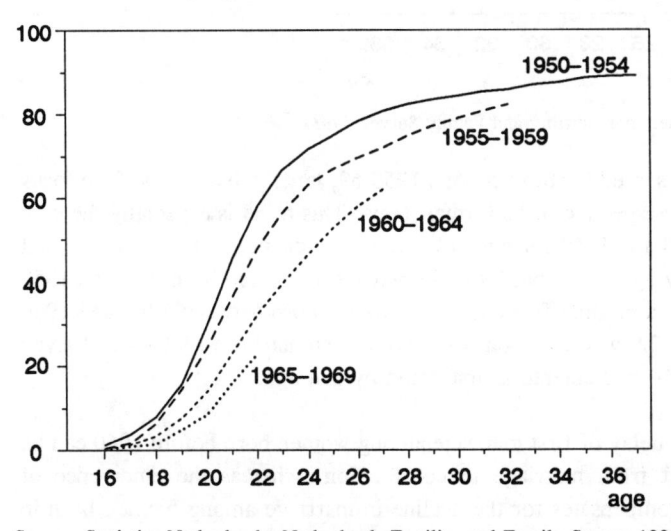

Source: Statistics Netherlands, Netherlands Fertility and Family Survey 1993.

---

[1] In graph 2, 5, 6 and 9 age has been calculated by subtracting year of birth minus 1 from the year in which the event of interest (marriage, divorce or childbirth) minus 1 occurred. In graphs 3,4, 7 and 8, age is equal to the age a woman has in the month at which the event occurred.

In graph 3, the decline in marriage across the cohorts 1950-69 is again visible. If cohabitation is added to these figures, however, it becomes clear that the decline in marriage was almost completely offset by the rise in cohabitation.

4. **Cumulative proportion of women who have ever entered a first union, by age and birth cohort, in percentages**

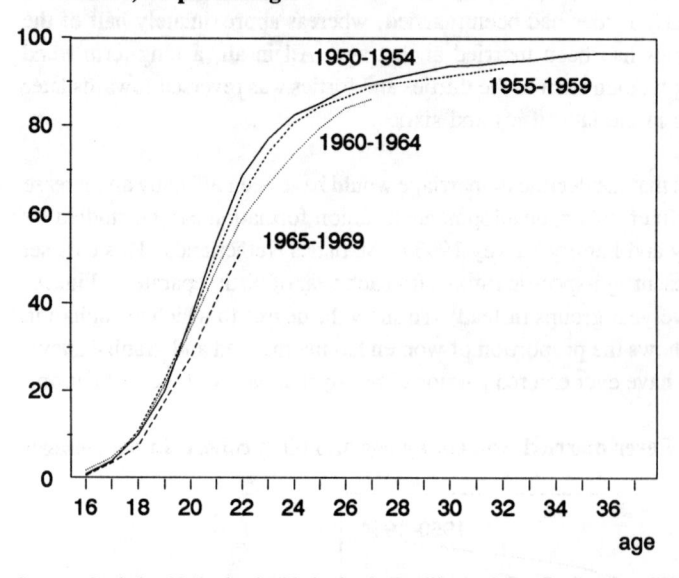

Source: Statistics Netherlands, Netherlands Fertility and Family Survey 1993.

The delay of first marriage, observed for birth cohorts 1950-69, largely disappears if the focus is on the entry into a union, irrespective of its formal status. This trend is especially the case for women born between 1950 and 1959 for whom there was no change in the incidence and timing of union formation. By age 25, about 80 to 85 percent of women born between 1950 and 1964 had entered a first union. Only five out of ten women born between 1965 and 1969 had entered a first union by age 22, whereas about six out of ten women born 1960-64 and seven out of ten women born 1950-54 had entered a first union by that age.

To sum up, it appears that the delay of first marriage among women born before 1960 can be entirely interpreted as a shift from marriage to cohabitation, whereas the emergence of cohabitation no longer fully compensates for the decline in marriage among women born in the sixties, at least at younger ages.

Union dissolution
In the Netherlands, divorce legislation changed in 1971 and the numbers of divorces started to rise (graph 5). They increased rapidly until the mid-eighties and then stabilized at a level of about 28 to 30 thousand per year.

Cohort experiences of women in the Netherlands   61

5. Number of divorces per ten thousand married women, by calendar year

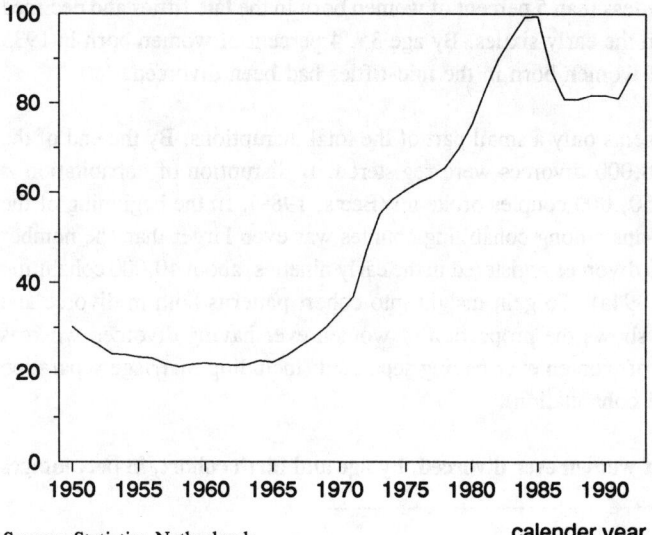

Source: Statistics Netherlands

The trends in divorce are also documented for female birth cohorts 1932-65. Not many women had ever been divorced by age 20 (graph 6).

6. Cumulative proportion of women ever divorced, at selected ages, by birth cohort, in percentages

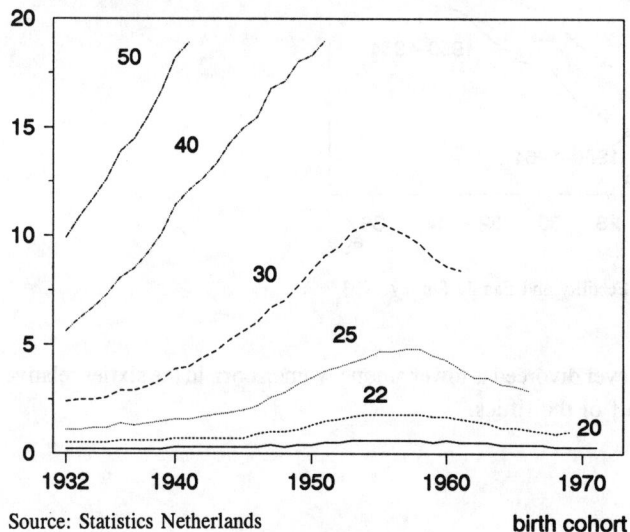

Source: Statistics Netherlands

By age 25, slightly more than 1 percent of women born in 1935 had experienced a divorce. This proportion rose to slightly less than 5 percent of women born in the late fifties and declined to about 3% of women born in the early sixties. By age 35, 4 percent of women born in 1935 as against about 15 percent of women born in the mid-fifties had been divorced.

The number of divorces represents only a small part of the total disruptions. By the end of the eighties for instance, about 28,000 divorces were registered. If disruption of cohabitation is added to these figures, about 50,.000 couples broke up (Beets, 1989). In the beginning of the nineties, the number of break-ups among cohabiting couples was even larger than the number of divorces. Besides the 30,000 divorces registered in the early nineties, about 40,000 cohabiting couples broke up (Manting, 1994a). To gain insight into cohort patterns both in divorce and in union dissolution, graph 7 shows the proportion of women ever having divorced whereas graph 8 shows the proportion of women ever having separated (including marriage separation and disruption of non-married cohabitation).

7. **Cumulative proportion of women ever divorced, by age and birth cohort, in percentages**

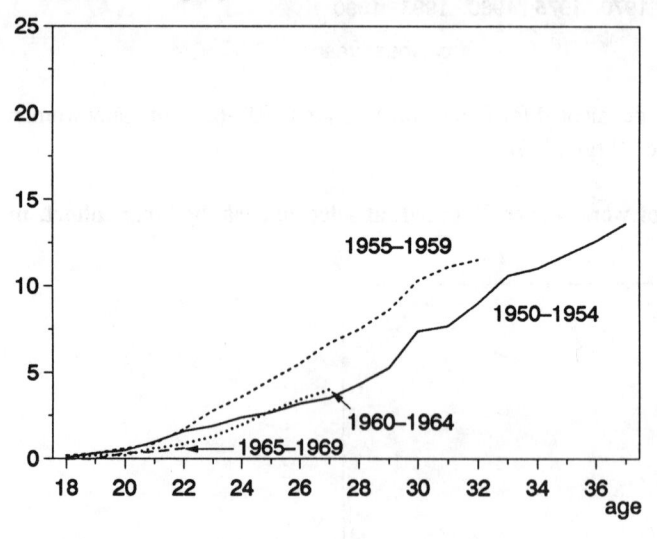

Source: Manting, 1994a, Netherlands Fertility and Family Survey 1993.

The proportion of women having ever divorced is lower among women born in the sixties relative to women born in the second half of the fifties.

8. **Cumulative proportion of women ever separated or divorced, by age and by birth cohort, in percentages**

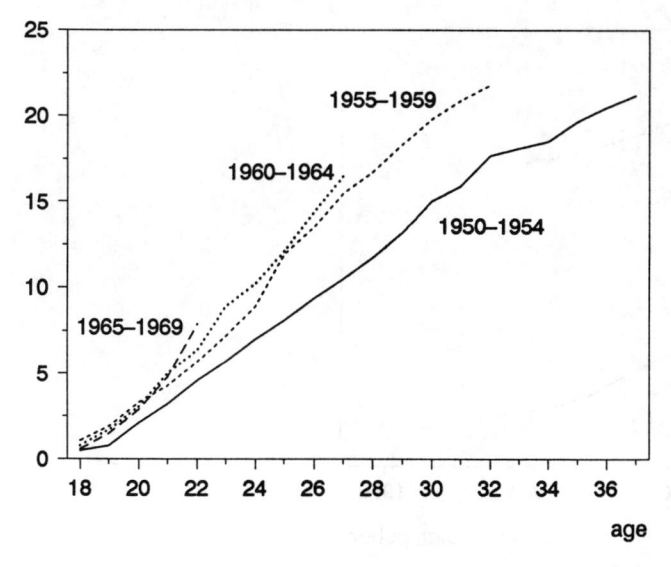

Source: Manting, 1994a, Netherlands Fertility and Family Survey 1993.

However, the proportions of women who have ever broken up increase rapidly across the birth cohorts. Whereas less than 5% of women in the early sixties had ever divorced by age 27, almost one out of six of these women had ever broken up by that age. Almost no women born in the late sixties divorced, but almost one out of twelve women of that cohort had broken up by that age.

All in all, divorce patterns across the cohorts show a non-monotonic pattern. The proportion of women ever having divorced rises for women born in the thirties, forties and fifties but falls for women born in the sixties. On the other hand, the number of women ever having broken up rises across the cohorts.

4.3 Cohort trends in fertility, education and work

Fertility
Developments in fertility are closely linked with marriage patterns. Graph 9 shows the proportion of women giving birth to a first child for selected ages and for the 1935-65 cohorts.

9. **Cumulative proportion of women who have given birth to a first child, at selected ages, by birth cohort, in percentages**

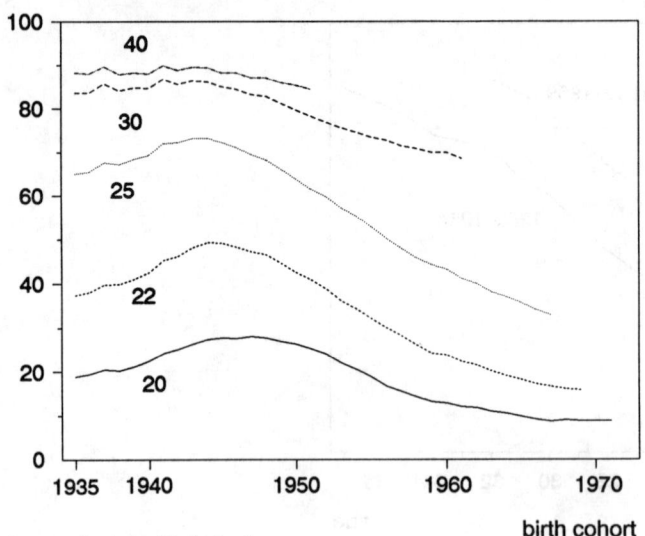

Source: Statistics Netherlands.

The proportion of women giving birth to a first child by age 20 increased from less than 20% (women born in 1935) to more than 25% (women born in the mid-forties). Women born in the fifties and sixties increasingly delayed entry into parenthood. About 10% of women born in the mid-sixties had given birth to a first child by age 20. By age 25, approximately half the women born in the forties had entered parenthood whereas only a third of women born in the early sixties had given birth to a first child.

The shift from early to later marriage occurred among women born in the mid-fifties, whereas the shift from early to later parenthood is discernible among women born in the mid-forties. According to Van de Kaa (1987, 1988), the availability of safe contraception (introduction of the pill in 1965) had much to do with the fact that fertility was postponed before marriage was delayed. At first, safe contraception allowed for an earlier marriage timing, because young couples could avoid births early in married life. An early marriage timing coincident with a later timing of parenthood occurred among women born in the mid-forties. Thereafter, safe contraception, together with long-term societal developments (see chapter 2), led to a shift from marriage to cohabitation, and thus to a postponement of marriage among women born in the mid-fifties and in later years.

Today, it is much more common to delay marriage until children are desired, or until a woman is pregnant. Table 1 shows the proportion of childless women, distinguished for cohabiting women, for married women who cohabited prior to marriage and for women who married without having cohabited before entry into marriage (calculated with the use of the Netherlands Fertility and Family Survey 1988; unweighed figures).

Table 1 Proportion of women (born 1950-69) who have no children, by several duration intervals of the union by legal status of the union (unweighted figures), in percentages

Childless at exactly:	1 year	2 years	4 years	10 years
Cohabiting women	97	94	89	67
Total (857=100%)	74	54	36	4
Married women who cohabited prior to marriage	96	89	66	18
Total (1062=100%)	99	95	81	30
Married women who did not cohabit prior to marriage	83	67	39	8
Total (2483=100%)	97	93	84	47

In this table, union duration is equal to years lived in cohabitation (cohabiting women), years lived in cohabitation plus marriage (married women who cohabited prior to marriage) and years lived in marriage (married women who did not cohabit prior to marriage). The first row shows the percentage of women who were childless at a certain union duration; the second row gives the proportion of women still observed at that duration.

For instance, 74% of the cohabiting women were observed after one year of cohabitation. Of those, 97% were childless at that time. Only a small proportion of the cohabiting women were observed after ten years (4%). The reason is that many cohabiting women marry after some time, many have separated, or are censored (see chapter 3).

Although the interplay has become more complex, this table shows that cohabiting women are more often childless than married women. Exactly four years after a union was entered, 89% of the cohabiting women were childless, whereas 81% of the women who married after a period of cohabitation were childless. Only 39% of the women who entered marriage directly were still childless at that time.

Education
A major factor put forward to explain developments in marriage and divorce over time has been the increase in educational achievement among women, as observed both in increasing educational enrolment and in increasing levels of education (chapter 2). First, education is one of the life domains that may interfere with the development of the union career, since it competes in time and energy or financial obligations. As a consequence, longer educational enrolment at ages

at which a marriage was customary will be accompanied by lower marriage frequencies at those ages.

Figures on educational enrolment are available for the cohorts 1940-64.

10. Proportion of women attending school, by age-group and birth cohort, in percentages

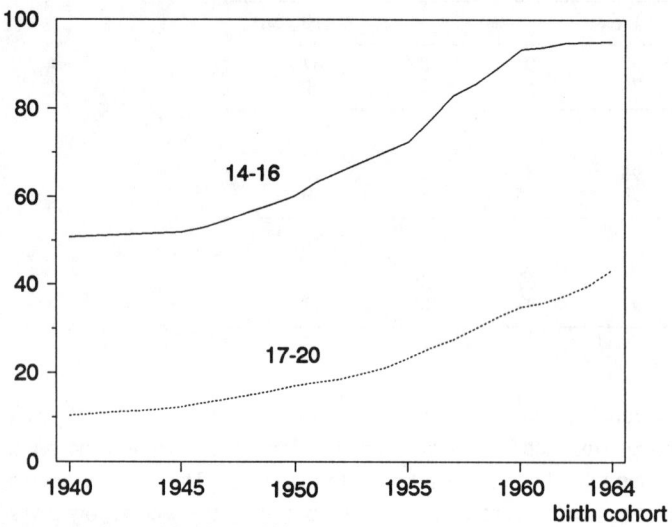

Source: Becker and Sanders, 1993.

Young women's educational enrolment at young ages (ages 14 to 16 and ages 17 to 20) rises steadily across the birth cohorts (graph 10). Educational participation between ages 17 to 20 is four times higher for women born in 1964 than for women born in 1940. About a tenth of women born in the early forties were attending school between the ages of 17 to 20. For women born in the mid-sixties, this figure was more than 40%.

Trends in final educational attainment are available for groups of cohorts born 1925-64.

Table 2 Educational attainment of female birth cohorts 1925-64 in the Netherlands

Educational attainment	1925-34	1935-44	1945-54	1955-64
primary education	42	25	18	12
lower level educational training	20	25	22	16
secondary education	11	11	10	8
medium level vocational training	18	25	29	36
pre-university education	2	2	3	6
high level vocational training	7	11	14	17
university degree	1	2	4	5

Source: De Jong Gierveld & Liefbroer, 1992.

Across the birth cohorts, the proportions of women with primary education only declines from 42% (birth cohorts 1925-34) to 12% (birth cohorts 1955-64). Whereas 7% of women born in 1925-34 have had a higher educational vocational training, 17% of women born in 1955-64 reached such a level. Further, differences between birth cohorts born 1925-54 and birth cohorts 1955-64 will be even larger in the future, since women born in 1955 or later may not have finished their education yet.

Labour force participation

Labour force participation as an indicator of women's independence is also seen as a major factor underlying changes in marriage and divorce. Labour force participation figures are available for women born between 1945 and 1965 (graph 11).

11. Proportion of women at work, by age-group and birth cohort, in percentages

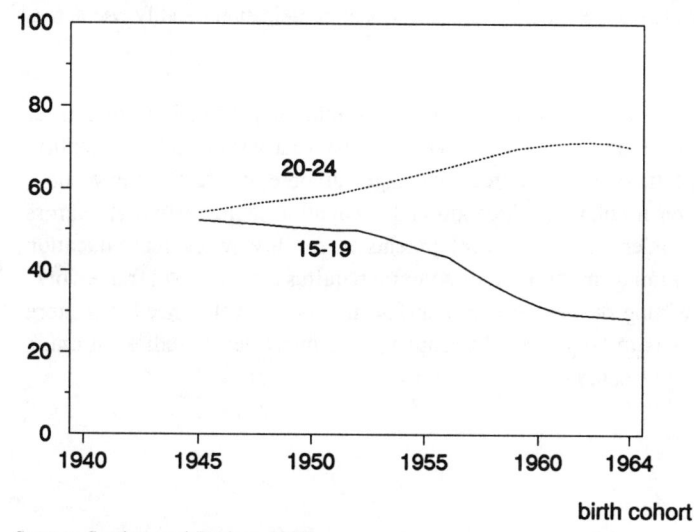

Source: Sanders and Becker, 1993.

Labour force participation declines linearly across the birth cohorts at younger ages (graph 8). About half the women born in 1945 participate in the labour market, whereas only 29% of women born in 1965 do so. This decline is brought about by prolonged school education. Participation in occupational careers increases among the cohorts, when they are in their early twenties. Between ages 20 to 24, participation rates rise from 54% (birth cohort 1945) to 70% (birth cohort 1964).

4.4   Summary

These macro level analyses give insight into long-term developments in several life domains for the Netherlands. Women born in the forties entered first marriage at a relatively young age: women born in the fifties and sixties progressively postponed entry into first marriage. This delay has not been completely offset by a rise in cohabitation.
Women born in the forties and fifties divorced more often than women born in the thirties. The incidence of divorce declined among women born in the sixties. If disruption of cohabitation is added to these figures, however, the likelihood of a disruption of a (non) married union increases rapidly across the cohorts.

Together with these developments, other life domains also changed. The numbers of women who entered parenthood was highest among women born in the mid-forties. Women born in the fifties and sixties progressively delayed entry into parenthood. The proportion of married women giving birth to a first child after several years of marriage is much higher than the proportion of cohabiting women entering parenthood. Whereas the majority of married women gave birth to a child within a few years after the wedding, only a minor proportion of the cohabiting women gave birth to a child.
Educational enrolment, educational achievement and occupational participation steadily rise across the birth cohorts.

The aggregate analyses presented above show that long-term inter-cohort trends in marriage, union formation, divorce and dissolution do not always run parallel with trends in fertility, education and labour force participation. Whereas marriage, divorce and fertility have non-monotonic trends across the birth cohorts, education and occupation increase linearly across the cohorts. Any attempt to understand how developments in fertility, work and education influenced cohort patterns in union formation and dissolution requires a micro level framework. An examination of the intertwining of these life domains at the micro level is needed if more insight into these relationships is to be gained. In chapters 5-7, micro level studies on union formation and dissolution are presented.

5 MOVING INTO A FIRST UNION

5.1 Introduction

Union formation has increasingly become a process of gradually moving-in. In earlier times, most women moved from living with their parents to living with their spouse. Nowadays, the variety of paths that can be followed in establishing a lasting union is large. Women more often live alone for a certain period of time or enter into cohabitation as a first step and marriage as a second step.

In chapter 2 it was hypothesised that both past and current life course experiences determine the route towards a lasting union. Life course experiences are defined as the product of both historical time (the wider context that offers opportunities for and imposes constraints on demographic behaviour) and personal time (the development of life goals by individuals). A general hypothesis is that birth cohorts differ in both the timing of entry into a union and the type of union chosen, because birth cohorts grow up in different historical periods. As a result, early life course experiences and the individual position with respect to various life domains at the moment a union is formed differ between birth cohorts.

Chapter 4 documented the earlier timing of marriage among women born in the forties and the later timing of marriage among women born in the late fifties and early sixties. Postponement of marriage has to a certain degree been compensated by the rise in cohabitation. For most women born in the beginning of the fifties, co-residence coincided with marriage. For only a few women, co-residence coincided with the new option of cohabitation. Women born in the beginning of the sixties grew up in a period of high marital instability. At the time they considered moving into a union, the negative consequences of marriage and divorce had become common knowledge. Presumably, this made them more careful in committing themselves to marriage. As a result, they entered into unions gradually, first through cohabitation, followed, perhaps, by marriage. The emergence of cohabitation did not, however, fully compensate the decline in marriage. For women born at the end of the sixties, the entry into a union by means of cohabitation has become 'a matter of course'. Very few have moved into marriage directly. Living alone for a prolonged period has also become more common among members of this cohort.

If cohabitation has changed from being an act against 'bourgeois' marriage to a strategy of entering into a union gradually (as documented in chapter 2), then the determinants of the process of moving into a union will have changed in meaning with historical time. The analyses below also examine separately the occurrence of cohort changes in the meaning of the determinants of entry into a union, into marriage and into cohabitation.

With the passage of individual time, children become more socially, economically and psychologically independent of their parents. As a result, past life course determinants weaken in strength as time passes. The notion stemming from life course theory, that individual characteristics and positions may have non-constant influences with the passage of time (Runyan, 1984) implies that one should allow for a varying meaning of past and current life course determinants of union formation across personal time. Whether determinants change in meaning with the unfolding of the life course, is also examined.

In short, it is hypothesised that both early life course experiences and the life course position at the moment union formation is considered provide the determinants of both the type and the timing of union formation, and that the role of these determinants changes in meaning across historical and personal time. The test for these hypotheses is summarized in research question two:

How have past and current individual life course experiences influenced first union formation?
- How have they influenced the (timing and type of) entry into a first union?
- Are there signs of a change in impact of these determinants over personal and historical time, and if so, how does the impact change?

In chapter 2, a conceptual framework was presented that guides this study of union formation and dissolution. In this chapter, the relationships between the bordered areas in this conceptual framework (see below) are examined into more detail.

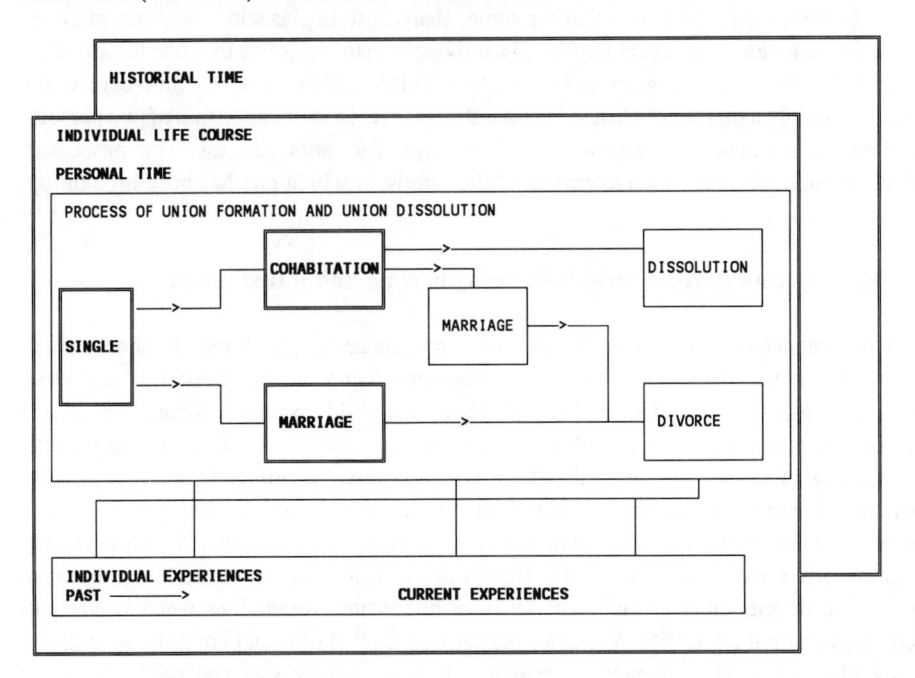

```
┌─────────────────────────────────────────────────────────────┐
│      HISTORICAL TIME                                        │
│  ┌───────────────────────────────────────────────────────┐  │
│  │ INDIVIDUAL LIFE COURSE                                │  │
│  │ PERSONAL TIME                                         │  │
│  │  ┌─────────────────────────────────────────────────┐  │  │
│  │  │ PROCESS OF UNION FORMATION AND UNION DISSOLUTION│  │  │
│  │  │                                                 │  │  │
│  │  │           ┌──────────────┐                      │  │  │
│  │  │           │ COHABITATION │──>──┐  ┌───────────┐ │  │  │
│  │  │      ┌───>└──────────────┘     │  │DISSOLUTION│ │  │  │
│  │  │      │         ┌──────────┐    │  └───────────┘ │  │  │
│  │  │ ┌────────┐     │ MARRIAGE │──>─┘                │  │  │
│  │  │ │ SINGLE │     └──────────┘                     │  │  │
│  │  │ └────────┘                                      │  │  │
│  │  │      │    ┌──────────┐           ┌─────────┐    │  │  │
│  │  │      └───>│ MARRIAGE │────>──────│ DIVORCE │    │  │  │
│  │  │           └──────────┘           └─────────┘    │  │  │
│  │  └─────────────────────────────────────────────────┘  │  │
│  │                                                       │  │
│  │  ┌─────────────────────────────────────────────────┐  │  │
│  │  │ INDIVIDUAL EXPERIENCES                          │  │  │
│  │  │ PAST ─────────>          CURRENT EXPERIENCES    │  │  │
│  │  └─────────────────────────────────────────────────┘  │  │
│  └───────────────────────────────────────────────────────┘  │
└─────────────────────────────────────────────────────────────┘
```

This chapter is organized as follows. It starts with a theoretical background that generates expectations concerning which past and current life course experiences influence first union formation and how they do so (section 2). Following the temporal sequence of the life course of individuals (see also, Bracher et al., 1993; Hoem and Hoem, 1992; Klijzing, 1992), there is a discussion of the role first of the past, and then of more recent experiences. In section 5.2.1 concrete hypotheses concerning effects of past life course experiences that are thought to be of importance for union formation - living in the parental home, parental divorce, religion, family size, age of the respondent's mother and home town - are formulated. Section 5.2.2 discusses elements of the more current life course experiences thought to play a substantive role in union formation: education, work and fertility. Attention then shifts to possible varying meanings of these determinants with personal and with historical time. The empirical part of this chapter first presents empirical evidence of relationships between past life course experiences and union formation, and second, empirical findings of the effects of current life course experiences on union formation.

5.2 Theoretical background

The assumption that marriage has decreasingly become 'the' marker of first union formation (Bumpass, 1990) leads to the notion that for some, shared life begins with entry into marriage but for others with entry into cohabitation. Since living together implies that one has to incorporate the daily life needs and wishes of the partner within one's own to a certain degree, co-residence is certainly a marker of change in commitment level in the relationship of two persons. Entrance into co-residence is a crucial step in the union formation process. This process is, first of all, influenced by the characteristics of the family in which one has been brought up.

5.2.1 Past life course experiences influencing moving into a first union

Children are influenced by family structures, the consequences of which may be short term or long-term, direct or indirect. Economic interpretations focus on the transfer of economic resources from parents to children and the effects on the children's life course. The amount of financial transfer from parents to children is generally indicated by variables such as parental educational level, income, age, marital status and family size. Sociological interpretations of how childhood experiences influence the later life course focus on the mechanisms of socialization, social control, status attainment and parental supervision (Thornton, 1991). Socialization offers children an attitudinal framework of reference through a complex set of processes. The development of an 'own' set of attitudes and orientations when young puts children on a certain track of life. Variables indicating the level of social control, supervision, or quality of parental environment are parental divorce, family size and mother's age at childbearing. There is evidence that innovative behaviour, such as cohabitation, tends to emerge in larger cities (De Feijter, 1991). The home town in which a woman grew up is thus an important measure, too. In the Netherlands, religious denomination has traditionally been a very important factor influencing the later demographic life course.

The discussion below concentrates on aspects that can be examined using the Netherlands Fertility and Family Survey 1988 of Statistics Netherlands: living in the parental home, parental divorce, religion, age of respondent's mother at childbearing, family size and home town. Expectations as to how these determinants influence union formation have been formulated, and a discussion follows as to how these determinants vary in meaning with historical and personal time.

Past life course experiences: *Parental divorce*
The economic interpretation of parental divorce focuses on the financial set back following divorce. The children of divorced parents are likely to have been brought up in more poverty than the children of intact parental families. Many single parent families depend on Social Security (Van Delft et al., 1988). According to Michael and Tuma (1985), who view the relationship between childhood experiences and marriage from an economic viewpoint, unproductive family circumstances lead to early marriage. Parental divorce, as an indicator for

such unproductive environments, lead then to faster marriage. In the opinion of Thornton (1991), children growing up in a one-parent family due to parental divorce are exposed to a lower level of social control and social supervision. They seem to take over adult responsibilities at an earlier age. Because they mature faster than children not experiencing parental divorce, they are more likely to form a union at early ages. Because experiences of the marital break up of their parents make children more reluctant to make a strong commitment, children from divorced parents prefer cohabitation more than children from intact families. From studies in which children have been followed up into their adult years, evidence has been found for long-term effects of parental divorce on children's behaviour (Kiernan & Chase-Lansdale, 1993). These children are more likely to be less well educated, to have lower income levels and to leave home at earlier ages (Kiernan & Chase-Lansdale, 1993). Research in the United States and in Britain shows that such daughters become women who are more likely to cohabit and marry at young ages (Kiernan & Chase-Lansdale, 1993; McLanahan & Bumpass, 1988; Thornton, 1991) and that they more often prefer cohabitation to marriage (Thornton, 1991).

The hypothesis that can be derived from the above is that *daughters of divorced parents have a higher risk of union formation, a higher risk of cohabitation but a lower marriage risk.*

Past life course experiences: *Living in the parental home*
Historically, most women left home to marry. In the past decades however, more and more women have left home to live alone for some while (Mulder and Manting, 1993). The reasons for leaving home to live alone are closely related to the wish to live independently, or are related to factors linked with other life domains, such as education (Mulder and Manting, 1993). Women living alone for some while are thus less inclined to form a union, especially a marital one, than women living at home, either because they wish to live alone, or invest in other time and energy consuming activities, such as education. This hypothesis is one of selectivity. First of all, women who live alone are selective in that they might have a clear preference to autonomy. Living as a single allows young people to be independent and autonomous, free from parental supervision (Goldscheider & Waite, 1987). Secondly, they are selective in that they have the skills to live independently. 'This would weaken the encouragement of marriage based on specialization and the division of labor (Becker, 1981)' (Goldscheider & Waite, 1987: 507-508). Thirdly, they leave home to live alone by necessity for reasons of education. Each of these reasons leads to lower risks of cohabitation and marriage. Another explanation proposed by Liefbroer (1991b) for the higher inclination of women living with their parents to form a union is that parents have more means of influencing the behaviour of children living in the parental home. Since parents presumably favour family life, they are likely to influence their children to form a union, especially a marital one. On the basis of these theories, one would expect women living with their parents to have a higher risk of union formation than women living singly.

On the other hand, one would expect that people living alone would have a better opportunity of forming a union gradually. Because they have a housing unit of their own, they have a better opportunity to move into cohabitation (Liefbroer, 1991b) through the process of gradually moving in, as described by Rindfuss and VandenHeuvel (1990). Women who live alone have a better opportunity to start a union formation by sharing for one or more nights, followed by living together more or less permanently, and finally, by giving up one or both separate housing unit(s). It would therefore seem likely that women living alone would have a higher rate of entering into cohabitation than women living with their parents. Since the period of living alone tends to change people's attitudes towards attaching more value to independence and autonomy (Goldscheider & Waite, 1986) this would be a second motivation to assume that persons who live alone prefer cohabitation more often than marriage.

On the basis of these arguments, the following hypothesis is formulated: *young women living at the parental home run a higher risk of union formation and of marriage, but a lower risk of cohabitation.*

Past life course experiences: *Having a religious denomination*
For a very long time, marriage was the only acceptable form of shared life within Christianity (Liefbroer, 1991b). Although secularization leads to a diminishing role for religion, many studies, in many countries, still report the importance of the religious background of women for entry into marriage (For the Netherlands, Liefbroer, several publications; Manting, 1991; for US, Michael & Tuma, 1995; Haurin, 1992; Thornton, 1991; for Australia, Santow & Bracher, 1993) and for entry into cohabitation (For the Netherlands, Liefbroer, 1991a). Women with a religious affiliation have a more positive attitude towards marriage (Halman, 1991). Moreover, church membership in the Netherlands is very crucial for the way one looks upon primary relationships, sexual permissiveness, voluntary childlessness and other issues related to primary relationships (De Feijter, 1991). Although the interest lies mainly in a division between women with or without a religion, a further distinction in the empirical examination is also made between Roman Catholics and others, because Catholics seems to be much less traditional than Calvinists (Halman, 1991). Liefbroer (1991a) showed that the religious affiliation of parents led to a lower risk of cohabitation among persons born in 1961.

It is expected that *women with a religious affiliation have a higher inclination to form a union and to marry but a lower risk of cohabitation.*

Past life course experiences: *Being brought up in a small family*
The economic interpretation of the number of siblings with whom a child has been brought up is that the more children are present in the parental family, the lower are the material resources. Assuming that parents use their resources to influence their children's life course, family size is seen as an indicator of the amount of money, time and energy parents may give to each child separately (Waite & Spitze, 1981). It is possible that children in a small family may be stimulated more to invest in other life domains, such as education and work, at the expense of early marriage. Moreover, women growing up in smaller families may be brought up in an environment that favours marital and family life less than women growing up in larger families. As a consequence, women from larger families will value marriage most highly (Santow & Bracher, 1993). This type of explanation can also be readily applied to explain that women brought up in smaller families are less likely to form a union and more likely to enter into cohabitation, assuming that women brought up in smaller families have a greater urge for

independence. Studies investigating the relationship between family size and entry into marriage show different empirical results. Sometimes it is found that marriage rates rise with family size (for Australia, Santow & Bracher, 1993; for the US, Michael and Tuma, 1985). On the other hand, Waite and Spitze (for the US, 1981) and Blossfeld and Huinink (1991) found no significant influence of family size on marriage patterns, whereas Marini (for the US, 1985) found a negative impact of family size on the timing of marriage. Despite these empirical findings, the hypothesis elaborating on the above theoretical explanations is followed. The theoretical notions predict *that women who were brought up in a small family have a lower union and marriage rate but a higher rate of cohabitation.*

Past life course experiences: *Having a young mother*
The mother's early childbearing has important effects on the life course of children (Thornton, 1991). The mother's age at childbirth of the respondent serves as an indicator of the 'readiness of the mother for parenthood'. According to Thornton (1991) and Haurin (1992), children of young mothers have fewer social, psychological and economic resources than do children of older mothers and relative deprivation is associated with lower parental home quality. Assuming that a lower parental home quality leads to a higher rate of union formation, children having a young mother are more likely to form a union. Another, more positive explanation, is that young mothers have more positive attitudes towards their daughters' early union formation. It is also possible that, since they are younger, they have more liberal attitudes and they object less to cohabitation than do older mothers.
The hypothesis following from this argument is that *women who have relatively young mothers have a higher risk of union formation and cohabitation, but a lower marriage risk.*

Past life course experiences: *Growing up in a small town*
Growing up in a small town probably means that these women are exposed to a more family-oriented environment. Moreover, a small town offers fewer attractive alternatives (Kobrin & Waite, 1984). New demographic behaviour, such as living as cohabiting couples used to be, began to emerge in large cities (De Feijter, 1991). People living in smaller cities have lagged behind.
It is expected then that *women who grew up in a small city more often form a union or a marriage, but have a lower rate of cohabitation.*

Historical changes in the meaning of past life course experiences to moving into a first union
Individualization and secularization are thought to be important long-term trends influencing union formation (chapter 2). Individualization refers to men and women increasingly striving for independent living, individual self-fulfilment, and establishing one's own personal life. Several types of 'new' demographic behavioural outcomes, such as unmarried cohabitation, sexual intimacy before marriage, having children outside marriage, are phenomena that have become increasingly accepted among all subgroups within the population, whether older and younger. As a result of these long-term trends one would expect factors such as religious affiliation (De Feijter, 1991) or family background would decreasingly influence the individual life course.

Such a conclusion was drawn after studying behaviour that had become mainstream behaviour. The conclusion does not hold for behaviour that has become more exceptional through the years (Latten, 1992). That social differentiation decreases when cohabiting couples are compared with married couples seems to result from the fact that most people cohabit and marry. What would happen if not only mainstream behaviour, but also more deviant options were examined? Recently De Jong Gierveld and Liefbroer (1992), investigating whether this mechanism was present in the case of the relationship between educational attainment and union formation among women born between 1945 and 1959, showed that educational attainment indeed weakens in strength for entry into cohabitation. Is this also the case for other determinants? A recent study in Norway, comparing people born in 1945 with people born in 1960 showed that a few past and current life course determinants influence persons born in 1960 more strongly with regard to marriage, but, regarding cohabitation, they did not influence people born in 1960 any differently from those born in 1945 (Blom, 1992). Is this also the case for the Netherlands, and for women born between 1950 and 1969 as well?

A side effect of individualization and secularization is the occurrence of pluriformity; in addition to the standard options, more deviant options increasingly emerge. Pluriformity means that factors indeed weaken in strength for behaviour that becomes more standard through time, but increase in importance either for options becoming less standard through time, or for new options. Direct entry into marriage (that is to say, entry into marriage without a prior period of cohabitation) is an example of behaviour that has become decreasingly standard across the cohorts (women born between 1950 and 1969) examined in this study; cohabitation is an example of behaviour that has become more standard across these birth cohorts. Hence, it is expected that past life course experiences increasingly affect a selection into marriage, but decreasingly affect a selection into entry into cohabitation.

In Chapter 4 it was shown that more women enter into cohabitation instead of marriage. The majority of women born in the fifties entered a first union by marriage, whereas the majority of women born in the sixties entered a union by cohabitation. Among women born in the fifties, determinants influencing entry into marriage should thus have a similar impact on entry into a union, because entry into a union is mostly equivalent to entry into marriage. Among women born in the sixties, however, determinants influencing entry into cohabitation should have a similar impact on entry into a union, because entry into a union coincides more often with entry into cohabitation. This means that one should expect determinants to change in their effect on union formation across the cohorts, from the effects they have on marriage to the effects they have on cohabitation.

The expectation, to be referred to as the *historical change hypothesis*, is that:
- Past life course experiences influence entry into *marriage directly* less among older birth cohorts but more among more recent birth cohorts.
- Past life course experiences influence entry into *cohabitation* more among older birth cohorts and less among recent birth cohorts.

- Among the earlier cohorts, the effect of past life course experiences on *union formation* is similar to the effects past life course determinants have on direct entry into marriage. Among the later cohorts, the effects on union formation is similar to the effects these determinants have on cohabitation.

A weakening strength of past life course experiences with the passage of individual time
Entry into a union is highly age-specific. Age has a normative, a psychological, a social and a biological component (Papastefanou, 1990) affecting the timing of union formation. As time goes on, individuals mature - biologically and psychologically - and become ready for an intimate sexual relationship with a partner. The transition to marriage and, today, the transition to cohabitation form part of the transition period from youth to adulthood (Blossfeld & Nuthmann, 1990; Marini, 1985; Willekens, 1991). This period represents the movement from economic dependence and participation in the family of origin to economic independence and the establishment of a family of procreation (Marini, 1985). Age has legal implications, as in the coming of age, and the age of consent. Additionally, there is a normative consensus concerning the ideal age of marrying, having children, and other behaviour. People have a sense of behaviour being 'on' and 'off' time.

With age, individuals become more socially, psychologically and economically independent of their parents, and so parental influence on their children's life course declines. Current daily life experiences become more important for entry into a union than past life course experiences. Past life course experiences may set individuals on a certain track of life, but later life course experiences modify earlier ones (Liefbroer, 1991a). That past life course experiences influence the later life course and that the impact of past life course experiences presumably decline because of current experiences are assumptions stemming from life course theory. If age is seen to be a broad indicator of biological, social and economic changes, then the influence of past life course experiences weakens in strength with age.

Therefore, the expectation, to be called the *life course change hypothesis*, is that:
- the influence of past life course experiences on the process of first union formation declines in impact with age.

In the scheme below, all the expectations formulated above have been summarized. The third column indicates the general expected effect of a certain determinant on entry into a first union, entry into marriage or cohabitation. For instance, the expectation is that women living at home have a higher rate of entering into a first union, and a higher rate of marriage, but a lower rate of cohabitation. The fourth column shows the historical change hypothesis for union formation, marriage and cohabitation separately. It is expected, for instance, that living at home differentiates entry into a marriage less among the earlier birth cohorts (+) but more among the later ones (++). And it differentiates entry into cohabitation more among earlier birth cohorts but less among later cohorts (from - to 0). Further, because the impact of living at home among earlier birth cohorts resembles the effect on marriage (+), but among later cohorts it resembles the effect on cohabitation (0), the effect of living at home changes from having a positive (+) to having no substantial influence (0) across the cohorts. The fifth column shows the life course change hypothesis. The expectation is that, for instance, the positive impact of living in the parental home on both union formation and marriage declines (from + to 0) with age.

Scheme 1   Summary of hypotheses: past life course experiences and moving into a first union

		Main expected effect	Historical change hypothesis	Life course change hypothesis
Parents divorced	marriage	-	- -> --	- -> 0
	cohabitation	+	+ -> 0	+ -> 0
	union	+	- -> 0	+ -> 0
Living in parental home	marriage	+	+ -> ++	+ -> 0
	cohabitation	-	- -> 0	- -> 0
	union	+	+ -> 0	+ -> 0
A religious affiliation	marriage	+	+ -> ++	+ -> 0
	cohabitation	-	- -> 0	- -> 0
	union	+	+ -> 0	+ -> 0
Being brought up in a small family	marriage	-	- -> --	- -> 0
	cohabitation	+	+ -> 0	+ -> 0
	union	-	- -> 0	- -> 0
Having a young mother	marriage	-	- -> --	- -> 0
	cohabitation	+	+ -> 0	+ -> 0
	union	+	- -> 0	+ -> 0
Growing up in a small town	marriage	+	+ -> ++	+ -> 0
	cohabitation	-	- -> 0	- -> 0
	union	+	+ -> 0	+ -> 0

Explanation:
A minus sign (-) indicates a lower risk of union formation, marriage or cohabitation.
A positive sign (+) indicates a higher risk of union formation, marriage or cohabitation.
A zero (0) indicates no significant impact on the risk of union formation, marriage or cohabitation.
The arrow indicates a changing meaning across birth cohorts (from cohort 1950-54 to 1965-69) or with age (from 16-18 to 22 and above).

5.2.2 Current life course experiences influencing moving into a first union

In addition to past life course experiences, current life course experiences may influence entry into a union. A major factor put forward to explain changes in union formation is the growing independence of women, to be observed in their longer educational investment, higher educational attainment and higher labour force participation (Blossfeld and Huinink, 1991; Diekmann, 1990; Hoem, 1986; Liefbroer, 1991b, Waite and Spitze, 1981). Individual changes in education and work influence entry into a union. Besides developments in these life domains, changes in the individual fertility domain are also important in union formation. The following section first discusses the expected effects of education, work and fertility on union formation, marriage and cohabitation. Attention is then given to possible variations of these effects with historical and personal time.

Current life course experiences: *Educational enrolment*
Education is a life domain that interferes with the unfolding of the union career, since it competes for the time and energy required in establishing a long-lasting union. Moreover, the increasing educational enrolment of women prolongs the phase of uncertainty about the future. Insecurity about the future causes delay in marriage (Oppenheimer, 1988) and, possibly, delay of cohabitation too. This combination of longer enrolment and later marriage may also be a consequence of the fact that students have less money to spend, less time for a relationship and are less inclined to commit themselves to marriage (Hoem, 1986, page 127). Other explanations of a lower marriage rate among students point to the societal norm that young people still enrolled in education should not marry (Blossfeld and Huinink, 1991, Waite and Spitze, 1981). All these explanations lead to the expectation that women students have a lower union formation rate, both for marriage and for cohabitation, than women not undergoing education. Empirical results in several countries report that women students do indeed have a lower rate of first marriage (Blossfeld and Huinink, 1991, Hoem, 1986, Liefbroer, 1991b) and a lower rate of union formation and cohabitation (Liefbroer, 1991b). It is postulated *that women attending college or university have a lower union, marriage and cohabitation risk.*

Current life course experiences: *Educational achievement*
Education might not only affect union formation through enrolment at a certain time, but also through the level of educational attainment achieved (Blossfeld & Huinink, 1991; Hoem, 1986). Highly educated young adults attach greater value to independence and autonomy than young adults with low educational attainment, so they marry later (Liefbroer, 1991b). The level of education may also be viewed as an indication of attachment to the labour market; the higher the level of education, the higher the attachment to an occupational career and the greater the economic independence of women (Blossfeld and Huinink, 1991). Since high economic independence reduces women's gains from marriage, high levels of education should lead to a lower marriage rate. De Feijter (1991) and Latten (1992) showed that, in the beginning of the seventies, when cohabitation started to emerge, highly educated women tended to cohabit more often than less well educated women. In contrast with these cross-sectional findings, however, several longitudinal studies (Blossfeld and Huinink, 1991, Hoem, 1986, Liefbroer, 1991b) found that the level of education did not significantly delay marital timing, provided that the dynamic measure of the educational status - educational enrolment - was included in the model. This would mean that education influences union formation only temporarily, via enrolment rather than via attainment. Despite the empirical findings of these longitudinal studies, it is believed that educational attainment may have an additional effect by increasing the number of alternatives open to women, even after they have left higher education. Even after controlling for educational enrolment, women with a higher educational level delay entry into parenthood more than women with a lower educational level (Vermunt, 1991) and a higher educational level

might also delay entry into marriage. Therefore, it is expected that *highly educated women have a lower risk of first union formation and of marriage, but a higher risk of cohabitation.*

Current life course experiences: *Labour force participation*
Economic theories postulate that the rising earning power of women lowered the 'gains of marriage' (Becker, 1981). Historically, women gained economic support through marriage (from the husband) whereas men gained support with regard to domestic services (from the wife). The rise in the earning power of women, through increasing education and labour force participation, has disturbed this traditional sexual division of labour, thereby reducing the material advantages to women of marriage. One would thus expect that work leads to a lower inclination to marry, and probably also to a lower inclination to form a union.
Work may have another, indirect, effect on entry into a union, especially a marital one. In the Netherlands, having children generally coincides with leaving the labour market. Working women tend to have a lower rate of first childbirth (Vermunt, 1991). It might therefore also (indirectly) lower the rate of marriage, since having children and entry into marriage are closely intertwined. The expectation should thus be that working women have a lower inclination to marry than women who are not gainfully employed.
Work might also be interpreted as being an indicator for attaching a relatively high value to independence. If working women value independence and autonomy more than women who are not gainfully employed, then working women should be less eager to marry, but more inclined to enter into cohabitation. The expectation is that *working women form a union at a lower rate, that they have a lower marriage risk, but that they enter into cohabitation at a higher rate.*

Current life course experiences: *Fertility*
Apart from developments in women's occupational and educational careers, changes in fertility play a role in marriage, too. Historically, marriage invariably preceded the birth of a child. Although the linkage between marriage and having and rearing children is on the decrease, it is still very close. Because marriage and having children are still strongly linked, it is expected that *pregnant women have a higher risk of union formation, marriage and cohabitation.*

Historical changes in the linkage of current experiences to union formation
As in the influence of past experiences, it is expected that current life course experiences become increasingly important in explaining the differentiation of entry into marriage, whereas they become decreasingly important in explaining the differentiation of entry into cohabitation. De Jong Gierveld and Liefbroer (1992) showed that, for the Netherlands, for women born between 1945 and 1959, the effect of educational attainment indeed weakens in impact on cohabitation, but grows in impact on marriage. Its effect on union formation is expected to change from a positive to a negative impact. The impact of fertility, however, may perhaps be different, given the increasing numbers of women who have children born out of wedlock. Since the linkage between fertility and marriage - although still very strong - is on the decrease, pregnancy may probably have a declining impact on entry into (direct) marriage.

The *historical change hypothesis* postulates that:
- work and education influence entry into *marriage directly* less among older birth cohorts but more among more recent birth cohorts.
- fertility influences entry into marriage directly more among older cohorts than among younger cohorts
- work and education influence entry into *cohabitation* more among older birth cohorts and less among recent birth cohorts.
- among the earlier cohorts, the effects of current life course experiences *on union formation* will be similar to the effects these determinants have on marriage. Among the later cohorts, the effect of current life course experiences on union formation will be similar to the effects these determinants have on cohabitation.

Changing meaning of current life course experiences with the passage of individual time
Recently, researchers have seriously questioned overall abstinence from marriage (e.g. Blossfeld & Huinink, 1991; Oppenheimer, 1988). There are several explanations why marriage, and possibly entry into a union, has been increasingly postponed. First of all, the longer educational enrolment of women extends the period of living without a partner. Since marriage most often occurs after leaving the educational system, increasing educational enrolment has been pointed out as one of the main forces underlying the postponement of marriage. Put simply, the longer one stays in college, the more is marriage delayed (Blossfeld, 1991; Lesthaeghe, 1992). Oppenheimer (1988) challenges the idea that the desire to marry has declined as the result of increased female labour force participation. She is convinced that the greater economic independence of women causes a temporary delay in marriage rather than an overall reduction in the numbers of people marrying. She assumes that, since marriage is no longer a means for women to acquire their financial independence, quality demands for a 'suitable' marriage partner have risen. The result is a more careful and critical search period. A longer search period also means that marriage is concluded at higher ages than ever before. Although she does not neglect the possibility that a side effect of a longer search period is that some women may eventually abstain from marriage, the basic assumption of her search theory is that women progressively delay marriage, but they do not abstain from it.

Another explanation of the marriage delay is that women, confronted with a huge number of options, postpone decisions involving a high level of irreversibility: 'The biographic theory interprets the decline in marriage and fertility rates as the consequence of the attempt to avoid or to delay the risk involved in long-term commitments within biographically relevant choices' (Birg, 1990;147). People increasingly opt for flexibility in the life course in order to avoid crucial life events involving a high level of commitment and a high level of emotional, social and financial costs associated with undoing these commitments (Mulder and Manting, 1993). Marriage involves a higher level of commitment than cohabitation in that it creates legal barriers to divorce. Consequently, marriage is postponed until later in the life course.

If current life course experiences delay entry into a union, entry into marriage or entry into cohabitation, then it may also be the case that current life course experiences initially hampering

a union formation at lower ages stimulate entry into a union at higher ages. Chapter 4 reported that the declining numbers of marriage seemed to be more the result of a delay than an overall decline. A large proportion of unmarried men and women, both younger and older, assume that they will marry at some time in the future (Statistics Netherlands, 1994). If a larger majority eventually form a (marital) union, then it is likely that determinants that initially hamper union formation, stimulate the process at later ages. On the basis of the above, the hypothesis (to be referred to as *catching up*) is that
- work, educational enrolment, as well as educational attainment, hamper a union at earlier ages, but stimulate entry into a union, marriage or cohabitation, at later ages.

The expectations are summarized in the scheme below.

Scheme 2 Summary of hypotheses: Current life course experiences and moving into a first union

		Main expected effect	Historical change hypothesis	Catching up hypothesis
Studying	marriage	-	- -> --	- -> +
	cohabitation	-	- -> 0	- -> +
	union	-	- -> 0	- -> +
High educational level	marriage	-	- -> --	- -> +
	cohabitation	+	+ -> 0	+ -> -
	union	-	- -> 0	- -> +
Employed	marriage	-	- -> --	- -> +
	cohabitation	+	+ -> 0	+ -> -
	union	-	- -> 0	- -> +
Pregnancy	marriage	+	++ -> +	+ -> -
	cohabitation	+	+ -> 0	+ -> -
	union	+	++ -> 0	+ -> -

Explanation: See Scheme 1 (chapter 5).

5.3 Empirical findings of the process of first union formation

This section describes the procedure to eliminate those determinants playing no statistically significant role in union formation. Several multivariate models have been estimated. One contains all relevant past life course determinants; another, all current life course determinants. Furthermore, multivariate models including both past and current life course determinants have been estimated to check whether past life course determinants lose their impact after controlling for more current experiences. Multivariate hazard analyses have been carried out by means of the log rate model (see chapter 3 for a discussion of the advantages and disadvantages).

The dependent variable in the analyses is the hazard rate of first union, further divided into the hazard rate of marriage and the hazard rate of cohabitation. The (monthly) hazard rate of union formation is the rate with which entry into a union occurs within a month, given that it has not occurred previously. An inspection of the age at which a union is formed showed that women do not form a union before age 16 (with the exception of a very few women constrained to form a union at age 16 exactly). The clock, measuring time (in units of months) in the process of first union formation, starts at age 16 and stops at the moment a union is formed (irrespective of its legal status) or, when a union has not (yet) been formed at the moment at which the interview was held (see chapter 3 for an explication). The estimated model is a competing risk model, because single women are at risk of two competing events: cohabitation and marriage. At the moment women enter a first union by marriage, they are no longer exposed to the risk of unmarried cohabitation. Similarly, at the moment women enter a first union by nonmarried cohabitation, they no longer run a risk of entering into their union by marriage. Three quarters of the nearly six thousand women in the sample had formed a first union: three out of ten women entered into cohabitation, four out of ten women married directly. The average duration (starting at age 16) was 6.7 years (cohort 1950-54; 6.5 years (cohort 1955-59); 6.3 years (cohort 1960-64) and 4.2 years for the youngest cohort (1965-69). This is the average observed duration, which is less than the average time for which women live without a partner after the age of 16, because some observations were censored at the time the interview was held.

5.3.1 Methodological procedure

Table 1 shows the coding of the variables, together with the (monthly) hazard rates of entry into a union, entry into marriage and entry into cohabitation of all categories of the covariates. The coding of the variables derives from practical motivations, such as the avoidance of categories with too few observations. For instance, because it was decided to examine cohorts that are relatively young at the time the interview was held (18 to 37 years), the age categories have been divided into 16-18, 19-21 and 22 and above (See chapter 3 for a detailed discussion). No further distinction has been made for ages 22 and above to avoid too many zero observations for the youngest birth cohort (1965-69). More than half of the women born in the fifties had formed a first union before age 22; more than three quarter of these women had entered into a union at age 22. For women born in the sixties, somewhat less than half the women born in 1960-64 and about a quarter of the women born in 1965-69 had entered into a union before age 22. At age 22, about two thirds of women born in 1960-64 had formed a union, in contrast with rather more than a quarter of women born in the late sixties.

Table 1 shows the univariate results. The first column gives the hazard rate of first union formation, the second the hazard rate of cohabitation, and the third the hazard rate of marriage. For instance, the rate of entering into a union at ages 16 up to 18 is 0.0029. The hazard rate of union formation is much higher at ages 22 and above, namely 0.0206.

Table 1 Monthly hazard rates of first union formation, distinguished to union type, time dimensions, past and current life course determinants (univariate results)

	All unions	Cohabitation	Marriage
average	0.0104	0.0045	0.0058
Age t			
1. 16-18	0.0029	0.0014	0.0015
2. 19-20	0.0152	0.0061	0.0091
3. >= 21	0.0206	0.0095	0.0111
Birth cohort			
1. 1950-54	0.0119	0.0031	0.0088
2. 1955-59	0.0119	0.0048	0.0071
3. 1960-64	0.0100	0.0059	0.0041
4. 1965-69	0.0054	0.0039	0.0015
Parents divorced t			
1. no	0.0102	0.0043	0.0059
2. yes	0.0139	0.0100	0.0039
Parental home t			
1. living in parental home	0.0057	0.0018	0.0039
2. living outside parental home	0.0247	0.0128	0.0118
Religion i			
1. no religion	0.0111	0.0071	0.0040
2. roman catholic	0.0099	0.0033	0.0066
3. other religion	0.0102	0.0031	0.0071
Parental size family			
1. <= 2 children	0.0107	0.0043	0.0064
2. > 2 children	0.0094	0.0050	0.0043
Age difference with mother			
1. <= 25	0.0117	0.0058	0.0059
2. > 25	0.0099	0.0041	0.0058
Size of municipality of residence when aged 6 to 16			
1. >= 400,000	0.0112	0.0067	0.0044
2. >= 100,000	0.0104	0.0055	0.0049
3. < 100,000	0.0103	0.0040	0.0062
Educational level i			
1. low	0.0128	0.0044	0.0084
2. middle	0.0096	0.0043	0.0053
3. higher	0.0080	0.0053	0.0027
Occupational status t			
1. unemployed	0.0126	0.0052	0.0074
2. studying	0.0024	0.0018	0.0006
3. employed	0.0153	0.0062	0.0091
Pregnancy (at least three months) t			
1. no	0.0101	0.0045	0.0055
2. yes	0.0379	0.0058	0.0321

t = time-varying covariate, i = situation at time of interview
(the sum of the hazard rate of marriage and cohabitation does not always equals the hazard rate of union formation because of truncation).

These results have to be interpreted with caution, because these calculations have yet to be controlled for other relevant, factors affecting union formation.

Multivariate models

In order to assess the statistical significance of these past life course covariates in the presence of other relevant past life course factors, a *first multivariate model* containing all past life course covariates, birth cohort and age has been estimated. The first objective was to test whether, in accordance with the expectations, these determinants had a significant impact on union formation. All past life course experiences have a significant impact either on entry into a union or on entry into cohabitation or marriage. Appendix chapter 5 shows the results of the tests implemented.

The inclusion of a covariate describing whether women have experienced parental divorce led to a huge number of cells containing no observations at all, since relatively few women have experienced a parental divorce. It was therefore decided to exclude this covariate from the multivariate model. The relationship between parental divorce and union formation is thus limited to that of the univariate results presented in table 1. Table 1 shows that the children of divorced parents have, as expected, a higher union formation rate, a much higher rate of entering into cohabitation, and a lower marriage rate than women from intact families.

Tests on a *second multivariate* model, including birth cohort, age and current life course experiences, namely pregnancy, occupational and educational status, and educational level attainment showed that all these determinants have a significant impact on union formation. An estimation problem arose with pregnancy. Many cells contained no observations at all when the pregnancy covariate was included in the model. This is because only a few women became pregnant while single (chapter 4). Pregnant women have a five times higher rate of marriage than women who are not pregnant. Because of the many zero cells, it was decided to exclude this covariate in further analyses.

Finally, it was expected that current life course experiences are likely to overrule the influence of past life course experiences. Liefbroer (1991a) showed that social background influences the process of first union formation only slightly differently after controlling for more current positions a person may acquire. In order to understand whether the effects of past individual experiences become statistically insignificant after controlling for the current educational and occupational status, several other *multivariate* models containing a few past and current life course determinants simultaneously were estimated. This was to test whether the significant impact of past life course experiences disappears after controlling for more recent experiences. All past life course experiences proved, however, to be significant, before and after controlling for these later life course determinants (see Appendix chapter 5).

Two separate multivariate models are, therefore, presented: one containing all past life course determinants (with the exception of parental divorce); another containing all current life course experiences (with the exception of the covariate describing the pregnancy status).

5.3.2 Empirical findings: past life course determinants influencing moving into a first union

In the previous sections, expectations were formulated with regard to the overall impact of a determinant on union formation as well as expectations with regard to changes in meaning of these determinants with historical and personal time. Before presenting their cohort and age variations, the main impact of these determinants is discussed: on entry into a union, on entry into marriage directly and on entry into cohabitation. Table 2 tabulates parameter estimates of a multivariate model containing main effects of past life course experiences only.

Table 2 Main effects of past life course experiences on first union formation: parameter estimates

Entry into first:		marriage b	exp(b)	cohabitation b	exp(b)	union b	exp(b)
mean		-5.49	0.004	-5.22	0.005	-5.21	0.01
risk	marriage					0.13*	1.14
	cohabitation					-0.13*	0.88
age	16-18	-1.03*	0.36	-0.71*	0.49	-0.91*	0.40
	19-21	0.56*	1.75	0.29*	1.33	0.45*	1.57
	22 or more	0.47*	1.61	0.42*	1.53	0.45*	1.58
birth cohort	1950-54	0.55*	1.74	-0.52*	0.59	0.09*	1.09
	1955-59	0.37*	1.45	-0.08*	0.92	0.10*	1.10
	1960-64	-0.15*	0.86	0.22*	1.25	-0.01	0.99
	1965-69	-0.77*	0.46	0.38*	1.46	-0.17*	0.84
parental home	at home	-0.29*	0.75	-0.80*	0.45	-0.49*	0.61
	not at home	0.29*	1.33	0.80*	2.23	0.49*	1.64
religion	none	-0.34*	0.71	0.43*	1.53	0.02	1.03
	roman catholic	0.16*	1.17	-0.12*	0.89	0.02	1.02
	other	0.18*	1.20	-0.30*	0.74	-0.04	0.96
parental family size	0-1 children	-0.09*	0.92	0.03	1.03	-0.03	0.97
	2 or more children	0.09*	1.09	-0.03	0.97	0.03	1.03
age difference with mother	<= 25	0.12*	1.13	0.21*	1.23	0.16*	1.17
	25 or more	-0.12*	0.88	-0.21*	0.81	-0.16*	0.85
home town	>= 400,000	-0.11*	0.90	0.15*	1.16	0.02	1.02
	>= 100,000	-0.05	0.95	0.04	1.05	-0.01	0.99
	< 100,000	0.16*	1.17	-0.19*	0.82	-0.01	0.99

*: b/se(b) > 1.96

The first column shows the effect of the covariates on entry into a marriage, the second the relative risk (the multiplier with which the hazard of a certain category deviates from the average hazard rate). The negative parameter of age 16-18 (-1.03) means that women at that age have a lower risk of marriage; it is 0.36 (second column) times lower than the average risk of union formation.
The third and fourth columns show parameter estimates and relative risks for entry into cohabitation; the fifth and sixth for entry into a first union.

Starting with *entry into marriage directly*, the first marriage risk is lowest when women are 16 to 18 years old, highest when women are 19 to 21 years old and again lower when women are older than 21 years. The parameter estimates of the marriage risk at ages 21 and above should be interpreted with caution, since they reflect the experiences of women in a large age range (21-37). On the other hand, the multivariate models in which entry into a union was censored after age 25 or after age 27 showed similar parameters (Appendix chapter 3). The similarity of the parameter estimates before and after censoring derives from the fact that so many women have already formed a union at age 22. As expected, rates of marriage decrease across the cohorts. Cohort 1950-54 has a 1.74 times higher risk of marriage than average; cohort 1960-64 has a 0.86 times lower risk of marriage than average. It was expected that a period of independent living would move women away from marriage. In contrast, singles move into marriage faster than women living in the parental home. Perhaps the unexpected finding of singles moving into marriage at so quickly is related to the fact that only the main effect is examined, not the interactions with age. This is discussed in more detail with the presentation of the empirical results testing the life course change hypothesis.
Religion, family size and home town have the hypothesised effects: Religious women have a much higher marriage rate than non-religious women; women brought up in a small family have a somewhat lower risk of marriage than women brought up in a larger family; and finally, women in smaller cities marry at a higher rate than women in larger cities. The higher rate of women brought up in a small family supports the idea that women with more siblings have been brought up in a more family and marriage oriented environment. A marriage rate that is lower the higher the size of the municipality indicates that social and economic alternatives to marriage rise with community size. In contradiction with the expectation that young mothers would favour cohabitation for their children more than marriage (resulting in a relatively low risk of marriage), women with a relatively young mother have a higher marriage risk.

Hazard rates of *entry into cohabitation* rise with age. In accordance with the hypothesis, relative risks of cohabitation increases across the cohorts from 0.59 to 1.46 times higher than average. It was expected that women living independently would move into cohabitation at a much higher rate than women living at home. This is indeed the case. Women living independently have a 2.23 times higher risk than average, while women living in the parental home have a 0.45 times lower risk of cohabitation. Also, in accordance with the hypothesis, it is clear that religious women have a lower risk of cohabitation than women without a religious affiliation. Differences between type of denomination are not very large. Roman Catholics have a 0.89 times lower risk of cohabitation, while women from another denomination have a 0.74 times lower risk of cohabitation. It was expected that women brought up in a small family would be more likely to enter into cohabitation. Although the risk is indeed somewhat higher, the difference is not statistically significant.

The relationship between age of mother and entry into cohabitation is also as expected. Women with a relatively young mother are more likely to enter into cohabitation than those with a relatively older mother. And finally, size of municipality does indeed influence entry into cohabitation according to the hypothesis. Living in a large town leads to a 1.16 times higher risk of entry into cohabitation than average. The results of religion should be interpreted with caution since this variable, although labelled as a determinant of women's past, is measured at the time of interview. It is possible that a few women have changed their religious affiliation during their life course (and, with relevance for this analysis, after entry into a union). On the other hand, analyses of first union formation with another data set including the religion in which one was brought up instead of religion measured at the time of interview revealed similar results in that women brought up in a non-religious environment had a much higher rate of cohabitation and a much lower rate of marriage than women brought up in a religious environment (Manting, 1991).

Finally, the model of *first union formation*, shows that the risk of marriage is somewhat higher (positive parameter of +0.13) than the risk of cohabitation (a negative parameter of -0.13). At early ages, the risk of a union formation is much lower than at later ages. As expected, women born in the sixties had a lower risk of forming a union than women born in the fifties.

The remaining findings for union formation are rather surprising. First of all, in contradiction with the expectation, women living at home have a lower risk of forming a union than women living alone. It was expected that women living independently would value independence and autonomy more than people living at home and that they would thus have a lower risk of union formation. Secondly, religious affiliation has no impact at all on the risk of a union. Non-religious women and women with a religious denomination have similar union rates. Since so many studies have shown that religious people differ in different types of demographic behaviour from non-religious people, this is a remarkable finding. Moreover, the family size in which a woman was brought up seems to have no importance for her inclination to form a union. The expectation was that people brought up in a small family would have less favourable family attitudes resulting in a lower risk of union formation. Finally, the home town in which one grew up does not discriminate entry into a first union, although it was expected that women growing up in larger cities would have a lower rate since new innovative behaviour, such as living alone, was thought to emerge in larger cities.

Having a young mother is the only covariate that has the expected influence. Women with a relatively young mother have a 1.17 times higher risk of union formation than average. The fact that these findings are largely in contradiction with the hypotheses was, at first sight, somewhat surprising. On reflection, however, the explanation is quite simple. Religion does not influence union formation, because it has a positive impact on entry into marriage and a negative impact on cohabitation. The overall result is that religion does not really influence entry into a first union. A similar explanation can be given for home town. Because women who were brought up in a small town have a high rate of marriage but a low rate of entry into cohabitation, home town does not influence union formation. Since some determinants influence entry into cohabitation in the opposite way from that of entry into marriage, their overall impact on union formation disappears. In other words, the overall influence of past life course determinants on union formation is the result of opposite influences on marriage and cohabitation.

In short, findings confirm expectations formulated to explain differentiation with regard to past life course experiences in marriage and cohabitation risks to a large extent. The findings do not, however, confirm the hypothesised effects of these determinants of the process of first union formation as a whole. Before discussing this in detail, the empirical evidence is examined for their possible changes with time.

The scheme below summarizes the findings.

Scheme 3 Summary of findings: Main effects of past life course factors on moving into a first union

		Main expected effect	Main effect: findings
Parents divorced (univariate results)	marriage	-	-
	cohabitation	+	+
	union	+	+
Living in parental home	marriage	+	-
	cohabitation	-	-
	union	+	-
A religious affiliation	marriage	+	+
	cohabitation	-	-
	union	+	0
Being brought up in a small family	marriage	-	-
	cohabitation	+	0
	union	-	0
Having a young mother	marriage	-	+
	cohabitation	+	+
	union	+	+
Growing up in a small town	marriage	+	+
	cohabitation	-	-
	union	+	0

Explanation: See scheme 1 (chapter 5).

Historical change?
If the historical change hypothesis postulating that determinants vary in meaning across the birth cohorts is correct, then the interactions between determinants and birth cohort should differ

significantly. Tests on the multivariate model do indeed show that a number of determinants vary significantly with birth cohort. The results of these tests are given in Appendix chapter 5. Many determinants appear to vary significantly with historical time: not only for union formation (all determinants, except age of mother), but also for the process of marriage and cohabitation separately (all determinants, except age of mother and family size).

It was believed that determinants may change in meaning with historical time, because both marriage and cohabitation changed in meaning. In this section the historical change hypothesis is examined in more detail. Table 3 shows the cohort change of relative risks of marriage for all past life course experiences. These risks are calculated from a multivariate model, controlling for all relevant significant effects (Appendix chapter 5, table 1 and table 3). After controlling for interaction effects, the parameter estimates of the main effects (table 2) of the past life course determinants did not really change.

For the process of entry into marriage directly, the historical change hypothesis postulates that *determinants have an increasing effect on the marriage risk*. If this is so, then relative risks in table 3 will be more equal to 1 among older birth cohorts than among more recent birth cohorts. A relative risk of 1 for a certain birth cohort and for a certain covariate means that members of a specific cohort who belong to a certain category do not differ in the rate of members of that specific cohort who belong to the baseline category. This means that a covariate does not influence the hazard rate.

Table 3   Relative risks of entry into marriage

Birth cohorts:	1950-54	1955-59	1960-64	1965-69
at home relative to not at home	0.5	0.4	0.4	0.2
roman catholic relative to none	1.3	1.6	1.9	4.3
other religion relative to none	1.3	1.5	2.2	12.2
a small family relative to a large family	0.7	0.9	0.8	0.6
having a young mother relative to old mother	1.4	1.4	1.4	1.4
small home town relative to medium	1.5	1.5	0.9	1.7
small home town relative to big	2.0	1.6	0.8	1.1

The marriage risk for women born in 1950-54 living at home is 0.5 times lower than the marriage risks of women of that cohort living independently. For women born later, the differentials between persons living at home or not are larger. For instance, for women born in the first half of the sixties, the marriage risk is 0.4 times lower for people living at home than for those living independently. For women born between 1965-69, differentials between those living either at home or away from home is even larger. This means that living at home increasingly affects entry into marriage and so it supports the historical change thesis.

In accordance with the historical change thesis, differences associated with religion also become larger across the cohorts. Religion matters significantly less among those born in the early fifties than for those born in the early sixties.

Although the effect of family size on marriage varies across the birth cohorts, it only supports the historical change hypothesis for the three youngest cohorts. Women born between 1950 and 1954 into a small family have a 0.7 times lower risk of marriage than women of that cohort born into a larger family. For women born between 1955-69, the effect of family size increases with the cohorts. Since the interaction effect of family size with birth cohort and type of union was insignificant, these findings have to be interpreted with caution. Being brought up in a small family (relative to a larger family) leads to a 0.9 times lower risk of marriage for women born 1955-59, but a 0.6 times lower risk among the youngest cohort.

The effect of the age of the mother remains stable across the cohorts, in contrast with the historical change thesis. Also in contradiction with expectations, living in a small town relative to growing up in large cities decreasingly discriminates entry into marriage (with the exception of the youngest cohort). Members of cohort 1950-54 who grew up in a small town had a 1.5 times higher risk of marriage, while members of cohorts 1960-64 who grew up in a small town have a 0.9 times lower risk of marriage.

In short, the historical change hypothesis is supported for the case of three determinants: living at home, religion and family size (to a certain extent).

The notion that *past life course experiences decreasingly differentiate the process of cohabitation*, since it has become such common behaviour to enter into cohabitation, is supported by only two covariates (table 4).

Table 4 Relative risks of entry into cohabitation

Birth cohorts:	1950-54	1955-59	1960-64	1965-69
at home relative to not at home	0.1	0.1	0.2	0.2
roman catholic relative to none	0.4	0.4	0.6	0.8
other religion relative to none	0.3	0.4	0.5	0.5
small family relative to larger family	0.9	1.2	1.0	0.8
young mother relative to older mother	1.4	1.4	1.4	1.4
small home town relative to medium	0.9	0.8	0.5	0.9
small home town relative to big	1.0	0.8	0.4	0.5

The differences in risk between those living at home and those living independently become smaller, although still quite large. Women born in the fifties have a 0.1 times lower risk of entry into cohabitation when they live at home relative to those not living at home. For women born in the sixties, this figure is 0.2.

Supporting the historical change hypothesis, religion decreasingly discriminates entry into a cohabitation, although differences between women without a religious affiliation and Catholic women are still rather large among the younger cohorts. Roman Catholics have a 0.4 times lower risk of cohabitation among women born 1950-54 (relative to non-religious women) and a 0.8 times lower risk among women born in the sixties.

In contrast with the historical change thesis, the effects of neither family size nor age of mother weaken across the cohorts. Family size does not have a linear cohort change in its impact on cohabitation, whereas the effect of age of mother does not change at all. Finally, home town has the opposite effect of what was expected. Among women born in the early fifties, the size of the town in which one was brought up does not really matter for the risk of cohabitation (relative risks of 0.9 and 1.0) whereas women born in the early sixties and brought up in a small town have a 0.5 times lower risk of cohabitation relative to those who brought up in a town of medium size. In short, only the changing effects of religion and living at home support the historical change thesis.

The historical change hypothesis, specific for the process of first union formation, postulated that *among the earlier cohorts, the effects of past life course experiences on union formation are similar to the effects these determinants have on entering marriage directly. Among the later cohorts, the effects of past life course experiences on union formation are similar to the effects these determinants have on cohabitation.* Empirical evidence testing this hypothesis is presented in table 5.

Table 5   Relative risks of entry into a first union

Birth cohorts:	1950-54	1955-59	1960-64	1965-69
at home relative to not at home	0.2	0.2	0.3	0.2
roman catholic relative to none	0.7	0.8	1.0	1.9
other religion relative to none	0.6	0.8	1.0	2.5
small family relative to larger family	0.8	1.0	0.9	0.7
young mother relative to older mother	1.4	1.4	1.4	1.4
small home town relative to medium	1.2	1.1	0.7	1.3
small home town relative to big	1.4	1.1	0.6	0.8

The union risk for women living at home relative to those who do not live at home does not really change across cohorts. Women living at home have a 0.2 times lower risk of union formation than women living independently. And that remains more or less so, irrespective of year of birth. Its stable impact across the cohorts is the result of two countervailing tendencies. The influence of this determinant on marriage increased but that on cohabitation decreased with birth cohorts.

The effect of religious affiliation changes from a negative via a neutral to a positive effect. The positive impact on the youngest cohort should be interpreted with caution, because of this cohort's relative youth. In the former section, it was made clear that religion had no significant impact on entry into a union. Here we see that this is the result of the changing effect of this covariate across the cohorts. Religion does not have a significant impact for women born between 1960-64, neatly fitting into Liefbroer's (1991a) findings for cohort 1961. But this does not really support the historical hypothesis, which expected a positive impact of religion on the early and a negative impact on the later cohorts. The influence of family size does not have a linear cohort change. Also, the effect of having a young mother does not significantly change across cohorts. The town in which a woman grew up did not matter for entry into a union (table 2): just like having no religion. Growing up in a small town (relative to the three largest Dutch cities) changes from having a positive to a negative effect. Growing up in a small city used to influence entry into a union positively but it has a negative impact among the women born in the sixties.

The findings presented in table 5 show that cohort changes in the impact of past life course determinants on union formation are the result of a shift from marriage to cohabitation. Because the determinants have a differential impact on those two processes, the impact of past life course determinants changes across the cohorts.

All in all, cohort variations are not always as expected. The changing effects of religious affiliation and living at home support the historical change hypothesis for both cohabitation and marriage. Yet, although the evidence does not always support the hypothesis, it supports the general notion that variations across historical time should be taken into account if the dynamics in the processes of union formation are to be understood. For instance, the fact that religion does not matter for union formation is correct - but only for those born in the early sixties. In addition, to conclude that the expectation that the municipality in which one grew up matters for union formation was not supported (table 2), is incorrect once one controls for the changing meaning of this covariate across time. As time goes by, the relationships between the determinants and union formation change. One has then always to be aware of the time dimension in the study of social change, since conclusions drawn with regard to the underlying causes for union formation tend to vary heavily with year of birth. Another time dimension in union formation is ageing. The meaning of ageing for union formation is now discussed.

Past life course experiences: weakening in strength with the passage of personal time?
The 'life course' hypothesis postulates that past life course experiences have a diminishing impact with the passage of personal time. It was expected that many other important individual changes might occur, increasingly overruling the impact of former experiences. Age is an indicator of all these individual changes not controlled for in the analyses above, such as maturation, and biological ageing. One might interpret ageing as a broad indicator of individual life course for which no control has been made. Table 6 shows the relative risks of determinants having a changing impact with age. If the relative risks are closer to 1 in ages 22 and above than ages 16-18, then there is support for the 'life course' hypothesis.

Table 6   Relative risks of entry into marriage

Age:	16-18	19-21	22 +
at home relative to not at home	0.1	0.4	1.0
roman catholic relative to none	1.6	1.9	2.7
other religion relative to none	2.4	2.5	3.2
small family relative to larger family	0.6	0.8	0.9
young mother relative to older mother	1.8	1.3	1.3
small home town relative to medium	1.2	1.3	1.5
small home town relative to big	0.8	1.5	1.9

Support for the life course hypothesis in the process of marriage is found for the three covariates: living at home, family size and having a young mother (table 6). Differentials between those either living at or away from home decrease with age. At ages 16-18, those living at home have a 0.1 times lower risk of marriage than those living independently. At ages 22 and above, the risks of those either living at or away from home are equal. The effects of religion do, however, increase with age. Roman Catholics have a risk 1.6 times higher than non-religious women while relatively young, but a 2.72 times higher risk after age 22. This implies that non-religious women tend to lag behind at early ages, and that this gap becomes larger with age. In accordance with the life course change thesis, family size decreases in impact from 0.6 to 0.9. The effect of the age of the mother also decreases with age. The effect of home town, however, increases with age. Women living in a small town marry more than women living in a medium size municipality at young ages, but even more at later ages.

Table 7 Relative risks of entry into cohabitation

Age:	16-18	19-21	22 +
at home relative to not at home	0.1	0.2	0.4
roman catholic relative to none	0.4	0.4	0.7
other religion relative to none	0.4	0.5	0.5
small family relative to larger family	0.8	1.0	1.1
young mother relative to older mother	1.8	1.3	1.3
small home town relative to medium	0.7	0.7	0.9
small home town relative to big	0.4	0.7	0.9

Support for the life course hypothesis for entry into a cohabitation is to a large extent confirmed. First, the differences between those living at or away from home decrease with age. Second, the differences between religious and non-religious women decrease with age. Furthermore, the effect of the age of the mother decreases with age. Finally, home town decreasingly affects entry into cohabitation. The effect of small family size, however, changes from having a negative to a positive effect.

Table 8 presents the results for the process of overall union formation.

Table 8 Relative risks of entry into a first union

Age:	16-18	19-21	22 +
at home relative to not at home	0.1	0.3	0.6
roman catholic relative to none	0.8	1.0	1.3
other religion relative to none	0.9	1.0	1.3
small family relative to large	0.7	0.9	1.0
young mother relative to older mother	1.8	1.3	1.3
small home town relative to medium	0.9	1.0	1.1
small home town relative to big	0.6	1.0	1.3

In accordance with the life course thesis, several covariates differentiate entry into a union more at early than at later ages: living at home, family size and having a young mother. For instance, living at home at younger ages hampers a union 0.1 times more relative to those living independently at that age. At age 22 and above, women living at home have only a 0.6 times lower union risk. Furthermore, women brought up in a small family have a 0.7 times lower rate of union formation at early ages but a similar rate of union formation at ages 22 and above.

In contrast with the life course thesis, the effect of religion changes from negative to positive. Roman Catholics have a rate of union formation 0.8 times lower at early ages and 1.3 times higher at later ages. The negative sign of the effect of a small home town changes into a positive sign with age.

All in all, the life course hypothesis is supported: the age of the mother, living at home, family size (not for entry into cohabitation), hometown and religion (both for entry into cohabitation only) diminish in impact with age. Before evaluating the consequences of the empirical findings presented here, the empirical findings with regard to the more current life course experiences are presented.

5.3.3 Empirical findings: Current life course experiences influencing moving into a first union

In this section, the influence of education and work on union formation are reviewed. First, the main effect of determinants on union formation, marriage and cohabitation are described. The empirical evidence testing the historical and life course change hypothesis is then presented.

Table 9 shows the parameter estimates of current life course experiences for union formation, marriage and cohabitation, without controlling for relevant interaction effects.

Table 9 Main effects of current life course determinants on first union formation: parameter estimates

Entry into first:		marriage b	exp(b)	cohabitation b	exp(b)	union b	exp(b)
mean		-5.92	0.003	-5.51	0.004	-5.59	0.004
risk	marriage					0.13	1.14
	cohabitation					-0.13	0.88
age	16-18	-1.00*	0.37	-0.97*	0.38	-0.99*	0.37
	19-21	0.47*	1.60	0.28*	1.32	0.39*	1.48
	22 or more	0.53*	1.70	0.70*	2.01	0.60*	1.82
birth cohort	1950-54	0.46*	1.58	-0.56*	0.57	0.02	1.02
	1955-59	0.35*	1.42	-0.04	0.96	0.11*	1.12
	1960-64	-0.11*	0.90	0.25*	1.28	0.02	1.02
	1965-69	-0.70*	0.50	0.36*	1.43	-0.15*	0.86
occupational status	unemployed	0.53*	1.71	0.13*	1.14	0.29*	1.34
	studying	-1.14*	0.32	-0.46*	0.63	-0.71*	0.49
	employed	0.60*	1.82	0.33*	1.39	0.42*	1.52
education	low	0.47*	1.60	-0.01	0.99	0.25*	1.28
	medium	0.09*	1.09	-0.14*	0.87	-0.05	0.95
	high	-0.56*	0.57	0.14*	1.15	-0.20*	0.82

*: b/(se(b)) > 1.96

As expected, students have a much lower rate of marriage, cohabitation and union formation. Their risk of marriage is 0.32 times lower; of cohabitation, 0.63 times lower; and union, 0.49 times lower than average.

In addition, educational attainment influences the processes. Highly educated women have a much lower risk of marriage, a higher rate of cohabitation and a lower union rate. This is in accordance with the expectation that highly educated women attach more value to independence, which presumably leads to a lower inclination to form a union, especially marriage. It was expected that educational attainment would therefore have an effect in addition to educational enrolment. This is indeed so. These findings are, however, in contradiction with findings for Sweden (Hoem, 1986) the Netherlands (Liefbroer, 1991b) and for Germany (for marriage only: Blossfeld & Huinink, 1991). These researchers have found that educational attainment no longer significantly influenced the process of marriage and/or union formation, after controlling for educational enrolment. They concluded that it was enrolment more than achievement that influenced the process of marriage and/or cohabitation. That these studies did not find a significant impact of educational level, after controlling for enrolment, might result from the fact that, in these studies, both educational attainment and educational enrolment were operationalized as time-varying covariates. As such, educational attainment correlates highly with educational enrolment. In this study, educational attainment is measured at the time of interview. The disadvantage is that one might sometimes measure the situation after, and not before, entry into a union. On the other hand, since students have such a low risk of union formation, most women have finished their education before entering into a union.

Since the rise in women's earning capacity is seen as one of the most important forces for the declining attractiveness of marriage, it was expected that working women would have lower rates of marriage. Because working women probably value independence more than unemployed women, it was thought that working women would be more eager to enter into cohabitation. Lower union formation rates, especially marital ones, were expected because work competes with having children; having and wanting children is still an important motivation for marriage.

In contrast with these expectations, working women have an even higher rate of marriage than women who are not gainfully employed (table 9). Not only do working women have a somewhat higher rate of marriage. They also have a higher rate of cohabitation and union formation. These findings do not confirm Becker's expectation (1981) that working women would be less likely to form a marriage. Perhaps working women have a higher rate of marriage because they are more attractive partners than those not gainfully employed.

The findings are summarized below.

Scheme 4 Summary of findings: main effects of current life course experiences on moving into a first union

		Main expected effect	Main effect: findings
Studying	marriage	-	-
	cohabitation	-	-
	union	-	-
High educational level	marriage	-	-
	cohabitation	+	+
	union	-	-
Employed	marriage	-	+
	cohabitation	+	+
	union	-	+
Pregnancy (univariate results)	marriage	+	+
	cohabitation	+	+
	union	+	+

Explanation: See Scheme 1 (chapter 5).

Historical change?

The historical change hypothesis postulates that *current life course experiences increasingly discriminate entry into marriage*. Table 10 shows the relative risks for work and education for each birth cohort. These relative risks are calculated from the parameters of a multivariate model containing all the relevant interactions (see Appendix chapter 5, table 4 and 5). The effects of work and education presented in table 9 did not really change after controlling for these interactions.

Table 10 Relative risks of entry into marriage

Birth cohort:	1950-54	1955-59	1960-64	1965-69
studying relative to employed	0.3	0.2	0.2	0.1
studying relative to unemployed	0.3	0.2	0.2	0.1
employed relative to unemployed	1.0	1.0	1.2	1.0
high education relative to low	0.2	0.3	0.2	0.4
high education relative to medium	0.6	0.7	0.5	1.3

The historical change hypothesis postulating that direct entry into marriage becomes increasingly differentiated among the more recent cohorts is only supported for students relative to working women (table 11). Compared with working women, students have a 0.3 times lower risk of marriage among women born in the early fifties and a 0.1 times lower risk of marriage among women born in the end of the sixties.

Work relative to unemployment does not, however, change in meaning. What is more, once one controls for other relevant interaction effects as well, the positive impact of work on union formation disappears. This may seem strange, but, as we see when the life course hypothesis is examined, the explanation is simple.

The evidence with regard to educational level is also inconsistent with the hypothesis. Differences between higher and lower educated women become smaller, instead of larger. Differences in marriage rate between women with a relatively high and an average education does not change in meaning linearly across the cohorts.

The historical change hypothesis postulates that the effect of current life course determinants decreasingly influences entry into cohabitation.

Table 11   Relative risks of entry into cohabitation

Birth cohort:	1950-54	1955-59	1960-64	1965-69
studying relative to employed	0.8	0.5	0.5	0.4
studying relative to unemployed	0.8	0.6	0.6	0.4
employed relative to unemployed	1.1	1.1	1.2	1.0
high education relative to low	2.4	1.7	1.3	0.8
high education relative to medium	1.7	1.4	1.2	0.8

The hypothesis is largely supported for educational attainment, but not for being a student, nor for being in work (table 11). First of all, the differentials between working and studying women increase instead of decrease. Students of cohort 1950-54 have a 0.8 times lower rate of cohabitation than working women, but students of cohort 1960-64 have a 0.4 times lower rate. The cohort change is thus the opposite from that expected.

The differences between working and unemployed women are absent and this remains so, irrespective of the year of birth. The historical change hypothesis is not supported.

More highly educated women of cohort 1950-54 had a 2.4 times higher risk of cohabitation than less well educated members of this cohort; more highly educated women of birth cohort 1960-64 have only a 1.3 times higher risk of cohabitation than less well educated members of that cohort. This is in line with the historical change hypothesis.

Finally, the empirical findings of cohorts changes in the impact of current life course determinants on entry into a union are presented in table 12.

Table 12 Relative risks of entry into a first union

Birth cohort:	1950-54	1955-59	1960-64	1965-69
studying relative to employed	0.5	0.3	0.3	0.2
studying relative to unemployed	0.5	0.3	0.3	0.2
employed relative to unemployed	1.0	1.1	1.2	1.0
high education relative to low	0.7	0.6	0.3	0.4
high education relative to medium	1.0	0.9	0.6	1.1

Because the effect of being a student becomes increasingly important across the cohorts both for entry into marriage and cohabitation, it is not surprising that students, relative to working women, increasingly abstain from entering into a union. Students of cohort 1950-54 have a 0.5 times lower risk than those at work, while students of cohort 1960-64 have a 0.2 times lower rate of entering into a union. Once again, work, relative to unemployment, does not change in effect over time. Working women have a risk as high as women not gainfully employed. This is not only the case for women born in 1950-54, but also for women born in 1965-69.

The differences between educational levels become larger, too. Highly educated women born in 1950-54 have a 0.7 times lower risk of union formation than less well educated members of that birth cohort, while highly educated women of cohort 1960-64 have a 0.3 times lower risk of union formation than less well educated members of cohort 1960-64.

All in all, there is certainly support for the notion that factors change in meaning across historical time. The change is not however always in line with the expected direction in which the impact of determinants was thought to develop over time.

Current life course experiences: catching up?

The 'catching up' hypothesis postulated that determinants initially hampering marriage eventually stimulate it. If this is the case, the relative risks (comparing one category with another category within a covariate) should change from below 1 to more than 1 (table 13).

Table 13 Relative risks of entry into marriage

Age:	16-18	19-21	22 +
studying relative to employed	0.2	0.2	0.3
studying relative to unemployed	0.1	0.2	0.5
employed relative to unemployed	0.7	1.2	1.6
high education relative to low	0.1	0.3	0.4
high education relative to medium	0.6	0.7	0.9

Students have a 0.2 times lower risk of marriage than working women. At ages 22 and above, their marriage rate is still 0.3 times lower. Although differentials become smaller with age, students still have a much lower rate at older ages, in contrast with the life course change hypothesis.

Working women relative to unemployed women have a lower rate of marriage at younger ages, but a higher rate of marriage at older ages.

Although differences between educational level decline with age, more highly educated women do not really catch up at later ages. Compared with women of a lower educational level, more highly educated women have a 0.1 times lower marriage rate at younger ages, but they still have a (0.4 times) lower rate at older ages.

Table 14   Relative risks of entry into cohabitation

Age:	16-18	19-21	22 +
studying relative to employed	0.4	0.4	0.8
studying relative to unemployed	0.3	0.5	1.3
employed relative to unemployed	0.7	1.2	1.6
high education relative to low	0.5	1.1	1.5
high education relative to medium	0.9	1.1	1.4

Developments in the relationships of work, study and educational attainment are more or less similar to those described above. However, differentials in risks are much lower than observed for the two processes described above. Differences between the risks of cohabitation for working women and students almost disappears by age 22 and more. Working women have a lower rate of cohabitation at early ages, and a higher rate at later ages. Once again, this supports the life course hypothesis. In this case, changes in the effect of educational level also support the life course hypothesis. More highly educated women have a lower rate of cohabitation at younger ages, but a higher rate of cohabitation at older ages.

Table 15   Relative risks of entry into a first union

Age:	16-18	19-21	22 +
studying relative to employed	0.2	0.3	0.5
studying relative to unemployed	0.2	0.3	0.8
employed relative to unemployed	0.7	1.2	1.6
high education relative to low	0.3	0.6	0.8
high education relative to medium	0.7	0.9	1.1

Students postpone entry into a union much more at younger ages. At older ages, students still have a lower inclination to form a union, but their rate resembles the rate of working women more closely. The differences between students and working women become smaller with the unfolding of the life course.

Highly educated women tend to postpone entry into a union more than the less well educated. At older ages, the impact of higher education, relative to women with an average level of education, is positive. Thus, for higher education relative to average levels of education, the catching up hypothesis is, to a certain extent, supported.

Previously, it became clear that work stimulates entry into a union. After controlling for the relevant interaction effects, work does not have a significant cohort change in impact on union formation. Here we see that that is the result of controlling for the interaction of work and age. Working women generally have a higher rate of union formation, but not so much at younger ages. While young, working women postpone entry into a union much more than women who are not gainfully employed. In accordance with the hypothesis, work hampers a union at lower ages, but stimulates it at later ages.

All in all, some support is found for the life course hypothesis that determinants change from having a positive to having a negative impact on union formation.

5.4   Summary

The analyses presented above show that past life course experiences are important for entry into marriage directly, entry into cohabitation and entry into a first union.

Having experienced parental divorce, living with parents, having a religious affiliation, being brought up in a small family, having a young mother and growing up in a municipality of a certain size are all factors exerting an important influence on entry into cohabitation and marriage. If the impact on entry into marriage is a positive one, then the impact on entry into cohabitation is generally a negative one (with the exception of the age of the mother and living at home). The effects of most of these influences were as expected, although living at home and the age of the mother proved to be exceptions. It was expected that singles would move into marriage at a much lower rate than women living at home, but the reverse proved to be the case.

If daughters have a relatively young mother, which means that their mothers formed a union at a relatively young age, then they also have a higher rate of cohabitation and of marriage.

Because of the differential impact of past life course determinants on cohabitation and marriage, past life course determinants (religion, family size and home town) do not always influence entry into a union as such. In addition, further inspection showed that religion and home town had no significant impact on union formation, because the effect of religion and growing up in a small town changes from positive to negative over the cohorts. In general, there was much support for the notion that the factors vary in meaning, although change was not always in the hypothesised direction. It was expected that past life course determinants would affect direct entry into marriage increasingly and into cohabitation decreasingly. This was indeed so for the covariates living in the parental home, religious affiliation, family size (only for entry into marriage), but not for home town or the age of the mother.

The life course hypothesis postulated that past life course determinants had a decreasing influence with personal time. This is indeed the case for many determinants: living at home, brought up in a small family (with the exception of cohabitation), having a young mother, and, only for cohabitation, home town and religion. The findings are summarized below.

Scheme 5 Summary of findings: past life course experiences influencing moving into a first union

		Main expected effect	Main effect: findings	Historical change hypothesis	Historical change: findings	Life course change hypothesis	Life course change: findings
Parents divorced	marriage	-	-	- -> --	x	- -> 0	x
	cohabitation	+	+	+ -> 0	x	+ -> 0	x
	union	+	+	- -> 0	x	+ -> 0	x
Living in parental home	marriage	+	-	+ -> ++	- -> --	+ -> 0	- -> 0
	cohabitation	-	-	- -> 0	-- -> -	- -> 0	-- -> -
	union	+	-	+ -> 0	- -> -	+ -> 0	-- -> -
A religious affiliation	marriage	+	+	+ -> ++	+ -> ++	+ -> 0	+ -> ++
	cohabitation	-	-	- -> 0	-- -> -	- -> 0	-- -> -
	union	+	0	+ -> 0	- -> +	+ -> 0	+ -> ++
Small family size	marriage	-	-	- -> --	- -> --	- -> 0	-- -> -
	cohabitation	+	+	+ -> 0	- -> -	+ -> 0	- -> +
	union	-	0	- -> 0	- -> -	- -> 0	- -> 0
Having mother under 25	marriage	-	+	- -> --	+ -> +	- -> 0	++ -> +
	cohabitation	+	+	+ -> 0	+ -> +	+ -> 0	++ -> +
	union	+	+	- -> 0	+ -> +	+ -> 0	++ -> +
Living in small town	marriage	+	+	+ -> ++	+ -> 0	+ -> 0	+ -> ++
	cohabitation	-	-	- -> 0	- -> --	- -> 0	-- -> -
	union	+	0	+ -> 0	+ -> -	+ -> 0	- -> +

Explanation: See scheme 1 (chapter 5).
no observation: x

Current life course experiences also play an important role in the direct entry into marriage and entry into cohabitation. For current life course experiences, a positive impact on marriage also means a positive impact on cohabitation (with the exception of educational level). This is the opposite from what was found for the relationship between past life course determinants. Pregnant women have a much higher rate of marriage, cohabitation and union formation. Students are not only less likely to marry, they are also less likely to enter into cohabitation. They are in any case less likely to form a union. Working women, relative to women who are not gainfully employed, have a higher rate of marriage, but also a higher rate of cohabitation. Work stimulates entry into a union. Educational attainment proves to be an exception. A higher level of education stimulates entry into cohabitation, but hampers entry into marriage. Because the effect of higher education on marriage is much greater than its impact on cohabitation, it leads to a much lower rate of union formation.

Some of these relationships vary with historical time, although work proves to be an exception, because the impact of work remains stable across the cohorts. The negative impact of being a student on marriage, cohabitation and union formation increases across the cohorts. The changing effect of educational level supports the historical change hypothesis for entry into cohabitation: the effect decreases. In general, the varying meaning of current life course experiences does not support the historical change thesis. The catching up hypothesis is supported by the empirical findings for the case of work, since it hampers entry at early ages and stimulates entry at later ages. This hypothesis is also supported for the case of educational level (for cohabitation only), but not for the case of study. The findings are summarized below.

Scheme 6 Summary of findings: Current life course experiences influencing moving into a first union

		Main expected effect	Main effect: findings	Historical change hypothesis	Historical change: findings	Life course change hypothesis	Life course change: findings
Studying	marriage	-	-	- -> --	- -> --	- -> +	-- -> -
	cohabitation	-	-	- -> 0	- -> --	- -> +	-- -> -
	union	-	-	- -> 0	- -> --	- -> +	-- -> -
High educational level	marriage	-	-	- -> --	-- -> -	- -> +	-- -> -
	cohabitation	+	+	+ -> 0	+ -> 0	+ -> -	- -> +
	union	-	-	- -> 0	- -> --	- -> +	-- -> -
Employed	marriage	-	+	- -> --	0 -> 0	- -> +	- -> +
	cohabitation	+	+	+ -> 0	0 -> 0	+ -> -	- -> +
	union	-	+	- -> 0	0 -> 0	- -> +	- -> +
Pregnancy (univariate results only)	marriage	+	+	++ -> +	x	+ -> -	x
	cohabitation	+	+	+ -> 0	x	+ -> -	x
	union	+	+	+ -> 0	x	+ -> -	x

Explanation: See scheme 1 (chapter 5).
no observation: x

5.5 Evaluation

The analyses reported here shed light on the process of moving into a first union. As anticipated, past and current life course experiences strongly influence moving into a cohabitation and marriage. For a few determinants, a positive impact of past life course determinants on entry into cohabitation means a negative impact on entry into marriage. As a result, these determinants do not always influence the process of total union formation.

The process of moving into a union has been observed for women born between 1950 and 1969. Entry into a first union is progressively lower across the cohorts, at least at younger ages. Women born in the sixties have a lower rate of union formation than women born in the fifties. During the period in which these women grew up, a shift occurred within the process of union formation. It became less standard to form a union by marriage and more standard to enter it by cohabitation. As a result of this shift from marriage to cohabitation, determinants vary highly in their impact on union formation across the cohorts. If one had studied these processes for women born between 1960 and 1964 only, one could have concluded that religion has no important impact on union formation. If only the women born 1955-59 had been studied, it would have been concluded that home town and family size do not affect the process of union formation. And, had just the women born in the first half of the fifties been studied, one would have concluded that religion and a large size of the municipality in which one grows up had, a negative impact on union formation. The empirical findings for the youngest cohort (1965-69) must be interpreted with caution, since only a quarter of them has ever formed a union. These findings support the notion, stemming from life course theory, that an individual life course is embedded in a historical context. To gain insight into the process of union formation, one must be aware of the historical context in which social behaviour is studied. Yet, although empirical findings were supportive for the general notion that determinants vary in meaning with historical time, it did not always support the hypothesised change in the direction postulated in the historical change thesis.

The relationship between past life course determinants and moving into a union is not only historic-specific, it also varies with a woman's age. A distinction is drawn between age categories 16 to 18, 19 to 21 (the ages when most women form a union) and ages 22 and above. The last category covers a broad age range, but it should be borne in mind that almost three quarters of the women had entered a union by the age of 23. This study cannot however trace the process of union formation for all women. At younger ages, several past life course determinants exert much more influence on entry into marriage, cohabitation or entry into a union, than at later ages. Although past life course determinants influence these processes even after controlling for more recent current life course experiences, they diminish in impact with age. These findings support another notion stemming from the life course theory that stipulates that past life course experiences are increasingly mediated by more current experiences. In this case, past life course determinants were not greatly mediated by the more current experiences examined in this study.

Yet, as women grew older, the impact of past life course determinants decreased with age, which supported the life course change thesis.

In contrast with past life course determinants, current life course determinants not only affect entry into marriage and cohabitation to a high degree, but also entry into a union. This is mainly caused by the fact that, if a current life course determinant has a negative impact on marriage, it also has a negative impact on cohabitation. As a result, it has a negative impact on union formation as a whole. It is generally thought that women's increasing female economic independence has influenced a number of demographic developments, including the declining attractiveness of marriage (Becker, 1981). This expectation that their growing economic independence leads to women's lower rates of marriage, has not been confirmed. Recently, this notion has been called in question. Oppenheimer, for instance, argues that increasing economic independence has led to a delay of marriage rather than an overall decline. Results show that this notion is supported in that work hampers marriage, cohabitation and union formation at younger ages, but stimulates it at later ages. Oppenheimer's (1988) explanation for the positive impact of having a job on marital timing might thus be better suited than Becker's (1981) explanation. Oppenheimer suggests that 'Young people's uncertainty about what kind of work they will be engaged in during their mature adult years makes it difficult to estimate what long-run socioeconomic position accompanies any potential match' (Oppenheimer, 1988: 573). Having a stable work career reduces the uncertainties of the traits of the potential mate and leads to an earlier timing of marriage. Another explanation of a positive link between work and marriage is the fact that a stable financial situation has often been considered to be a prerequisite for marriage. Perhaps working women marry at a higher rate because they feel more settled than students. A strategy towards settling down should be followed more by working women than by students. Working women are presumably more ready to make long-term commitments, such as marriage, than women still enrolled in education.

Students are more likely to follow a strategy towards retaining flexibility (Mulder & Manting, 1993). Presumably, they place a high value on keeping options open and postpone decisions involving a high level of commitment. Marriage involves a higher level of commitment than cohabitation in that it creates legal barriers to union disruption. Students are indeed more likely to delay entry into cohabitation and, especially, entry into marriage.

After controlling for age, work does not really influence entry into a union. The impact of work did not change across the cohorts. This does not support the historical change thesis.

Linked with the rise in labour force participation is the longer investment in education. Longer educational enrolment is a prerequisite for labour force participation. The findings presented in this chapter show that it is more educational enrolment than labour force participation that has stimulated the declining attractiveness of marriage. Students have been increasingly less likely to enter into marriage or cohabitation. A longer investment in education has surely influenced the postponement of union formation. In addition to educational enrolment, educational achievement also affects the processes. Highly educated women have a lower rate of entering into a union and a lower rate of marriage, but a higher rate of cohabitation.

Differences between students and non students tend to decrease with age. Students are less likely to form a union when they are young. In addition, women who have left the educational system, are much more likely to enter into a union, marriage or cohabitation. This is also evident for the case of educational attainment. The negative effect of educational attainment is especially strong at early ages, but less so at later ages. Once again, educational achievement is important for explaining differentiation in union formation, but differences become smaller as a woman grows older. These findings suggest that students and women with a higher level of education have not (yet) caught up when they grow older. The negative impact of work at younger ages changes into a positive impact at later ages. The empirical finding of work supports the catching up thesis.

6 MOVING INTO MARRIAGE DURING THE PERIOD OF COHABITATION

6.1 Introduction

For many women, household formation is characterized by two transitions. The first in the process of union formation is entry into a union. This process was studied in the previous chapter. The second is the entry into subsequent marriage. This chapter concentrates on the latter.

Many young people foresee a period of cohabitation, possibly followed by marriage. Cohabitation is most often a short-term living arrangement. For cohabiting women, marriage may either be a matter of convenience, motivated by the wish to have children, or practical or financial reasons, or it may be a passage of confirmation (Trost, 1979).

In the past decade, cohabitation has become a widespread phenomenon. At the beginning of the 1990s, there were almost half a million cohabiting couples (Statistics Netherlands, 1994). With time, the normative pressure to marry soon after cohabitation has diminished. Along with the rise in cohabitation, there has been a trend towards greater equality in terms of the obligations and rights of cohabiting couples relative to married ones. These tendencies might have diminished the necessity to marry soon after entry into cohabitation. As a consequence, underlying forces leading to marriage after a period of cohabitation must have changed over time. Comparatively little is known about the underlying structures motivating the marriage of cohabiting couples. Moreover, little attention has been given to historical changes in the meaning of these underlying determinants. This chapter sheds light on the changing causal structures underlying entry into subsequent marriage.

More specifically, this chapter concentrates on the relationships between past and current life course experiences and entry into subsequent marriage. It is believed that, if women are brought up in an environment that favours marriage highly, they will in turn have a higher inclination to marry, even though they entered into cohabitation first. It is, therefore, hypothesised that past life course determinants influence the likelihood of a subsequent marriage, even after a period of cohabitation. This chapter examines the varying impact of past life course determinants on entry into marriage after a period of cohabitation.

During the period of cohabitation, individuals may alter their life goals in reaction to current life course experiences. This motivation change may affect their likelihood to enter into a marriage. The decision to marry is still closely linked with the wish to have and rear children. Many cohabiting women view the arrival of children as an important motivation to marry (De Graaf, 1990; Manting, 1994b). In this chapter, it is not so much the wish to have children, but rather the actual changes in the fertility career that are considered in terms of their impact on subsequent marriage.

This chapter affords insight into the *third research question*:

How have past and current individual life course experiences influenced the entry into marriage of cohabiting women?
- How have they influenced the (timing of) entry into marriage?
- Are there signs of a change in the impact of these determinants over personal and historical time, and if so, how does the impact change?

This chapter examines the relationships between past and current life course determinants and the process of subsequent marriage: the bordered areas in the conceptual framework are examined.

Conceptual framework

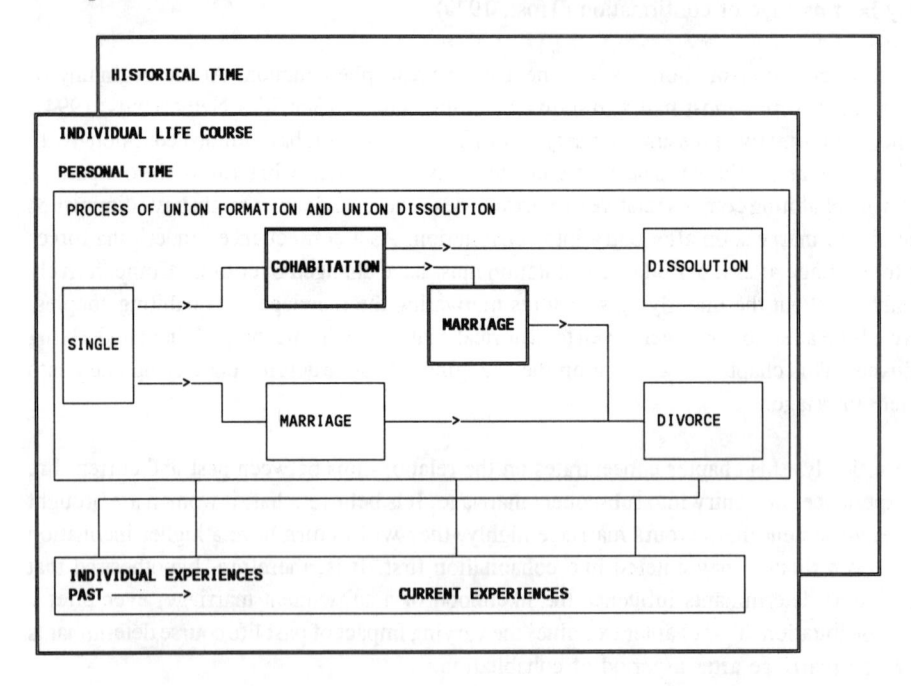

The following section starts with a short discussion of expected relationships between underlying forces and subsequent marriage. First of all, time plays a role in the transition into subsequent marriage. Secondly, the (changing) relationships between past life course experiences and subsequent marriage are discussed. Then, the (time-varying) relationships between current life course experiences and subsequent marriage are described. Thereafter, empirical results are presented. The chapter ends with a short discussion of the findings.

6.2 Time and moving into subsequent marriage

Cohabitation is generally a short-lived phenomenon. In West-Germany for instance, the median length of cohabitations started in the mid eighties was about 3 years. About 40 percent of the women starting to cohabit in the eighties in the Netherlands were still living together unmarried after 5 years (Blossfeld et al., 1993a).
The clock measuring personal time in the process of subsequent marriage starts the moment a woman begins to cohabit. After that moment, she runs the risk of either subsequent marriage or a break-up. The period may therefore end either at the interview date (no marriage or break-up having (yet) occurred), at the moment of breaking up, or at the moment of subsequent marriage. Women who had not (yet) married were treated as censored at the time of the interview (February 1988) and women who had experienced a dissolution were censored at the moment of breaking up.

Of the nearly six thousand women in this sample, almost two thousand entered their first union by cohabitation. More than half of them married, one out of six cohabitations ended in a break-up and somewhat more than a quarter of them was censored at the time of interview. The average (observed) duration of (first) cohabitation of women in the sample was 31 months. The average duration of cohabitation would have been more than that, since about a quarter of these unions were censored at the time of interview.

Personal time: *duration of cohabitation*
Becker (1981), in explaining the variation of marital stability with marital duration, pointed out that, during marriage, the amount of material assets not easily transferable to another partner increases with the duration of the marriage. A similar mechanism might also be present during the cohabitation phase. During the period of cohabitation, couples may invest in couple-related material assets, such as a house or a car, or they may 'invest' in children. Some couples may enter into marriage motivated by practical reasons, such as to acquire pension rights, to regulate obligations and rights with regard to children, and so on. Many enter marriage because marriage is considered to be a matter-of-course (Manting, 1944b). Entry into marriage is linked to a standard set of obligations and rights, whereas cohabiting couples must find out the rules for dividing property or for establishing financial support themselves, according to their personal wishes.
The longer a union endures, the more the emotional bonds become replaced by social or economic bonds (Trost, 1986). It seems that some couples who take marriage for granted marry soon after they have entered into cohabitation. Other couples, who do not take marriage for granted, may not marry at all or may postpone marriage in reaction to other individual developments. They might eventually marry because they feel confident enough about their

relationship, or because of a wish to have children, regulate property, ensure pension rights, and so on. It is therefore expected that *the risk of subsequent marriage is higher at early years of cohabitation but lower at later years of cohabitation*.

Historical time: *birth cohort membership*
Chapter 5 documented the rise of cohabitation with more recent birth cohorts. Apart from such a shift from marriage to cohabitation, it is likely for marriage to be increasingly postponed across cohorts. There are several explanations for this expectation. First of all, the normative pressure to marry soon after entry into cohabitation has diminished. Secondly, the relative advantages of marriage have declined. And thirdly, gradual moving into a union presupposes that entry into marriage is decreasingly considered at the start of cohabitation. All this may have increasingly led to a lower inclination to marry with more recent birth cohorts. It is therefore, expected that *the inclination to marry after a period of cohabitation declines across the birth cohorts*.

6.3 Past life course experiences influencing the moving into subsequent marriage

A general assumption in this study is that an individual's past life course affects the later life course. Chapter 5 documented the consequences of the individual past life course experiences for the process of first union formation. Women brought up in an environment that highly favours marriage will in turn be more likely to marry. Even though women brought up in a marriage-oriented environment may have entered into cohabitation first, they may nevertheless be more inclined to marry shortly after cohabitation than women who have been socialized in an environment stressing independence and freedom at the expense of traditional family attitudes. The following section briefly summarizes how past life course determinants influence the process of the marriage of cohabiting couples. This chapter analyses the impact of having been brought up in a small family, having experienced parental divorce, the municipality in which one grew up, and religious affiliation. In contrast with chapter 5, the covariate describing whether a woman lives in the parental home has been excluded, since this chapter focuses on cohabiting couples. Almost no women cohabit with a partner while living in the parental home.

Past life course experiences: *Parental divorce*
Many long-term socio-economic and psychological effects on the life courses of children derive from the experience of parental divorce (Kiernan & Chase-Lansdale, 1993), so that its influence on subsequent marriage is expected. Even after a period of cohabitation, the children of divorced parents may be more reluctant to enter into marriage. It is expected *that daughters of divorced parents have a lower rate of subsequent marriage*.

Past life course experiences: *Having a religious denomination*
Women without a religion affiliation have a higher rate of entering into cohabitation than women who have one, although these differences weaken in strength across cohorts. Religion is clearly

important for the values one associates with marriage, family and children. The expectation is that *women with a religious affiliation have a higher subsequent marriage rate than women without religious affiliation.*

Past life course experiences: *Being brought up in a small family*
Family size of origin has only a minor effect on entry into cohabitation. Being brought up in a small family has a negative impact on direct marriage. Children brought up in a small family will probably be more highly stimulated to invest in other life domains, such as education and work. This might not only lead to a lower inclination to marry directly, but it might also lead to a lower inclination to marry after a period of cohabitation. The expectation is that *women who grew up in a small family have a lower rate of subsequent marriage than women who grew up in a larger family.*

Past life course experiences: *Having a young mother*
Women with relatively young mothers are somewhat more likely to enter into cohabitation. This was explained by the fact that young mothers probably have fewer problems with cohabitation than older mothers. As such, the stimulus for women with relatively young mothers to marry after entry into cohabitation will be less strong. The expectation is that *daughters of young mothers have a lower rate of subsequent marriage.*

Past life course experiences: *Growing up in a small town*
Innovative behaviour generally starts in larger cities whereas those who live in a small city generally lag behind. In the seventies, living as a cohabiting couple without any inclination to marry was less tolerated in smaller than in larger cities (De Feijter, 1991). Women who grew up in small cities will therefore be more eager to marry than women who grew up in a large city. The expectation thus is that *cohabiting women who grew up in a small city have a higher rate of subsequent marriage than those who grew up in a large city.*

A historical change hypothesis
As has been said: the meaning of both cohabitation and marriage has changed over the years. Over time, the advantages of marriage relative to cohabitation have declined. The larger majority of the population (64 percent) no longer disapproves of cohabiting couples who have no intention to marry (SCP, 1992). Parents will decreasingly stimulate their children to marry soon after entry into cohabitation. Therefore, it is expected that *past life course experiences have a decreasing impact on entry into subsequent marriage across cohorts.*

A life course hypothesis
The longer a cohabitation period endures, the more the social and economic bonds with the partner are likely to increase. With a longer duration, daily life experiences will become of more relevance for current life course transitions than experiences in the past. If the past is mediated by more current experiences, and duration is interpreted as a global indicator of change in the individual live, than past life course experiences will decrease in meaning with the duration

of the union. The life course hypothesis for the process of first union formation postulated that past life course experiences weaken in strength over the life course (chapter 5). The life course hypothesis for entry into subsequent marriage postulates that past life course experiences become decreasingly important the longer the period of cohabitation takes. The expectation is *that past life course experiences influence the entry into subsequent marriage more at early years but less at later years of cohabitation.*

All formulated expectations with regard to the (changing) meaning of past life course experiences for the process of subsequent marriage are summarized below.

Scheme 1 Summary of hypotheses: past life course experiences and moving into subsequent marriage

	Main expected effect	Historical change hypothesis	Life course change hypothesis
Parents divorced	-	- -> 0	- -> 0
A religious affiliation	+	+ -> 0	- -> 0
Being brought up in a small family	-	- -> 0	- -> 0
Having a young mother	-	- -> 0	- -> 0
Growing up in a small town	+	+ -> 0	+ -> 0

A minus sign (-) indicates a lower risk of subsequent marriage.
A positive sign (+) indicates a higher risk of subsequent marriage.
A zero (0) indicates no significant impact on the risk of subsequent marriage.
The arrow indicates a changing meaning across cohorts (from cohort 1950-54 to 1965-69) or with duration (from shorter to longer).

6.4 Current life course experiences influencing the moving into subsequent marriage

The period of cohabitation may be short, but other individual experiences may nevertheless change in that time. Individual and couple-related changes may occur that may eventually stimulate women to marry. Other life domains, such as education, work and pregnancy, as well as changes within them, may influence the entry into subsequent marriage, just as they influenced entry into a first union. There are two other important factors thought to be important for subsequent marriage. There is considerable evidence that the timing of prior life events affects the later life course. For the process of subsequent marriage, age on entering cohabitation might be important. The presumed effect is discussed below. Furthermore, not only pregnancy, but also childbirth may have an impact on subsequent marriage. The difference in impact on subsequent marriage will also be discussed below.

Current life course experiences: *Educational enrolment*
Both educational attainment as well as educational enrolment were associated with a lower inclination to marry. Investment in education may lead people to postpone transitions having a high level or irreversibility (Mulder & Manting, 1993). It used indeed to be the case that students were much less eager to enter into a union, to marry or to cohabit. It is anticipated that this negative effect will be similar for the process of marriage after a period of cohabitation. Thus, it is expected that *students have a lower rate of subsequent marriage than women who have left education.*

Current life course experiences: *Educational achievement*
Educational attainment as a proxy for a higher attachment to values such as independence and autonomy leads to the expectation that highly educated women will postpone subsequent marriage more than women with a lower level of education. *Cohabiting women with a higher level of educational attainment probably marry at a lower rate than cohabiting women with a lower level of educational attainment.*

Current life course experiences: *Labour force participation*
Several cross-sectional studies comparing cohabiting and married couples have shown that those who are cohabiting work more often than those who are married (Klijzing, 1989; Latten, 1992). However, as chapter 5 showed, work has a positive impact on marriage (without controlling for changes across time). Although it might seem to contradict the cross-sectional findings that cohabiting couples more often work than married couples, the explanation is quite simple; differentials in labour force participation emerge after entry into a union rather than before it. It is quite likely that, during the period of co-residence, married women will leave the labour market at a higher rate than cohabiting women. This might be because married women start having children soon after marriage; childbirth coincides most often with leaving the labour market. In that case, differences in labour force participation between cohabiting and married couples would emerge after rather than before entry into a union. It might well be that work operates indirectly. Work leads to a lower rate of entry into parenthood and, because marriage and fertility are closely linked, work might also lead to a lower inclination to marry after a period of cohabitation. Work might also be seen as an indication of independence. If that is the case, work has a direct effect in that working women are less inclined to make a transition to marriage. The expectation is that *working women have a lower subsequent marriage rate than women who are not gainfully employed.*

Current life course experiences: *Fertility*
Historically, marriage invariably preceded the birth of a child, but nowadays this is no longer the case. Some women are pregnant when they marry, while others already have one or more children at the time of their marriage. The number of births out of wedlock has risen quite significantly during the past twenty years (Bosveld et al., 1991) and the proportion of non-marital conceptions followed by marriage within a couple of months has diminished over the years (Beets, 1991). The interactions between marriage and having children have become more

complex. Rindfuss and Parnell (1989, p. 461) formulated several links, some of which I have translated to the case of cohabiting couples. Some of these cohabiting couples will wait until the woman becomes pregnant, whereupon they marry. For a few couples, an accidental pregnancy may lead to a marriage that might otherwise not have taken place. Pregnancy could also lead to the dissolution of a cohabitation, should a strong disagreement arise concerning the desirability of having a child. Other cohabiting couples who wish to have children in the near future may decide to marry before the woman becomes pregnant. In the Netherlands, one third of the married women who cohabited prior to marriage said that they married because they were pregnant, or because they wanted to have children. Women married recently reported this reason more frequently than women who married some time ago (De Graaf, 1990).

The assumption that many cohabiting couples postpone marriage until the woman is pregnant implies that pregnant women will have a higher rate of subsequent marriage than cohabiting women who are not pregnant. There is indeed empirical evidence that cohabiting couples have a higher rate of subsequent marriage when the woman is pregnant (Manting, 1991). However, not all women marry when they are pregnant; some women have their children without getting married. At present, little is known about the impact of childbirth on entry into subsequent marriage. It is possible that some couples decide to marry when the woman is pregnant because entry into marriage automatically ensures certain obligations and rights for the sake of children. If cohabiting women do not marry when they are pregnant, why then should they marry at a later date? Perhaps these women decide to have and bring up their children outside marriage, and have already made such financial and juridical arrangements that make marriage no longer necessary. The hypothesis to be derived from the above is that *childbirth during cohabitation leads to a lower rate of subsequent marriage, while pregnancy may lead to a higher rate of subsequent marriage.*

Current life course experiences: *Age at cohabitation*
There is growing evidence that the timing and order of prior life events affects the future life course (Mayer & Tuma, 1990; Rindfuss et al., 1987). With regard to subsequent marriage, the moment at which cohabitation was entered may well be important. Women who started to cohabit at younger ages may possibly be less 'ready' to marry than women cohabiting at older ages. The expectation is *that women who started to cohabit at a relatively young age have a lower likelihood to marry subsequently than women who started to cohabit at older ages.*

A historical change hypothesis
Just as in the influence of past experiences, it is expected that the relationships between education, work and fertility become decreasingly important in explaining the differentiation of marrying soon after entry into cohabitation. Moreover, since having and rearing children without being married is increasingly tolerated, it is likely that the incidence of pregnancy and possibly childbirth might stimulate younger women to marry much less than women born earlier. The expectation is that *current life course experiences influence entry into subsequent marriage less among the more recent cohorts.*

A life course hypothesis

Work and study hampered entry into cohabitation and marriage at younger ages, but stimulated it at older ages. It is possible that this is also the case for the process studied here. It is expected that *students, working women or women with a high level of education or a young age at cohabitation may have a lower marriage risk at early years, but may catch up at later years of cohabitation*. There seems to be no reason for the impact of pregnancy and childbirth to vary in meaning with personal time. The hypothesis is that *pregnancy and childbirth do not change in meaning with union duration*.

All expectations with regard to the (varying) meaning of current life course experiences for subsequent marriage are summarized in the scheme below.

Scheme 2   Summary of hypotheses: current life course experiences and moving into subsequent marriage

	Main expected effect	Historical change hypothesis	Life course change hypothesis
Studying	-	- -> 0	- -> +
High educational level	-	- -> 0	- -> +
Employed	-	- -> 0	- -> +
Pregnant	+	+ -> 0	+ -> +
First child born	-	-- -> 0	- -> -
Young age at entry	-	- -> 0	- -> +

Explanation: see scheme 1 (chapter 6)

6.5   Selection procedure

The dependent variable is the hazard rate of subsequent marriage. It is the rate of marriage of cohabiting women, given that they had not married previously. To gain more insight into the relationship of the determinants and subsequent marriage, univariate results are given first, commencing with the univariate results of past life course determinants.

Past life course experiences
Table 1 shows the hazard rates of subsequent marriage, categorized according to past life course covariates. This table shows univariate results, so no control has been made for other relevant determinants.

Table 1 Monthly hazard rates of subsequent marriage among cohabiting women, distinquished according to time dimensions and past life course determinants (univariate results)

average	0.018
Duration t	
1. $\leq$ 3 years	0.019
2. > 3 years	0.015
Birth cohort	
1. 1950-54	0.020
2. 1955-59	0.018
3. 1960-64	0.015
4. 1965-69	0.017
Parents divorced t	
1. no	0.018
2. yes	0.016
Religion i	
1. no religion	0.016
2. a religion	0.020
Parental size family	
1. $\leq$ 2 children	0.019
2. > 2 children	0.018
Age difference with mother	
1. $\leq$ 25	0.019
2. > 25	0.018
Size of municipality of residence when aged 6 to 16	
1. $\geq$ 400,000	0.018
2. $\geq$ 100,000	0.017
3. < 100,000	0.020

t = time varying covariate, i = situation at time of interview

As expected, the risk of a marriage is indeed somewhat higher at early years of cohabitation. In accordance with the hypothesis, the marriage risk is lower for women born in the sixties.

Even in this table, with no control for other relevant determinants, the differences related to past life course experiences are very small. Contrary to expectation, being brought up in a small family, or having a relatively young mother, does not really seem to matter for the rate of subsequent marriage. Women who experienced the divorce of their parents have a slightly lower rate of entry into subsequent marriage. Women without religious affiliation have indeed, as expected, a somewhat lower rate of marriage. In accordance with the hypothesis, women brought up in a small town have a somewhat higher rate of marriage than women, brought up in larger cities. The non-linear change with increasing size of municipality, however, contradicts the expectation.

A *multivariate* model, simultaneously including all these past life course experiences and duration and cohort membership, has been estimated to test whether, in the presence of each other, these past life course determinants significantly influence the process of subsequent marriage. In the presence of each other, only religion - together with duration and birth cohort - has a significant impact on subsequent marriage (See Appendix chapter 6 for the log likelihood ratio test).

Because the historical change hypothesis postulates that determinants have a decreasing impact on subsequent marriage across more recent birth cohorts, a test was implemented to investigate whether the interaction effects of birth cohort with past life course determinants improved the fit of the model significantly. However, no statistically significant interaction effects of birth cohort with past life course experiences were found. The life course hypothesis postulates a diminishing role of determinants the longer the period of cohabitation. None of the past life course experiences vary significantly with union duration.

It was expected that women whose parents were divorced, who grew up in a small family, had a relatively young mother, or grew up in a large town would be less eager to marry after a period of cohabitation. On the contrary, experiences early in life do not significantly influence subsequent marriage. Only religious affiliation plays a substantive role in the process of subsequent marriage.

These findings clearly show that past life course determinants do not influence the later life course, at least not directly. This supports the notion, stemming from life course theory, that the influences of a woman's past on the present are mediated by more current life course experiences. In this case, entry into cohabitation is such a current experience. These findings are also in line with those presented in chapter 5, showing that past life course determinants diminish in impact as women grow older.

All in all, it would seem that early life course experiences set individuals on a certain track of life, but, once important life decisions have been taken, past experiences play no further substantial role in the life course. The only exception to this statement is the relationship between religious affiliation and subsequent marriage. Having a religious affiliation stimulates marriage. It is, however, likely that the relationship between religious affiliation and subsequent marriage will weaken in strength after controlling for more recent life course experiences, such as education, work and fertility. Whether the impact of religion is mediated by these current life course experiences is examined in section 6.6.

The empirical evidence supports neither the historical change nor the life course hypothesis: past life course experiences do not vary significantly with cohort or duration. Thus, past life course determinants used to hold no importance for entry into subsequent marriage and they still have no relevance. Also, past life course experiences have no impact, either at early duration of cohabitation or at later duration of cohabitation.

Current life course experiences

Table 2 shows the risks of entry into marriage for cohabiting women, categorized according to their occupational, educational and fertility status and age at union (univariate results).

Table 2 Monthly hazard rates of subsequent marriage among cohabiting women, distinguished according to current life course determinants

Educational level i	
1. low	0.021
2. middle	0.018
3. higher	0.015
Occupational status t	
1. unemployed	0.020
2. studying	0.009
3. employed	0.019
Children t	
1. no child	0.016
2. pregnant	0.100
3. first child born	0.014
Age at cohabitation	
1. <19	0.017
2. 19-20	0.019
3. 21 or more	0.018

t=time-varying, i= situation at time of interview

Less well educated women have a higher rate of marriage than more highly educated women, as expected. Also, students have much lower rates of subsequent marriage. In contrast with the expectation, whether a woman works does not really influence subsequent marriage. The role of being pregnant comes particularly to the fore for the process of subsequent marriage. Pregnant women have a much higher rate of entry into subsequent marriage than women who are not pregnant. Women with at least one child born during the period of cohabitation have a much lower rate of marriage, as expected. Finally, the non-linear change with increasing age at which cohabitation was entered contradicts the expectation.

To assess whether a determinant still has a significant impact after controlling for the other relevant determinants, a *multivariate* model including all these current determinants and duration and birth cohort membership simultaneously has been estimated. The tests of the multivariate model (see appendix chapter 6) in which the significance of all these covariates are tested in each other's presence show however that a few covariates do not contribute significantly to the differentiation in the likelihood to marry. Neither educational attainment nor age at start of cohabitation influence significantly the process of marriage in a multivariate setting. It was expected that more highly educated women would have a lower rate of marriage than less well educated women. This was indeed found without controlling for other relevant determinants (table 2). Yet, after controlling for work, educational enrolment and dynamics in the fertility career, educational level no longer plays a significant role in the process of subsequent marriage. Another analysis, undertaken with another data set, showed that educational level did significantly influence the process of subsequent marriage (Manting, 1991). But that model did not control for educational enrolment. Perhaps having been a student is more important in the process of subsequent marriage than educational achievement. Educational level does not vary significantly in impact either with birth cohort membership (historical change hypothesis) or with duration of the union (life course change hypothesis). In combination with the findings of chapter 5, one may conclude that educational attainment strongly affects the early life course, but not the later life course. Although educational attainment is highly important for entry into cohabitation, it does not influence entry into subsequent marriage.

In contrast with the expectation that women who start to cohabit at younger ages will have lower risks of subsequent marriage than women who begin to cohabit at older ages, the age at union does not significantly influence the process of subsequent marriage in a multivariate setting. Nor does its meaning change across the cohorts (historical change hypothesis), given that the interaction effect of birth cohort and age at start of cohabitation is also insignificant. Furthermore, its meaning does not vary with the duration of the union, which implies that no support is found for the life course hypothesis either.

The occupational status of women (working, unemployed, or studying) and the covariate measuring whether women are pregnant or have had a child affect subsequent marriage at a significant level. Before discussing the effects of these determinants in more detail, another multivariate model is presented that includes all past and current life course determinants having a significant impact on subsequent marriage. In the next section, parameter estimates are given of these determinants in the presence of all other relevant determinants. This model includes religion (the only past life course determinant strongly influencing the process of subsequent marriage), the occupational, educational and fertility careers. Duration and birth cohort membership are also included, since they both play a significant role in the process of subsequent marriage.

6.6 Past and current life course experiences and the moving into subsequent marriage

The log likelihood ratio tests carried out on a multivariate model including all significant past and current life course experiences showed that all these determinants have a significant impact on the entry into subsequent marriage in the presence of each other (Appendix chapter 6). Religion does therefore have a significant impact on subsequent marriage, even after controlling for more recent life course experiences. Once again, tests were implemented to investigate whether there is support for the historical change and the life course thesis. The interaction effects of birth cohort with religion, the occupational and fertility career were not statistically significant. This implies that empirical evidence does not support the historical change thesis. Moreover, neither were the interaction effects of duration and religion, occupational status and fertility status significant. This implies that no support is found for the life course thesis. The only exception is a significant interaction of cohort membership with duration of the union. Parameter estimates of the model including all main effects and the interaction of cohort membership and duration are presented below (table 3).

Table 3   Parameter estimates of the model of moving into marriage during the period of cohabitation

parameters		b	exp(b)
mean		-3.87 *	0.021
duration	=< 3 years	0.18 *	1.20
	more than 3 years	-0.18 *	0.84
birth cohort	50-54	0.12	1.13
	55-59	0.09	1.09
	60-64	-0.04	0.96
	65-69	-0.17	0.84
religion	none	-0.10 *	0.90
	other	0.10 *	1.11
occupational status	unemployed	0.22 *	1.25
	studying	-0.52 *	0.60
	employed	0.30 *	1.34
fertility	no children	-0.62 *	0.54
	pregnant	1.24 *	3.46
	a childbirth	-0.62 *	0.54
=<3 years and cohort	50-54	0.26 *	1.30
	55-59	-0.05	0.95
	60-64	-0.05	0.95
	65-69	-0.15	0.86
> 3 years and cohort	50-54	-0.26 *	0.77
	55-59	0.05	1.05
	60-64	0.05	1.06
	65-69	0.15	1.16

*: b/se(b) > 1.96   L2: 119   df: 131

The mean monthly hazard rate of this specific model is 0.021 (exp(-3.87)=0.021). The expectation that marriage rates will be higher during the first years of cohabitation is supported: in the first three years the risk was 1.2 times higher than the average rate.

In accordance with the expectation, more recent birth cohorts have a weaker desire to legalize their unions quickly by marrying than do earlier birth cohorts. The rate of marriage diminishes across the birth cohorts. Women born in the early fifties had a rate that was almost 1.3 times higher than women born at the end of the sixties (1.13/0.84). The decreasing rate of marriage across the birth cohorts is an indication of the fact that cohabitation has become a completely accepted way of living together; that normative pressures to marry have declined over the years, that a decline in the advantages of marriage relative to cohabitation has been accompanied with a diminishing necessity to marry among cohabiting women; that more and more women entering into a union gradually without any intention to marry.

Past life course experiences
The relevant influence of past life course experiences for subsequent marriage is limited to that of religious denomination. And even religion differentiates the risk of subsequent marriage only to a minor extent. Women without religious affiliation have a somewhat lower risk of subsequent marriage than women with a religious affiliation. This confirms the formulated expectation that women with a religious affiliation have a somewhat higher marriage risk, even after entry into cohabitation. It indicates that growing up in an environment in which marriage is highly valued leads to a higher inclination to marry, even after having first entered into cohabitation. Although religion is labelled as a determinant indicating women's past, religion is measured at the time of interview. This implies that religion should be interpreted with caution, since some women have changed their religious affiliation after they married.

Current life course experiences
Current life course experiences are especially important for the transition into subsequent marriage. Being a student leads to a marriage rate 0.6 times lower than average. The societal norm that students should not marry would seem still to hold. Alternatively, educational enrolment is a period of uncertainty during which people avoid long-term commitments such as marriage (Oppenheimer, 1988). Blossfeld and colleagues found a similar relationship between educational enrolment and entry into subsequent marriage for German cohabiting couples (Blossfeld et al., 1993a). Employed women have a marriage rate that is 2.2 times higher (1.34/.60) than that of students, while unemployed women also have a significantly higher marriage risk than students. Leaving the educational system leads thus to a much higher rate of entry into subsequent marriage.
These findings show that working cohabiting women do not have lower rates of marriage than non-working cohabiting females. On the contrary, their risk of marriage is even higher, although the differences are very small. This does not confirm the new home economics hypothesis formulated by Becker (1981), that the growing economic independence of women would lead to lower rates of marriage. Work stimulates entry into marriage: this was also the case for direct entry into marriage, although this effect only operates at older ages.

Pregnant females have a higher marriage risk than those who are not pregnant, as was expected. Women who are pregnant with their first child have a risk 6.4 times higher than that of childless women who are not pregnant. Apparently, in the Netherlands the link between having children and getting married is still very strong. Marriage remains a prerequisite for rearing children, since the rate of entry into subsequent marriage is much higher among pregnant women. There is still a great desire to legalize a union before a child is born. The marriage risk among unmarried mothers equals the marriage risk of childless, not pregnant women. Women who do not marry when they are pregnant have a much lower rate of marriage once the child is born. The rate of entry into marriage for a union which had not been legalized within a few months of the child being born was found to be much lower in the Netherlands than in Germany (Blossfeld, et al., 1991). This may be caused by the fact that the majority of the Dutch population does no longer disapprove of cohabiting couples raising their children out of wedlock.

Historical changes?
The historical change hypothesis postulates that covariates will decreasingly differentiate the process into subsequent marriage across the birth cohorts. Because of the stance taken by the Churches against cohabitation in the past, one should expect religious women born in the fifties to marry at a faster rate than religious women born in the end of the sixties. Yet there is no sign for a changing linkage between religion and marriage among cohabiting women. Furthermore, there are no signs for a significantly changing meaning of work, education and fertility on subsequent marriage either: no significant interaction effects of birth cohort and another variable significantly improve the fit. As a consequence, there is no indication whatsoever that the differential impact of religion, working status or fertility status on entry into marriage of cohabiting women has diminished over historical time. Women born in the fifties who have no religious affiliation, who are students, not gainfully employed or childless have a lower rate of marriage. For women born in the sixties, this is still so.

Life course changes?
The life course hypothesis postulating varying influences of determinants during the union is not supported by the empirical evidence presented above. Only the idea that marriage will be increasingly postponed has been supported. Women born in the fifties have an especially high inclination to marry soon after entry into cohabitation (interaction effect of birth cohort and duration).

Compared with the analysis of first union formation presented in chapter 5, the number of significant interaction effects is small. It could be concluded that this is the result of the smaller number of observations in this analysis relative to the one presented in chapter 5. The number of observations is still rather large, however, since the process of subsequent marriage has been examined for about two thousand women, half of them marrying. Moreover, in a previous analysis of the timing of marriage of cohabiting women where whether a woman had borne a child during the period of cohabitation had not been taken into account, three as opposed to just one interaction effects with duration were found to be significant, which also suggests that it was not the small number of observations that led to few interaction effects.[1]

---

[1] In that analysis, interactions of occupational status and religion with duration showed that working women (relative to women who were not gainfully employed) and women without a religion (relative to women with a religion) had a lower marriage risk at early union durations but a higher marriage risk at later durations of the union. The fact that these interactions are gone in the analysis presented in this chapter (this analysis controls for whether or not a women has a childbirth during cohabitation, whereas the previous analysis did not), must lead to the conclusion that working and non-religious women had lower marriage risks at early union durations in that analysis because they have a higher likelihood of a childbirth during the period of cohabitation.

6.7 Summary and conclusion

This chapter has examined the relationships between both past and current life course factors and the tempo at which women move into marriage after entry into cohabitation. This chapter clearly demonstrates that past life course experiences weaken in strength with the unfolding of the life course. It was thought that women who had experienced a parental divorce, who had no religious denomination, who were brought up in a small family and had a relatively young mother had a lower rate of subsequent marriage, whereas women, who had grown up in a small city would have a higher rate of subsequent marriage, especially at early duration of cohabitation. Contrary to these expectations, empirical evidence did not support the statistical significance of these relationships. Few past life course experiences play a substantive role in the process of marriage, once cohabitation has been entered. Religious affiliation stands out as the only past life course determinant which influences moving into subsequent marriage. Even after controlling for current activity and life course statuses, such as work and pregnancy, religious affiliation influences entry into marriage in a positive way.

The dynamics in the fertility career are of paramount importance for entry into subsequent marriage. Once a woman becomes pregnant, she is likely to marry soon. Yet, if legalization of a union does not follow soon after a woman becomes pregnant, the rate of subsequent marriage drops to a comparatively low level. The rate of subsequent marriage among mothers is as low as among childless couples. Some other life course experiences influence a moving into subsequent marriage too. Educational enrolment influences the process of marriage in the expected, negative, way. However, educational achievement does not affect subsequent marriage. In contrast with the view that the growing economic independence of women leads to postponement of marriage, even somewhat higher rates of marriage were found among working cohabiting women, although the differences between working and unemployed women were very small. The expectation that women who entered into cohabitation at a relatively young age would be more likely to postpone marriage than women who entered it at a relatively higher age was not confirmed. Life course theorists assume that the timing and order of past life course events influence the later life course. In this case, this assumption is not supported, because the timing of cohabitation does not significantly influence the timing of subsequent marriage.

Varying effects of above mentioned determinants on subsequent marriage with personal and historical time were not found. Past and current life course experiences do not change at all in their impact on entry into marriage. Thus, past life course experience have been and remain of no importance for entry into subsequent marriage. Religion has remained important for explaining differentiation in marriage risks of cohabiting women. Current life course experiences have not played a substantive role in the moving into subsequent marriage. Moreover, these factors have not had a differential impact with union duration.

The following scheme summarizes all findings described above.

Scheme 3 Summary of findings: past and current life course experiences influencing moving into subsequent marriage

	Main expected effect	Main effect: findings	Historical change hypothesis	Historical change: findings	Life course change hypothesis	Life course change: findings
Parents divorced	-	0	- -> 0	0 -> 0	- -> 0	0 -> 0
A religious affiliation	+	+	+ -> 0	+ -> +	- -> 0	0 -> 0
Being brought up in a small family	-	0	- -> 0	0 -> 0	- -> 0	0 -> 0
Having a young mother	-	0	- -> 0	0 -> 0	- -> 0	0 -> 0
Growing up in a small town	+	0	+ -> 0	0 -> 0	+ -> 0	0 -> 0
Studying	-	-	- -> 0	- -> -	- -> +	0 -> 0
High educational level	-	0	- -> 0	0 -> 0	- -> +	0 -> 0
Employed	-	+	- -> 0	0 -> 0	- -> +	0 -> 0
Pregnant	+	+	+ -> 0	+ -> +	+ -> +	+ -> +
A first child born	-	-	- -> 0	- -> -	- -> -	- -> -
Young age at entry	-	0	- -> 0	0 -> 0	- -> +	0 -> 0

Chapter 5 showed that past life course determinants directly influence behaviour early in life, influencing union formation at younger ages. However, with the passage of time, past life course experience weakened in strength. This chapter shows that past life course experiences no longer influence the later life course, once cohabitation is entered. This implies that the impact of the individual's past operates only indirectly via its influence early in life on moving into a first union. Past life course determinants are mediated by more current experiences. In this specific case, entry into cohabitation is such a current experience.

Religious affiliation is an exception to this general mechanism. First of all, religious affiliation becomes increasingly important for moving into a first union with the passage of time (chapter 5) and religion is important for moving into subsequent marriage once a union has been formed. Thus, on top of its effect on the first transition in the union career (entry into cohabitation), it affects the second transition (from cohabitation to marriage). In short, religious women have a lower likelihood of entering into cohabitation. Having entered into cohabitation, religious women marry at a higher rate than non-religious women.

Chapter 5 showed that work influences moving into a union to a minor extent. Working women postpone entry into a union at younger ages and caught up later in life. Once again, no support was found for the notion that work, seen as an indication of female economic independence, is of the utmost importance for explaining the historical decline in marriage rates. It is the longer investment in educational achievement - a prerequisite for gaining economic independence - that is the more important factor in the decline in marriage rates. Being a student reduces the subsequent marriage risk importantly on top of the negative impact, especially early in life, on entry into cohabitation (chapter 5). Educational attainment influences subsequent marriage only indirectly, through its impact on the entry into a union. A high level of educational achievement has a negative impact on moving into cohabitation early in life, but has a positive impact on moving into cohabitation later in life. Once cohabitation has been entered, educational achievement no longer influences entry into subsequent marriage in a direct way.

It seems to be mainly enrolment in the educational system rather than work or educational achievement, that might be seen to support the notion that growing female economic independence has led to the declining attractiveness of marriage (at least, among cohabiting women).

That educational enrolment is of primary importance for moving into subsequent marriage supports the notion, stemming from life course theory, that changes in one life domain cannot be explained without taking changes in other life domains into account. The role of varying statuses in the fertility career also clearly demonstrates the importance of studying subsequent marriage with reference to changes in other life domains. Evidently, changes in the fertility career are closely linked with changes in the union career. The incidence of a pregnancy among cohabiting couples highly stimulates entry into marriage. Those who decide not to marry when the female partner is pregnant have a low rate of subsequent marriage after a child is born. This implies that cohabiting couples who wish to rear children within marriage are most likely to marry at the moment the woman becomes pregnant rather than after the child is born. That marriage and rearing children is closely linked is clearly demonstrated.

Women who entered into cohabitation at a relatively young age did not postpone marriage significantly more or less than women who entered into cohabitation at a later age.

Finally, besides these intra-cohort differentials in the risk of subsequent marriage, inter-cohort differentials are clear. It was thought that younger birth cohorts would encounter less normative pressure to marry soon after entry into cohabitation. Moreover, since cohabitation and marriage have become more equal in terms of rights and obligations, the need to move into marriage might have declined across the cohorts. The fact that recent birth cohorts do indeed have a much lower rate of subsequent marriage than earlier birth cohorts might also be seen as an indication for increasing numbers of women entering into a union gradually and who do not really consider marriage at the start of cohabitation. The effect of cohort membership remained significant after controlling for other important determinants. This suggests that, on top of inter-cohort compositional changes of the determinants included - work, educational level, educational enrolment, pregnancy and childbirth and religion - year of birth determines one's further life course. Alternatively, other compositional differentials, not controlled for in this study, cause a lower inclination to marry among the more recent birth cohorts.

In contrast with the previous chapter, past and current life course experiences have a constant effect over personal and over historical time. This was an unexpected finding. The only statistically significant interaction effect was an interaction between cohort membership and duration of the union. This indicates that, especially during the first years of cohabitation, the marriage risk decreases among those born more recently.

7 THE BREAK UP OF FIRST UNIONS

7.1 Introduction

Union instability has increased over the years. The annual number of disruptions of unmarried and married couples was about 50,000 at the end of the eighties (Beets, 1989) and about 70,000 at the beginning of the nineties (Manting, 1994a). In this study the standpoint taken is that the process of moving out of a union should be analysed from the moment a union is formed, and not, as is generally done, from the moment of marriage. The reason for studying the break up of unions from the moment of co-residence is that this point in time marks the real beginning of testing a relationship in daily life situations. This does not automatically mean that a union's legal status at and during the union are believed to be unimportant in the study of disruption. On the contrary. It is asserted here that, to understand more about the breaking up process, the consequences of (developments in) legal status for union stability should be examined. If cohabitation is perceived as a way of gradual entry into a union, then distinguishing legal status at the start of a union is important for understanding differentials in disruption. Marriage after a period of cohabitation might be an act symbolizing a couple's feeling that a long lasting mutual commitment is being expressed. If that is so, stability will probably be greater once marriage is entered. This chapter studies the break-up of couples from the moment a woman starts living with a partner, taking into account any change from cohabitation to marriage.

It is hypothesised that women who have been brought up in an environment favouring marriage have a lower inclination to break up. The implication is that past life course determinants influencing union formation might also influence union break-up. In accordance with life course theory, the assumption is made that developments in union stability can only be fully understood with reference to (changes in) other life domains. Current life course experiences, such as education, work and fertility, are thought to play a substantive role in the break up of couples. In addition to past and current life course experiences, several time dimensions play a role in the study of break-up. The further assumption is therefore made that, apart from year of birth and union duration, several other personal and historical time dimensions are of significance to this event.

Historical changes in the patterns of marriage and cohabitation have been documented in the previous chapters. Underlying determinants might also influence the union dissolution of the different cohorts in dissimilar ways. In this chapter, the support for a historical change thesis is therefore examined. Historical changes in the patterns of underlying forces affecting union disruption are postulated.

In accordance with the life course change hypothesis formulated for union formation, this chapter also studies to what extent past and current life course experiences change in their impact on union dissolution with the duration of the union.

In short, it is hypothesised that both early life course experiences and the life course position of a woman during the years of shared life provide determinants for union stability, and that the role of these determinants may change with historical and with personal time. The test for these hypotheses is summarized in research question four:

How have past and current individual life course experiences influenced first union dissolution over time?
- How have they influenced the (timing of a) union dissolution?
- Are there signs of a change in the impact of these determinants over personal and historical time, and if so, how does the impact change?

The last part of the framework of chapter 2 (the relationship between the bordered areas in the framework below) is studied in more detail.

Conceptual framework

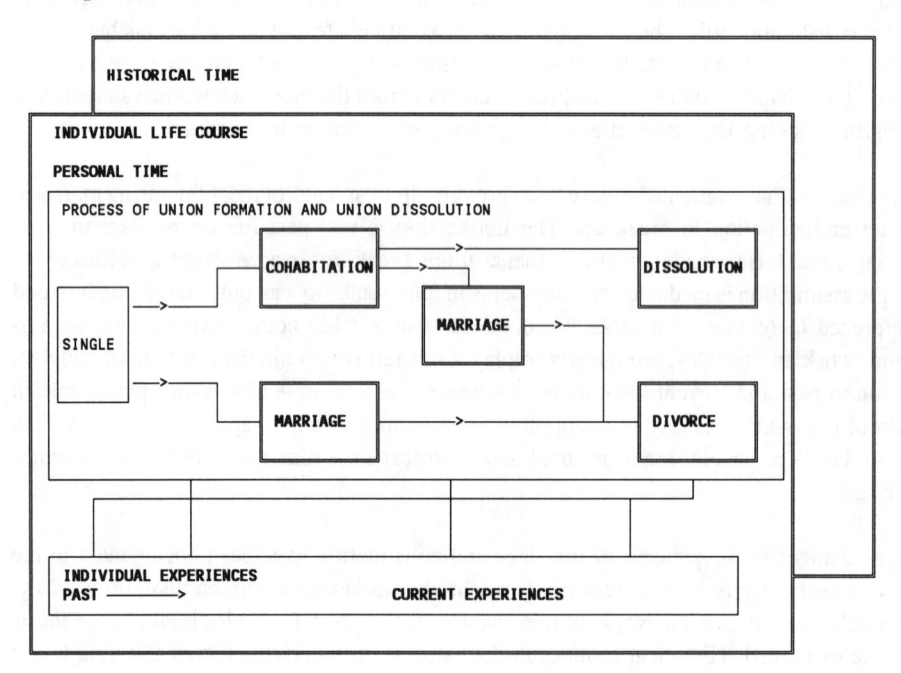

This chapter is organized as follows. First, the close link between movement in and out of a union is discussed. There follows, second, the role of time in the disruption process (section 7.2.2); third, the role of early life course experiences; fourth, the role of more immediate experiences (sections 7.2.3 & 7.2.4). Finally, several multivariate models representing this temporal movement in time over the life course are analysed to examine the impact of determinants in combination with each other (section 7.3). The chapter ends with a summary and a discussion.

7.2 Theoretical background

Long-term social developments have led to a steady rise in divorce rates over the years. The growing importance of individual self-fulfilment, a weakening of normative and religious guidelines, and an increasing tolerance of divorce have been accompanied by a growth in marital instability. Improved standards of living, growing female economic independence and simplification of the divorce laws have lowered the (financial) barriers to break-up. Many studies have provided insight into individual and couple-related circumstances affecting marital stability. Comparatively little is known about the dissolution behaviour of cohabiting couples and the underlying forces that affect their break-up. The next section begins with a discussion of the role of union status in union dissolution. Then, the relationship between several time dimensions and the process of disruption are discussed, followed by a section on past and more recent individual life course experiences. In these sections, separate hypotheses are formulated for each determinant.

7.2.1 The close link between movement into and out of a union

Several studies have shown that women who cohabit before marriage are more at risk of divorce than women who did not cohabit before marriage (Bracher et al., 1993; Bumpass, 1990; Klijzing, 1992; Manting, 1993; Schoen, 1992; Teachman et al., 1991). However, most of these studies examined the process of divorce from the time a marriage was entered and not from the start of cohabitation. Whether these differences persist when the break-up process is considered from the onset of co-residence is the key question. Relatively little is known about the dissolution process as it applies to cohabiting couples. Some recent longitudinal studies on the disruption of marriage and cohabitation have shed light on the processes involved. A Dutch multivariate event history analysis of union disruption indicated that union status had no significant impact on union disruption (Klijzing, 1992). Others show that cohabiting couples in the Netherlands have a much higher union instability than married couples (Beets, 1989b, Manting, 1994a). Results for the United States (Teachman et al., 1991) and for Sweden (Hoem & Hoem, 1992), however, showed that cohabiting couples had very high disruption risks, whereas married couples who had cohabited before marriage had a somewhat lower risk, and couples married without previous cohabitation had the lowest disruption risk of the three groups.

If cohabitation is a means of gradual entry into a union, and if cohabitation is sometimes entered into with no intention of forming a long-lasting relationship, then it is likely that cohabiting couples will decide to break up during this process of gradually moving-in more often than those entering marriage directly. Many cross-sectional studies show differences between cohabiting and married couples in the ways they perceive their relationship, attaching less value to the permanence of their union, and formulating different conditions of what a good relationship should be (Lesthaeghe et al., 1992; Statistics Netherlands, 1994; Van der Avort, 1987; Wiersma, 1983). These results provide further evidence for an expected greater instability among cohabiting couples. The incidence of dissolution might be higher among those cohabiting than among those married directly. If transition to marriage after a period of cohabitation is a sign for increased feelings of confidence about the relationship or 'survival' of the trial period, then union stability will be higher once marriage is entered. It is expected that *cohabiting women have the highest dissolution risks, that currently married women who cohabited prior to marriage have a somewhat lower risk than cohabiting couples, and that currently married women who did not cohabit prior to marriage have the lowest risk of union dissolution.*

Scheme 1   General hypothesis on legal status and first union dissolution

union status:	General expected effect
cohabiting	+ +
cohabiting -> married	+
married directly	-

Explanation:
A minus sign (-) indicates a lower risk of union dissolution
A positive sign (+) indicates a higher risk of union dissolution

7.2.2   The time dimension and movement out of a first union

It is common to study developments in divorce for one or more marriage cohorts and for union duration. Several other time dimensions also seem to play a role. Studies for the United States (Thornton & Rodgers, 1987) and for Finland (Lutz et al., 1991) show that aggregate developments in divorce can be explained in terms of age better than in terms of marital duration. Moreover, they showed that developments are sometimes better interpreted in terms of calendar periods than in terms of the year in which a marriage ended. In this chapter, attention is given to several of these time dimensions. The first historical time dimension considered is, naturally, birth cohort. The second is union cohort (the calendar period in which a union was entered). Further, attention is given to period effects. Personal time dimensions considered include age at union formation, the (time-varying) age of a woman during the union and the (time-varying) duration of the union.

Historical time

Chapter 4 documented the rise in the divorce rate over the past few decades. It also became apparent that younger birth cohorts experience union disruption more frequently than older cohorts. The reason is the more frequent cohabitation of younger cohorts. If cohabitation is indeed more unstable, then later cohorts should experience more disruptions, because they cohabit more often. Further, it might also be the case that instability of cohabitation has increased across the cohorts. If cohabitation is increasingly a means of gradual entry into a relationship, then it is likely that the instability of cohabitation will increase with historical time. As a result, disruption of cohabitation should be higher among more recent birth cohorts than among women born earlier. The general expectation is that the risk of a disruption will rise with historical time, partly because of a shift from marriage to cohabitation and partly by an increasing disruption rate among cohabiting women. Birth cohort membership is one indicator of historical time: the year in which a union is observed, or the year in which a union was formed, are other indicators of historical time. Developments across all three dimensions are studied.

Historical time: *Birth cohort*

Chapter 4 documented the higher incidence of separation among the more recently born. Cohort changes in disruption may occur because new cohorts have other expectations and values about relationships than older ones. Because later cohorts have grown up in a period of high marital instability, they will in general be less eager to commit themselves than were earlier cohorts and will often have entered into a union more gradually than their predecessors. This factor may lead to a higher instability rate among those born more recently. Several studies have shown that year of birth determines future marital instability (for Australia, Bracher et al., 1993) or future union instability (for the U.S., Schoen, 1992; for Sweden, Hoem & Hoem, 1992; and for the Netherlands, Klijzing, 1992). Partly as a result of a shift from marriage to cohabitation, it is hypothesised that *younger birth cohorts have higher rates of disruption than older birth cohorts. Relative to (subsequently and directly) married couples, the disruption risk of cohabiting couples increases even more across the birth cohorts.*

Historical time: *Union cohort*

Traditionally, divorce patterns have been studied across a series of marriage cohorts (marriages entered into in the same year, or in the same historical period). Trends across union cohorts will probably be similar to birth cohort trends. In that case, the more recently a union is formed the more union instability should rise, because women enter into a union today more gradually than they did in the past. It has been a general finding for a very long time that the divorce risk has increased across more recent marriage cohorts (for Canada, Balakrishnan et al., 1987; for Germany, Sweden and Italy, Blossfeld et al., 1993b; Diekmann & Klein, 1991; for Norway, Kravdal, 1988; for the US, Morgan & Rindfuss, 1985; Teachman, 1982). Thus, it is hypothesised that *more recent union cohorts have higher rates of disruption than earlier union cohorts. Relative to (subsequently and directly) married couples, the disruption risk of cohabiting couples increases even more across the union cohorts.*

Historical time: *Calendar year*
Divorce rates rose from the sixties up to the mid eighties. Not much is known about the historical developments of the disruption of cohabiting couples. Given that the incidence of cohabitation has increased with the years, and the belief that cohabiting couples separate more often, an ongoing increase in the dissolution risks across the calendar years is likely to be found. Period effects might occur, regardless of year of birth or period in which a union was entered. For instance, simplification of the divorce law in 1971 affected all married couples alike. Because, given the advantages and disadvantages of contemporary society, women decide upon (or are forced into) a break-up, period effects might become visible. It is expected that *dissolution rates are much higher today than they were in the past. Relative to (subsequently and directly) married couples, the disruption risk of cohabiting couples increases even more across the calendar years.*

Personal time
Several personal time dimensions play a role in the breaking up process of a union. The number of years lived with a partner, the individual age of a woman, or the age at which a union was formed might help determine union stability. It was argued that the separation risks to cohabiting couples would increase through historical time. For the personal time dimensions, it is not expected that these determinants affect the disruption rate of cohabiting and married couples differently. If, for instance, a personal time characteristic has a negative impact on union disruption, then it is expected that the effect of this determinant on disruption will be similar for both cohabiting and for married couples.

Personal time: *Union duration*
The stability of a union may vary with the years lived in a union. Theories of why (marital) stability varies with duration lead, however, to inconsistent expectations of how stability varies with personal time. Diekmann and Klein (1991) formulated their 'sickle model'. Co-residence is, in a way, a learning process. Partners become used to each other's habits and wishes, and the 'stock of sins' grows rapidly in the first years of marriage. The authors assume that divorce risks slow down during the later years of marriage. The main reason for the reduction would be that partners learn to cope with each other, becoming used to each other, making fewer mistakes, forgiving and forgetting former 'sins'. An alternative theory, leading to increasing union instability, is the "theory of accumulated irritations". Trussell and colleagues (1992) assume that '...partners become increasingly frustrated with each other's shortcomings and behaviour (until the straw finally breaks the camel's back)' (Trussell et al., 1992: 58). Here, the risk of a disruption would become stronger with increased union duration. Yet another explanation leading to a similar expectation, is that partners have a higher likelihood of growing apart the longer a union endures. Other experiences may, in the long run, drive couples apart. Yet Trussell's 'theory of growing acceptance' assumes an opposite relationship between duration and the risk of a dissolution. Because 'persons come to accept their partner's faults, realizing that .... there is no Mr Right or Ms Right' (page 58), the dissolution risk decreases linearly with union duration. A final, economic, explanation points to the effects of accumulation of shared assets (Becker, 1981). Assets, especially those like house or children, are union-specific

and not easily transported from one partner to another. Accumulation of such assets will increasingly hamper a break-up. Given that accumulation of assets is in general lower among cohabiting than among married couples (Mulder and Manting, 1993), this last explanation should lead to a divergent trend in union dissolution risks with increased duration for each union status separately. Specifically, the difference between the disruption risks of cohabiting and married couples will become higher with increased duration of the union, because of the cohabiting group's lower level of union-specific investment.
Empirical findings suggest that duration effects are generally not important (Bracher, et al., 1993; Trussell et al., 1992). Aggregate (Dutch) population statistics show that, after controlling for presence of children, divorce risks rise with marital duration (Tas, 1986).
These theoretical notions lead to different expectations about the variation of the risk with increasing union duration. It is difficult to identify the most fruitful explanation. Therefore, no expectation in respect of union duration have been made. The variation of stability with union duration is simply examined, because it is clear that there is every reason to suspect that union stability varies with union duration.

Personal time: *Age at union*
Several explanations have been provided for the higher marital instability of persons who marry at a young age. Those who marry when young are thought to be somewhat less experienced in dealing with a (marital) relationship; age at onset can be seen as an indicator of "personal readiness for marriage" (Morgan and Rindfuss, 1985, page 1059); young people probably have fewer financial, economic or social resources available to maintain a marital relationship; and a low age at marriage indicates a shorter search period for an 'eligible' mate, leading to less compatible matches and so to higher divorce rates (Becker, 1981). Research in a great number of countries has shown that the higher the age at marriage, the lower the chances of a divorce (Bracher et al. (1993); Diekmann & Klein (1991); Klijzing (1992); Morgan and Rindfuss (1985); Teachman et al. (1991); Trussell et al. (1992)). Assuming that the relationship between age at union formation and union dissolution is similar to that of the relationship between age at marriage and divorce, *a young age at entry into a union is expected to be linked to a higher risk of dissolution of a first union.*

Personal time: *Age*
Age at union is a point-in-time factor. It refers to the moment of union formation and ignores the fact that people age after a union is formed. As people grow older, their attitudes, norms and beliefs change. Ideological values are rather unstable when people are young (Alwin, 1991). It is possible that, with an increase in an individual's age, the stability of the union is more highly valued (Booth et al., 1987). Another explanation is that, as people become older, their attachment to each other as a consequence of the bonds of finance, property, children and so on increases. If people change with age, then union stability might also change with individual ageing. Age, as a time-varying factor instead of a point-in-time determinant, determines union stability. Given the assumption that the relationship between age and the dissolution of first

unions is similar to the relationship between age and divorce, the hypothesis is that *the risk of a dissolution will diminish with increasing age*.

Most studies have only incorporated a few of the above time dimensions. A few studies focusing on unravelling the effects of all these different types of time dimensions in the presence of each other show inconsistent results. Sometimes birth cohort is shown to have the strongest influence on divorce (Bracher et al., 1993), sometimes calendar year seems to be more important when explaining divorce than marriage cohort (Lutz et al., 1992) or birth cohort (Thornton & Rodgers, 1987). Trussell and colleagues (1992) found that increasing dissolution risks can be explained better in terms of union cohort than in terms of birth cohort.

With regard to personal time dimensions, it has sometimes been shown that the effect of age is greater than that of age at marriage (Lutz et al., 1991; Thornton & Rodgers, 1987), and that sometimes age at marriage is more important than age (Bracher et al., 1993). Duration is generally not important in the presence of age or age at marriage (Bracher, et al., 1993; Lutz et al., 1991; Thornton & Rodgers, 1987). This chapter explores the relevance of each time dimension for union dissolution, controlling to a certain extent for the other time dimensions.

The hypotheses formulated with respect to time and union dissolution are summarized in the scheme below. For historical time dimensions, differential effects on disruption are expected for those who cohabit (coh), for those who are currently married after a period of cohabitation (coh-> mar) and for those who married directly (mar).

Scheme 2   Summary of hypotheses: Time and moving out of a first union

	General expected effect	
Recent birth cohort	coh	++
	coh -> mar	+
	mar	+
Recent union cohort	coh	++
	coh -> mar	+
	mar	+
Recent calender year	coh	++
	coh -> mar	+
	mar	+
Short duration		?
Young age at union formation		+
Young age		+

Explanation: See Scheme 1 (chapter 7)

7.2.3 Past life course experiences influencing movement out of a first union

In addition to time, past life course determinants also influence the break-up of unions. If the way a union is formed influences union dissolution, it is likely that these determinants will, at least indirectly, affect union dissolution because of their direct influence on union formation. But there may be direct influences as well. Determinants studied for their impact on union formation are also examined for their influence on union dissolution: parental divorce, religion, family size, age of mother at childbearing, and home town. A general assumption is that the relationship between past life course determinants and union disruption will not be different for cohabiting and married couples. The hypotheses formulated concentrate on the link between past life course determinants and union disruption, irrespective of the status of the union.

Past life course experiences: *Parental divorce*
Divorce studies have given much attention to the transmission hypothesis (Mueller & Pope, 1977), according to which the children of divorced parents themselves have a higher divorce risk. Women from divorced families may 'escape' the parental home sooner; one way of becoming independent is to cohabit as quickly as possible. Daughters of divorced parents do indeed have a higher rate of cohabitation than women from no-divorce families (chapter 5). This explanation points more to an indirect than a direct effect of parental divorce: via the early timing of a union. There are, however, further factors pointing to direct effects on later union instability of parental divorce. Daughters of divorced mothers will have learned that women are capable of managing family life without a husband (McLanahan and Bumpass, 1988). Such women might well be more likely to consider divorce when confronted with an unhappy marriage. Research in different countries show inconsistent findings. Sometimes it was found that the children of divorced parents run a higher risk of divorce themselves (for the US, Mueller and Pope, 1977; for Germany, Wagner, 1991), but in other studies this effect was not found to be significant (for Australia, Bracher et al., 1993; for the Netherlands, Klijzing, 1992). These inconsistent findings may derive from different effects of parental divorce across countries or across time. Despite these inconsistent findings, the hypothesis is that *women of divorced parents have a higher likelihood of disruption than women of parents who are not divorced*.

Past life course experiences: *Having a religious affiliation*
Dutch Protestants appear to have a more tolerant attitude towards divorce than Catholics, but those who do not belong to a church disapprove much less of divorce (Halman, 1991). Religious women will consider a divorce much less frequently than non-religious women when confronted with an unsatisfactory relationship. The likelihood of a lower rate of marriage break up amongst religious women (in most studies measured as Catholic) is a universal finding in studies of divorce and union dissolution (For Canada, Balakrishnan et al., 1987; for Germany, Diekmann and Klein, 1991, Wagner, 1991; for the US, Menken et al., 1991; Teachman, 1982; for the Netherlands, Klijzing, 1992, Manting, 1993; and finally for Sweden, Hoem & Hoem, 1992). It is therefore expected that *religious women experience a lower rate of disruption than non-religious women*.

Past life course experiences: *Being brought up in a small family*
If women brought up in a small family attach more value to independence and freedom than to family-oriented attitudes, they will consider divorce at an earlier stage than women from larger families. Some studies show, however, no effect of family size on divorce (for Australia Bracher et al., 1993; for the Netherlands, Manting, 1993). Indeed, one study showed lower rates of divorce for women brought up in a small family (for the US; Teachman, 1982). However, we have already seen that small family size was associated with a lower rate of marriage (chapter 5), giving support to the view that women who grew up in a small family tended to attach less value to marriage. This would imply that *women who were brought up in a small family experience a higher rate of dissolution.*

Past life course experiences: *Having a young mother*
Women with relatively young mothers have a higher rate of union formation. This occurrence was explained by the view that young mothers would not discourage their children from marrying or cohabiting at young ages. It may also be that young mothers, because they are younger, are more tolerant of a break-up in their children's relationships than older mothers. As such, one would expect that *women with relatively young mothers experience a higher dissolution rate.*

Past life course experiences: *Growing up in a small town*
Tolerance towards divorce used to be higher in larger cities than in smaller ones (De Feijter, 1991). The municipality in which one grew up may be associated with the level of tolerance towards disruption. This might affect union stability. It is expected that *women who grew up in a small town experience lower rates of disruption.*

Historical changes in the meaning of past life course experiences to union disruption
The definition of what constitutes a good marriage is highly period-specific. Today, material aspects such as housing, financial situation, living in with parents-in-law are perceived to be less important than more affective elements of a relationship such as love, intimacy, respect, loyalty and fidelity (Halman, 1991). In the sixties, about half the Dutch population believed that divorce should not be tolerated where there were children. At the beginning of the eighties, almost nobody disapproved of divorce when children lived at home (SCP, 1992). The number of people who considered those who were married to be happier than the unmarried declined rapidly through the years (SCP, 1992). If the perceived attraction of marriage diminishes with time, alongside the motivation towards, and increasing toleration of divorce, then the underlying determinants may also change in their impact.

Chapter 4 documented the rising number of women who have ever experienced a break up of a relationship. One fifth of women born in the beginning of the fifties had separated before they were forty. The more recent the birth cohort, the higher the number of women experiencing a disruption. If dissolution becomes more frequent, then this must also mean that more and more women, irrespective of their past life course experiences, will follow this pattern. The historical change hypothesis for cohabitation was that past life course experiences weaken in strength over time because cohabitation has become a widespread phenomenon. Break up has also become widespread, which should mean that the determinants weaken in impact over time. A study on the divorce of married couples in Australia (Bracher et al., 1993) showed that there was indeed some weakening in the strength of current life course determinants. The historical change hypothesis for the relationship between past life course experiences and union dissolution is that *past life course experiences have a decreasing impact on union dissolution.*

A changing meaning of past life course experiences to union disruption with the passage of individual time
A general assumption of this study is that past life course experiences influence the later life course. As people grow older, their early life course experiences will, however, diminish in importance for current behaviour. Effects of past life course determinants will be overruled by more recent experiences. The influence of parents diminishes when their children start living with a partner or husband. This fact was made clear in chapter 6. The longer a woman lives with a partner, the less influence will parents exercise on their daughter's life-style. The life course change hypothesis formulated for union formation stated that past life course experiences diminish in impact as the individual life course unfolds. This was indeed the case, at least for some of the determinants. The life course change hypothesis for union dissolution is that *past life course experiences should decreasingly exert influence on the process of union dissolution with union duration.*

All the expectations formulated above are summarized in scheme 3.

Scheme 3 Summary of hypotheses: Past life course experiences and moving out of a first union

	general expected effect	historical change hypothesis	life course change hypothesis
Parents divorced	+	+ -> 0	+ -> 0
A religious affiliation	-	- -> 0	- -> 0
Being brought up in a small family	+	+ -> 0	+ -> 0
Having a young mother	+	+ -> 0	+ -> 0
Growing up in a small town	-	- -> 0	- -> 0

Explanation:
A minus sign (-) indicates a lower risk of union dissolution.
A positive sign (+) indicates a higher risk of union dissolution.
A zero (0) indicates no significant impact on the risk of union dissolution.
The arrow indicates a changing meaning across cohorts or with duration (from shorter to longer).

7.2.4 Current life course experiences influencing movement out of a first union

Many individual and couple-related changes influencing the stability of a union occur during co-residence. Individual changes requiring examination are similar to those studied for union formation: education, work, and fertility. The role of educational achievement is also examined. Partner-related changes will, however, not be examined in this study. The main reason is that the data set available does not permit the testing of relationships between partner-related characteristics and union stability, since nothing is known of former partners.

These immediate life course determinants may have an indirect impact on union dissolution because of their influence on union formation. They may, however, also have a direct effect on union dissolution. It is believed that impact of these determinants on union disruption will be similar both for married and unmarried couples.

Current life course experiences: *Educational enrolment*
From an economic viewpoint, female educational enrolment should reduce the sexual division of labour. Becker (1981) suggests that this may lead to reduced advantage in the state of marriage. It should thus also lead to a higher disruption rate. Perhaps students will also experience a higher rate of disruption because they have less time and energy left to invest in their relationship. *It is expected that students will experience a higher rate of disruption.*

Current life course experiences: *Educational achievement*
Education may influence union dissolution through both enrolment and level of attainment. If highly educated young adults value independence and autonomy more than young adults with low educational attainment (Liefbroer, 1991), then highly educated women, confronted with a unsatisfying relationship, may be more ready to consider a disruption than less well educated women. The result may be a higher rate of dissolution among highly educated women. The level of education may also be viewed as an indication of degree of attachment to the labour market; the higher the level of education, the higher the attachment to an occupational career and the higher the level of economic independence of women (Blossfeld & Huinink, 1991). If economic independence of women reduces the advantage of a union and also the (financial) barriers to disruption (Becker, 1981), then the expectation will be that highly educated women experience a higher level of disruption. Empirical findings with respect to the relationship of educational achievement and union stability do not always show a higher disruption rate among highly educated people. Some studies find no impact of educational level on divorce (Bracher, et al., 1993), others find that higher educated women do indeed have higher levels of dissolution (Trussell. et al., 1992; Hoem & Hoem, 1992), have lower levels of divorce (Menken et al., 1981; Teachman, 1982, Morgan and Rindfuss, 1985, South and Spitze, 1986) or, have higher levels of divorce (Blossfeld et al., 1992). Despite these latter findings, it is hypothesised that *women with a higher level of education will have a higher level of disruption.*

Current life course experiences: *Labour force participation*
The economic independence of women has generally been seen as the major force behind rising divorce rates. Working women can afford to divorce or to separate because they can acquire (economic) independence by other means than staying in a unsatisfying relationship. Female economic independence, of which labour force participation is an indication, leads to higher marital instability because the financial barriers to disruption are lower (Becker, 1981). Moreover, if work is an indication of a higher attachment to independence, then this should also raise their level of disruption. That working women have a higher rate of disruption or divorce is supported by empirical findings (Bracher et al., 1992; Trussell et al., 1992; Wagner, 1991). As such, this would lead to the expectation that *working women have a higher rate of disruption*.

Current life course experiences: *Having children*
During marriage, a husband and wife invest in the care of children. Children are seen as marital-specific 'capital' that cannot easily be transported to any next marital partner (Becker, 1981). The consequence is that having children should lead to a lower disruption rate. In addition, the normal barriers to disruption are higher when children are involved. That childless couples generally have a higher disruption rate might also be the results of anticipative behaviour. Couples may postpone parenthood until each is confident enough about the relationship with the partner. Couples who feel insecure may postpone parenthood, whereas couples who feel confident that they will have a long-lasting relationship may decide to have children. Many empirical results support the hypothesis that married couples who have no children have higher rates of divorce than married couple with children (Bracher e.a., 1993; Diekmann & Klein, 1991). Further, the disruption risks of all (married and unmarried) unions are higher for childless women than for mothers (Hoem & Hoem, 1992; Trussel et al., 1992, Klijzing, 1992). Families with more than two children seem to have a somewhat higher dissolution risk (Hoem & Hoem, 1992; Klijzing, 1992). The hypothesis is that *childless women have higher risks of dissolution than women with children, and women with one child have a higher risk of dissolution than women with more children*.

Current life course experiences: *child born before or pregnant when a union was formed*
One of the examples of how an individual's past may affect the future life course is the incidence of a pregnancy or a first birth before marriage. An accidental pregnancy was traditionally associated with a forced marriage. It is widely acknowledged that the divorce risk among women pregnant at the time of their marriage is higher (Morgan and Rindfuss, 1985; Teachman, 1992). It can be seen as an indicator of the lack of 'readiness for marriage'. The individual women were not ready for either marriage or the husband, but had to marry because they were pregnant. Today, pregnancy before marriage occurs mostly among cohabiting couples, but less frequently among women living independently from their partners. Although chapter 1 showed that the close link between marriage and fertility is on the decrease, most children grow up within a marriage relationship. Moreover, if having and rearing children out of wedlock can also be seen as a sign of a higher attachment to independence and freedom of going one own's way, then

rearing children out of wedlock should have a higher rate of disruption. Thus, *it is expected that women who were pregnant before entry into a union or during the period of cohabitation have a higher disruption rate than women who have their children born within wedlock.*

Historical changes in the meaning of current life course experiences to union disruption
Individuals make a decision about a disruption in a given historical time, at a given moment in their (union) life course (Morgan and Rindfuss, 1985). Opinions about social issues change over time; for example, about the combination of work with marriage, work and having children, childlessness, rearing children outside wedlock. Such changes might well affect union stability over historical time.
Childlessness, for instance, used to be an involuntary situation: now, it is a voluntary one. In the mid sixties, a large proportion of Dutch people did not approve of married couples who chose to remain childless. Voluntary childlessness is today almost completely accepted (SCP, 1992). Childlessness used to be associated with a high risk of divorce. Carlsson and Stinson (cited in Morgan and Rindfuss, 1985) argue that, because the occurrence of childlessness has changed from an involuntary to a more or less voluntary condition, it will lead decreasingly to higher marital instability. The sense of 'disorder' of having children out of wedlock has also changed. It used to be an accidental, involuntary situation. Today, increasingly more couples wait until pregnancy takes place before they marry. Because of the weakening impact of involuntariness, the expectation might be that its effect will decline with historical time. Negative attitudes towards highly educated women who also maintain a stable job and rear children outside wedlock have also diminished over time. The impact of this factor on union disruption might thus also be on the decrease. The 'historical change thesis' for union dissolution thus postulates that *current life course experiences decreasingly influence union dissolution.*

A changing meaning of current life course experiences to union disruption with the passage of individual time
Despite the fact that more and more women do not leave the labour market at the moment of marriage, most women leave the labour market after childbirth. The relatively small number of women who remain in the labour market at later years of their union might be seen as an indicator of their urge for independence. Consequently, the impact of work might vary with the duration of the union. At early years of the union, practically all women work. At later years, only those who most value independence will work. The expectation is that *the impact of work becomes larger with increasing union duration.*

Morgan and Rindfuss (1985) as well as Kravdal (1988) found that the higher likelihood of divorce among women who had a child before marriage operated only for the first years of marriage. This finding implies that if a marriage survives to later years, the impact of situations in the first years of the union on divorce diminish. It might imply that the impact of childlessness or of the chronological order of marriage and fertility diminishes with an increase of union duration. To elaborate further, the expectation is that *the impact of childlessness diminishes with an increase of union duration.*

Scheme 4 Summary of hypotheses: Current life course experiences and moving out of a first union

	general expected effect	historical change hypothesis	life course change hypothesis
Studying	+	+ -> 0	+ -> 0
High educational level	+	+ -> 0	+ -> 0
Employed	+	+ -> 0	+ -> ++
Childlessness	++	++ -> 0	++ -> 0
One child	+	+ -> 0	+ -> 0
Pregnant or childbirth before entry into a union	++	++ -> 0	++ -> 0

Explanation: See Scheme 3 (chapter 7)

7.3 Empirical findings: selecting relevant past and current life course experiences

This section describes the procedure to eliminate those determinants that play no statistically significant role in explaining differentials of risks of union dissolution. First, the influence on union dissolution of time dimensions in their simultaneity is studied. A presentation of univariate results is followed by a description of multivariate results. The same procedure is followed for past and current life course determinants. First, univariate results are shown, and then multivariate results are discussed. This procedure leads to the selection of the most relevant determinants. Finally, the results of the final model, including all relevant determinants, are presented.

The dependent variable in the analyses is, once again, the hazard rate. The monthly hazard rate is the risk of a dissolution in a certain month, given that it had not previously occurred. Women run the risk of a dissolution of a first union the moment they enter into it. The assumption is that the break-up of couples will differ according to the possibly time-varying type of the union, so a distinction is drawn between current and past legal status. Women enter into a union through cohabitation or marriage, but some women may marry after a period of cohabitation. The starting time is the moment a woman experienced entry into cohabitation or marriage, because it is only after that event that she is at risk of a dissolution or a divorce. Duration is thus measured from the moment of entry. For women currently cohabiting, duration is equal to the duration of the cohabitation; for women who married directly, duration is equal to the duration of the marriage. For women currently married but who previously cohabited, timing counts first the period of cohabitation, and then the period of marriage. The period of observation ends at the interview date by censoring (no dissolution having yet occurred) or at the moment the union was ended by the death of the marital spouse (death of a cohabiting partner is not known) or at the moment of dissolution of cohabitation or at the moment of divorce of the married couple. There are two shortcomings in the data set. One problem is that the death of a partner is known for those who were married, but not for those who were cohabiting. Although it is a very unusual event for women in the sample, this means that the duration of cohabiting unions might sometimes be shorter than has actually been measured. Another shortcoming of the data set is that the disruption date of cohabiting couples is known, but not for all married couples. Although the date of divorce is known, the actual date of separation is not known for less than half the married couples. To examine the impact of using date of divorce instead of date of separation for married couples, two models were estimated: one multivariate model in which the end of marriage was defined by separation (assuming that persons separated six months before divorce in the case of these marital disruptions of which date of separation was unknown) and another model in which the end of marriage was marked by the moment of divorce. The results were almost similar (Appendix chapter 7). It has therefore been decided to use date of divorce for all married women. Of the nearly 4,500 women who entered into a first union, about 600 have experienced a disruption. About 300 cohabiting women separated; about 100 currently married women who had cohabited before marriage separated; and about 200 married women who did not cohabit before marriage separated.

Historical and personal time determinants

Univariate results
Table 1 shows (univariate) hazard rates of union dissolution, distinguished according to the three types of union status and the historical and personal time dimensions. The monthly hazard rate of a disruption (irrespective union status) is 15 per 10,000; the hazard rate of cohabiting women is much higher (0.0054) than that of married cohabitors (0.0013) and of directly married women (0.0008).

Dissolution rates rise enormously across the birth cohorts. The risk of dissolution for the youngest female birth cohort is five times higher than that for the oldest female birth cohort. The increasing tendency across the birth cohorts (column 2) is not always visible for each union status separately (columns 3-5). For example, cohabiting women of the 1950-54 birth cohort have a disruption risk of .0047 as against a risk of .0057 for cohabiting women born in 1960-64. For the currently married couples (who cohabited before marriage), the tendency is the opposite. The risk of a dissolution slightly decreases across the birth cohorts from .0015 (1950-54) to .0011 (1960-64). Whether this holds in a multivariate analysis remains to be seen. The age composition may, for example, disturb these observations. The higher risk of the directly marrieds of the younger birth cohorts is probably caused by the fact that those women are on average younger than the women of the earlier birth cohorts. When women are young, or when women have formed a union at a relatively low age, they have a higher divorce rate. Women aged 19 to 20 have a risk of 0.0031, whereas women aged 29 to 30 have a risk of 0.0009.

Table 1 Monthly hazard rates of dissolution of first unions distinguished according to union status and time dimensions (univariate results)

	All unions	Cohabiting	Married after cohanitation	Married directly
average	0.0015	0.0054	0.0013	0.0008
Birth cohort				
1. 1950-54	0.0011	0.0047	0.0015	0.0007
2. 1955-59	0.0015	0.0050	0.0012	0.0007
3. 1960-64	0.0026	0.0057	0.0011	0.0010
4. 1965-69	0.0054	0.0085	0.0028	0.0010
Union cohort				
1. < 1975	0.0010	0.0056	0.0022	0.0008
2. 1975-79	0.0014	0.0043	0.0012	0.0008
3. >= 1980	0.0021	0.0061	0.0008	0.0005
Calender year t				
1. < 1972	0.0016	0.0059	0.0065	0.0008
2. 1972-73	0.0018	0.0066	0.0000	0.0014
3. 1974-75	0.0012	0.0034	0.0017	0.0008
4. 1976-77	0.0013	0.0031	0.0029	0.0008
5. 1978-79	0.0014	0.0058	0.0007	0.0007
6. 1980-81	0.0016	0.0041	0.0020	0.0009
7. 1982-83	0.0018	0.0065	0.0017	0.0007
8. >= 1984	0.0015	0.0059	0.0010	0.0007
Union duration t				
1. within one year	0.0023	0.0054	0.0005	0.0003
2. year 1	0.0020	0.0043	0.0009	0.0011
3. year 2	0.0017	0.0056	0.0008	0.0006
4. year 3	0.0021	0.0081	0.0014	0.0010
5. year 4	0.0012	0.0054	0.0010	0.0006
6. year 5	0.0013	0.0050	0.0016	0.0008
7. year 6	0.0010	0.0017	0.0013	0.0009
8. year 7	0.0013	0.0054	0.0013	0.0010
9. years 9-10	0.0012	0.0059	0.0019	0.0008
10. years 11-12	0.0011	0.0093	0.0019	0.0008
11. years 13-14	0.0008	0.0222	0.0013	0.0006
12. years 15-16	0.0008	.	0.0019	0.0006
13. years 17 or more	0.0015	.	0.0029	0.0013
Age at union				
1. 16-18	0.0030	0.0085	0.0028	0.0017
2. 19-20	0.0013	0.0044	0.0013	0.0008
3. 20-24	0.0011	0.0047	0.0009	0.0004
4. 25-37	0.0017	0.0048	0.0005	0.0005
Age t				
1. 16-18	0.0044	0.0086	0.0054	0.0009
2. 19-20	0.0031	0.0060	0.0027	0.0015
3. 21-22	0.0022	0.0058	0.0014	0.0009
4. 23-24	0.0014	0.0044	0.0010	0.0007
5. 25-26	0.0014	0.0041	0.0016	0.0008
6. 27-28	0.0012	0.0062	0.0012	0.0005
7. 29-30	0.0009	0.0029	0.0011	0.0007
8. 31-32	0.0011	0.0056	0.0015	0.0007
9. 33-37	0.0010	0.0115	0.0011	0.0006

t = time-varying covariate, . = no observations

Rates also rise the later a union is formed. The dissolution rate is twice as high for those who entered into a union in the eighties than for those who did so in the seventies. The disruption rate of first unions increases across the union cohorts, whereas the risk of a divorce decreases. Whether this holds in a multivariate model containing other relevant time dimensions remains to be seen. The lower union divorce rate for the union cohort 1980-88 may, for instance, be caused partly by the fact that this cohort has on average a much lower union duration than union cohort 1975-79. Divorce rates are lower at earlier years, which may be a cause of the lower divorce rate for the 1980-88 cohort. Finally, dissolution rates do not really show a linear increase or decrease in trends across the years. This trend may be disturbed by the age composition that differs across calendar years.

Multivariate results
In this section, the results of a multivariate model, containing all these time dimensions simultaneously, is discussed. The results of table 1 have to be interpreted with caution, since these figures do not control for other relevant time dimensions. That is why a *multivariate* model including all these determinants simultaneously has been estimated. All temporal covariates were compressed into two to four categories, because it would not otherwise have been possible to estimate the influence of each covariate in the presence of all others. Average union duration differs a great deal between union statuses; 31 months in cohabitation, 67 months in the married status for currently married women (duration of cohabitation is not included in this measure) and 113 months for those directly married. It was the reason that union duration could not be broken down into more categories.

Model fit was guided by the above formulated theoretical concepts. The first step was to examine the impact of a determinant on the union dissolution risk. There is no significant period effect (table 2: no 5). Other determinants do have a significant impact on union disruption (nos. 1-4, 6-7).

It was expected that tendencies in disruption might differ between cohabiting and married couples. However, period effects were not significantly different for married and cohabiting couples, given that there was no significant interaction effect of calender year with union status. Nor is the impact of calendar year significant after controlling for age (nos. 8-11).

After controlling for union status, birth cohort does not significantly influence union dissolution. Although the expectation was that disruption rates would rise more among cohabiting couples relative to married couples, there is no indication of a significant cohort change in disruption for each union status separately, given that the interaction of birth cohort and union status is insignificant. Nor is the impact of birth cohort significant after controlling for age (nos. 12-15).

Table 2   Results of conditional loglikelihood ratio tests of a model of dissolution including temporal covariates and union status

Union duration (in months) in 3 categories (0-48, 49-84, > 85)
Age in four categories (0-20, 21-22, 23-24, > = 25)
Age at union in three categories (<19, < 21, > = 21)
Calender year in three categories (<1974, 1974-1979, > = 1980)
Union cohort in two categories (< 1980, > =1980)

	L2	df	ΔL2	Δdf
0 { }	925.6	2592		
1 {A} duration	876.4	2589	49.2	3*
2 {B} birth cohort	825.1	2588	100.4	4*
3 {C} age	827.1	2588	98.4	4*
4 {D} age at union	837.2	2589	88.4	3*
5 {E} calender year	921.5	2589	4.1	3
6 {F} union status	443.3	2589	482.3	3*
7 {G} union cohort	874.8	2590	50.8	2*
8 {E,F}	439.8	2587		
9 {E,F,EF}	436.4	2583	3.4	4
10 {E,C,F}	420.5	2584		
11 {C,F}	424.0	2586	4.5	3
12 {F} union status	443.3	2589		
13 {B,F}	434.1	2586	9.1	3
14 {B,D,F}	356.6	2584		
15 {D,F}	359.0	2587	3.6	3
16 {F} union status	443.3	2589		
17 {G,F}	443.3	2588	0.0	1
18 {G,F,GF}	425.3	2586	18.0	2*
19 {F} union status	443.3	2589		
20 {A,F}	440.3	2587	3.0	2
21 {A,F,AF}	436.2	2583	4.1	4
22 {C,F}	424.0	2586		
23 {C,D,F}	356.6	2584	67.5	2*
24 {D,F}	359.0	2587		
25 {C,D,F}	356.6	2584	2.5	3
26 {D,F,G}	357.1	2586		
27 {D,F,G,FG}	339.2	2584	17.9	2*
28 {D,F}	359.0	2587		
29 {B,D,F}	356.6	2584	2.4	3
30 {A,E,D,F}	354.5	2583		
31 {AE,D,F}	346.4	2579	8.1	4
32 {C,G,D,F}	354.1	2583		
33 {CG,D,F}	347.7	2580	6.4	3
34 {E,C,F}	420.5	2584		
35 {E,C}	424.0	2586	3.5	2

L2:   loglikelihood
df: degree of freedom
*:   conditional p < 0.01
{}:   indicates nul model
{A}:   indicates model including the main effect of covariate A only
{A,B,AB}:   indicates model including the main effects of covariates A and B and the interaction effect of A and B.

See chapter 3 for a description of the log likelihood ratio tests. An asterisk means that inclusion of a certain determinant (or interactions with certain determinants) contributes significantly to the fit of the model.

Table 1 showed that women born in the sixties have a much higher dissolution rate than women born in the fifties. The rate of disruption is almost five times higher for women born in 1965-69 than for women born in 1950-54. The fact that the effect of birth cohort is insignificant after controlling for union status can be interpreted as follows. Because younger birth cohorts are much more likely to be in an unstable union (that is, to cohabit or to be married after cohabitation) they have a much higher dissolution rate. If the fact that younger cohorts cohabit more often than earlier cohorts is controlled for, then year of birth does not significantly influence union dissolution. Women born in the sixties experience many more break-ups because they cohabit more often than do women born in the fifties. Moreover, cohabiting women born in the sixties do not have a higher rate of disruption than cohabiting women born in the fifties.

Union cohort does not significantly influence the process of dissolution either, after controlling for union status. Nevertheless, the different tendencies for cohabiting and married couples to be seen in table 1 are significant. The interaction effect of union cohort and union status is significant (nos. 16-18).

After controlling for union status, neither did duration contribute significantly to the fit of the model. The higher disruption rate at the first years of the union must thus be the result of a relatively high proportion of cohabiting women (with a high level of disruption) at early years of the union, whereas at later years of the union there are relatively high proportions of women who married directly (with a low level of disruption). Once this compositional shift in union status is controlled for, duration effects are no longer significant (nos. 19-21).

After controlling for union status, both age and age at union have a significant impact on union dissolution. Thus, the risk of disruption is significantly higher when women are relatively young or when women have formed a union at an early age. However, after controlling for age at union, the time-varying covariate of the individual's age is no longer significant, whereas after controlling for the age of the individual, age at union is significant (nos 22-35). This means that age at union explains differentiation in union disruption risk more than the time-varying age a woman has.

Some other checks have also been made, but this examination does not change all the results presented above (see Appendix 7). For the time-varying example of age, the conclusion must be that when an individual is very young, the dissolution risks are higher, but when the individual has reached the age of approximately 25 (see table 1), the older age of the individual is of no importance in the variation of the risks, whereas age at union still is still significant.

In summary, with union status controlled for, birth cohort, calendar year, and duration have no significant impact on union dissolution. After controlling for age at union, age no longer influences the level of disruption of unions significantly.

Past life course determinants
In this section, univariate results are first presented, followed by evidence of multivariate estimations. Table 3 gives a first rough indication of how past life course determinants influence union dissolution.

Table 3 Monthly hazard rates of dissolution of first unions distinguished according to union status and past life course determinants (univariate results)

	all unions	cohabiting	married after	married directly
Parents divorced t				
1. no	0.0014	0.0050	0.0013	0.0008
2. yes	0.0034	0.0100	0.0014	0.0007
Religion i				
1. no religion	0.0024	0.0056	0.0013	0.0014
2. roman catholic	0.0010	0.0050	0.0012	0.0005
3. other religion	0.0012	0.0052	0.0015	0.0007
Parental size family				
1. ≤ 2 children	0.0018	0.0060	0.0012	0.0007
2. > 2 children	0.0015	0.0052	0.0014	0.0008
Age difference with mother				
1. ≤ 25	0.0019	0.0059	0.0013	0.0010
2. > 25	0.0014	0.0052	0.0014	0.0007
Size of municipality of residence when aged 6 to 16				
1. $\geq 100,000$	0.0021	0.0054	0.0016	0.0012
2. $< 100,000$	0.0013	0.0054	0.0012	0.0006

t=time-varying, i= covariate is measured at time of interview

Three of the covariates reflecting elements of the respondent's past life course - size of municipality, divorced parents, religion - show a great diversity of total risk of dissolution. Children of divorced parents have a risk of 0.0034 as against a risk of 0.0014 for children whose parents did not divorce. Non-religious women have a rate that is twice as high as religious women, irrespective of denomination. Children who grew up in a large city have a higher rate of disruption than those who lived in a small town during their childhood[1]. These univariate analyses give a first indication about the validity of the hypotheses formulated. The differences in disruption risk between women who were brought up in a small or a large family are negligible. There are also no differences in disruption risks between women with a relatively younger or older mother. Home town is important for differentiating the divorce risk, but for the level of disruption of cohabiting couples, the town in which one is brought up is not important. Among the directly marrieds, women with no denomination have a higher divorce rate than women with a denomination.

---

[1]Home town was originally coded into three categories, as was done in the analyses presented in the previous chapters. Because the hazard rate did not differ between women living in a medium sized city and those living in a large city, this covariate was recoded into two categories.

Multivariate results

For the univariate findings presented in table 3, it remains to be seen whether these determinants still influence the process of union dissolution after controlling for union status. Because the life course hypothesis postulates an impact of determinants varying with personal time, union duration was included as one of the covariates to check whether the determinants have a varying influence according to union duration. Because the historical change hypothesis postulates that determinants may vary with historical time, two separate multivariate models were estimated to check whether determinants vary with either birth cohort or union cohort. The first model included birth cohort as a historical time dimension, together with the respondent's experience of a parental divorce, size of parental family, age of mother at childbearing, size of the municipality, religion (compressed to 'no religion' and 'a religion'), union status, union duration. The second model contained all these determinants too, but, instead of birth cohort, union cohort as a historical time dimension was included.

The results of the first multivariate model (table 4) show that all determinants significantly influence the risk of a dissolution (nos 1-4,6-8), with the exception of parental family size (nos 5).

After controlling for union status, age of mother no longer affects the level of union dissolution significantly (nos 9-15). Although it was hypothesised that determinants have a similar impact on disruption figures for both cohabiting and married couples, the differing impact of age of mother and family size on disruption of the three union statuses was also checked (this was done by testing the significance of the interaction of union status with a determinant). Age of mother and family size do not significantly interact with union type (nos 16-17). To check the historical change hypothesis, it was investigated whether these two determinants interacted significantly with birth cohort. They did not (nos 18-21). The life course hypothesis was not supported either: family size and youthful age of mother do not change in significance with union duration (22-25).

Table 4 Results of loglikelihood ratio tests of a model of union dissolution including past life course determinants, duration and birth cohort

	L2	df	ΔL2	Δdf
0 { }	1089.4	1152		
1 {A} duration of union	1040.2	1149	49.2	3*
2 {B} birth cohort	989.0	1148	100.4	4*
3 {C} parents divorced	1055.4	1150	34.0	2*
4 {D} religion	992.4	1150	97.0	2*
5 {E} parental family size	1084.6	1150	4.9	2
6 {F} age of mother	1078.1	1150	11.3	2*
7 {G} union status	607.1	1149	482.3	3*
8 {H} size of municipality	1063.7	1150	25.7	2*
{G}	607.1	1149		
9 {A,G}	604.1	1147	3.0	2
10 {B,G}	598.0	1146	9.1	3
11 {C,G}	594.8	1148	12.3	1*
12 {D,G}	590.1	1148	17.0	1*
13 {E,G}	607.0	1148	0.1	1
14 {F,G}	602.8	1148	4.3	1
15 {G,H}	599.1	1148	8.0	1*
second-order-effect of union status {G} and				
16 {E,G,EG}	605.1	1146	1.9	2
17 {F,G,FG}	600.2	1146	2.6	2
second-order-effect with birth cohort of women {B} and (controlling for union status {G})				
18 {B,E,G}	598.0	1145		
19 {BE,G}	596.3	1142	1.6	3
20 {B,F,G}	594.8	1145		
21 {BF,G}	593.7	1142	1.1	3
second-order-effect with duration {A} and (controlling for union status {G})				
22 {A,E,G}	604.0	1146		
23 {AE,G}	602.6	1144	1.4	2
24 {A,F,G}	599.9	1146		
25 {AF,G}	598.5	1144	1.3	2

* conditional p < 0.01

Determinants might not only vary with birth cohort as a representative of a historical time dimension, but also with union cohort. Therefore, another multivariate model, including union cohort instead of birth cohorts, was estimated (table 5). Neither age of mother nor family size interact significantly with union cohorts.

The multivariate findings show that the influence of family size and age of mother does not vary significantly with union cohort. In short, family size does not influence union dissolution. Women with a relatively young mother do indeed have a significantly higher dissolution rate, as expected, but the effect disappears after controlling for union status. Thus, this determinant influences union dissolution only indirectly through its influence on union formation, but it has no direct impact. Because children of young mothers most often choose to cohabit, they have a somewhat higher disruption risk.

Table 5 Results of conditional loglikelihood ratio tests of a model of union dissolution including past life course determinants (parents divorced, religion, parental family size {E}, age of the mother {F}, size of municipality), the union status, duration and union cohort

second-order-effect of union cohort {D} and (controlling for union status {G})	L2	df	ΔL2	Δdf
7 {D,E,G}	416.5	571		
8 {DE,G}	415.2	570	1.3	1
9 {D,F,G}	412.3	571		
10 {DF,G}	409.2	570	3.1	1

*: conditional $p < 0.01$

Past mediated by more immediate experiences

Before discussing the relationship of the remaining significant past life course determinants and union dissolution, another multivariate model is presented which explores to what extent past life course determinants lose their impact once more recent life course positions are introduced. One of the main assumptions of the life course perspective is that, after controlling for the current characteristics of the individual, the impact of early life course experiences on behaviour during the later life course will fall, because they will act mainly indirectly via earlier, relevant, behaviour. Bumpass and colleagues (1991) found that the experience of parental divorce was mediated through other covariates such as the respondent's age at marriage, education and cohabitation experience. They suggest that the inter-generational link in family disruption is strongly associated with demographic behaviours that in turn may affect the outcomes of the higher risk of divorce. If so, the expectation is that women coming from a divorced family have higher disruption risks, but that these mainly disappear after controlling for the individual's later life course position. This mechanism might also be relevant to the other three determinants significantly influencing union dissolution: religion, home town and parental divorce.

First, a multivariate model, including religion and home town (the remaining significant determinants) and a covariate measuring childbirth(s) as well as age at union, was estimated to check whether these two past life course determinants were mediated by the two current ones (age at union and childbirth). Religion still has a direct effect on the dissolution of a first union, but home town and the interaction of home town with union status no longer influence the union dissolution process significantly after controlling for the two current life course determinants (table 6).

Table 6 Results of loglikelihood ratio tests of a model of first union dissolution, including significant past life course determinants (religion {C}, home town {E}) and current determinants (children {B}, age at union {D}), union status {F}, union cohort {G} and duration {A}.

	L2	df	ΔL2	Δdf
1 {A,B,C,D,E,F,G}	552.6	851		
2 {A,B, ,D,E,F,G}	561.2	852	8.5	1*
3 {A,B,C,D, ,F,G}	556.4	852	3.8	1
4 {A,B,C,D,E,F,G,EF}	544.4	849	8.2	2
5 {A,B,C,D,E,F,G,AE}	551.9	849	0.7	2
6 {A,B,C,D,E,F,G,EG}	552.6	850	0.0	1

*: conditional $p < 0.01$

Moreover, the historical change hypothesis was not supported for home town: no significant interactions of these determinants with union cohort were found. Furthermore, neither is there support for the 'life course change thesis' postulating that past life course determinants might vary with personal time. Home town does not vary significantly with duration. Thus, the impact of home town on union disruption disappears after controlling for age at union and the individual fertility career.

Another model, including current life course determinants and parental divorce, showed that the impact of parental divorce was also mediated by the more immediate determinant. The influence of parental divorce and the interactions of parental divorce with union status, union duration and union cohort are not significant (table 7).

Table 7 Results of loglikelihood ratio tests of a model of first union dissolution, including determinants during the union life course (children {C}, age at union {E}), past life course determinants (religion {D}, parental divorce {B}) and duration {A}, union status {F} and union cohort {G}

	L2	df	ΔL2	Δdf
1 {A,B,C,D,E,F,G}	476.1	851		
2 {A, ,C,D,E,F,G}	481.2	852	5.1	1
3 {A,B,C,D,E,F,G,BG}	472.9	850	3.2	1
4 {A,B,C,D,E,F,G,AB}	469.8	849	6.3	2
5 {A,B,C,D,E,F,G,BF}	470.4	849	5.6	2

*: conditional $p < 0.01$

In summary, all past life course determinants turn out to play an insignificant role in the process of disruption, with the exception of religion. Family size does not influence the process of union dissolution at a significant level. The youthful age of the mother no longer significantly influences union stability, once controls for union status are introduced. Significant impacts of home town and parental divorce disappear after controlling for more current life course experiences (the age at which is union is formed and the individual fertility career). Before discussing these findings in more detail, the empirical findings of a model containing current life course experiences are presented.

Current life course experiences

In the next section, the influence of current life course experiences on the process of union dissolution is examined. First, univariate results are presented; and second, the results of a multivariate model. The univariate results are given in table 8.

Table 8 Monthly hazard rates of dissolution of first unions distinguished according to union status and current life course experiences (univariate results)

	all unions	cohabiting	married after cohabitation	married directly
Educational level i				
1. low	0.0013	0.0052	0.0015	0.0008
2. middle	0.0015	0.0059	0.0013	0.0006
3. higher	0.0021	0.0050	0.0012	0.0008
Occupational status t				
1. unemployed	0.0010	0.0069	0.0014	0.0007
2. studying	0.0027	0.0052	0.0014	0.0010
3. employed	0.0020	0.0052	0.0013	0.0009
Children				
1. no child t	0.0023	0.0053	0.0014	0.0010
2. child/pregnant before entry	0.0016	0.0127	0.0040	0.0013
3. first child born within union t	0.0010	0.0050	0.0014	0.0007
4. second child born within union t	0.0006	0.0087	0.0011	0.0004

t=time-varying, i= covariate is measured at time of interview

Women with higher educational levels have a dissolution rate of 0.021 whereas less well educated women have a risk of 0.013. Less well educated cohabiting women have, however, a more or less similar disruption risk to that of women with a high level of education. Furthermore, the risk of a divorce among those directly married is also similar for women with advanced educational levels (0.008) and for the less well educated (0.008). The implication of this finding is that the much lower, overall, risk of disruption of less well educated women is mostly the result of the fact that more of these women belong to the married group. Since married women have a much lower divorce risk, and since less well educated women tend to marry more frequently, their overall risk of a disruption is much lower than among better educated women.

As expected, students experience the highest risk of disruption, followed by working women. Unemployed women have the lowest risk (0.001). This is in accordance with the economic theories of marital disruption, which argue that economically independent women have a higher risk of disruption, because their gains from marriage and their barriers to divorce are lower. However, these differences in risk between working, studying and unemployed women disappear to a large extent when the disruption rates for each union status are examined separately. For example, the divorce risks of married women are almost the same regardless of whether the woman works, studies, or works in the household. Cohabiting women who are not gainfully employed have a somewhat higher risk of disruption than cohabiting women who do not work in the home.

The covariate fertility is coded into three time-varying categories (being childless, having one child, or having at least two children) and one constant category (having a child/ being pregnant at entry of union). Table 8 indicates that, in general, childless women are at greater risk of dissolution than mothers with one child, and women with one child are at greater risk than women with at least two children (with the exception of the high rate of disruption among cohabiting women with at least two children, but this result should be interpreted with caution given the small number of women in that category). Childless women have a lower risk of disruption that women whose children are born before entering into a union. That childless women are at greater risk of overall disruption is due mainly to the fact that many cohabiting women (with a high rate of disruption) are childless.

Multivariate findings
A multivariate model has been estimated containing all current life course determinants (table 9).

Educational level, occupational and fertility career influence the rate of a disruption significantly. However, after controlling for union status, educational level and occupational career no longer significantly improve the fit of the model (nos 10, 12). That work does not influence the level of disruption after controlling for union status must mean that working women have much higher disruption rates because they cohabit more often than unemployed women. The same conclusion can be drawn with respect to educational level. That educational level does not significantly influence the process of disruption after controlling for union status must mean that the effect of educational level on union disruption operates via the union status. Because highly educated women entered into cohabitation more often (chapter 5), and because cohabiting women have a much higher risk of disruption, highly educated women have a higher disruption rate.
Interactions between the educational level and occupational career with union status and union cohort are not significant. Both the life course and the historical change hypotheses are supported for the occupational and educational status in that this determinant varies significantly with union duration and with birth cohort. However, after controlling for individual fertility career, work no longer interacts significantly with birth cohort or with union duration. This implies that the presence of children and the compositional shift therein during the union or across the cohorts is more important than whether or not a woman works.

Table 9 Results of loglikelihood ratio tests of a model of first union dissolution, including the current life course experiences, union status, duration, birth cohort and union cohort

		L2	df	ΔL2	Δdf
0 { }		1153.4	2592		
1 {A}	duration	1104.1	2589	49.2	3*
2 {B}	birth cohort	1052.9	2588	100.4	4*
3 {C}	occupational status	1080.4	2589	73.0	3*
4 {D}	children	980.1	2588	173.3	4*
5 {E}	education	1136.0	2589	17.3	3*
6 {F}	union status	671.0	2589	482.3	3*
7 {G}	union cohort	1102.6	2590	50.8	2*
controlling for union status					
6 {F}		671.0	2589		
8 {A,F}		668.1	2587	3.0	2
9 {B,F}		661.9	2586	9.1	3
10 {C,F}		671.0	2587	0.1	2
11 {D,F}		639.3	2586	31.7	3*
12 {E,F}		669.6	2587	1.4	2
13 {G,F}		671.0	2588	0.0	1
second-order-effect with union status					
14 {C,F,CF}		662.5	2583	8.4	4
15 {E,F,EF}		664.8	2583	4.9	4
second-order-effect with duration					
16 {A,B,F}		657.3	2584		
17 {AB,F}		654.7	2578	2.6	6
18 {A,C,F}		667.7	2585		
19 {AC,F}		654.0	2581	13.6	4*
20 {A,D,F}		625.4	2584		
21 {AD,F}		620.1	2578	5.4	6
22 {A,E,F}		666.7	2585		
23 {AE,F}		663.7	2581	3.0	4
24 {A,G,F}		667.9	2586		
25 {AG,F}		667.8	2584	0.2	2
second-order-effect with birth cohort					
26 {BC,F}		661.8	2584		
27 {B,C,F}		645.8	2578	16.0	6*
28 {BD,F}		631.7	2583		
29 {B,D,F}		627.5	2574	4.2	9
30 {BE,F}		661.5	2584		
31 {B,E,F}		653.8	2578	7.7	6
32 {BG,F}		658.4	2585		
33 {B,G,F}		657.6	2582	0.8	3
second-order-effect with union cohort					
34 {CG,F}		671.0	2586		
35 {C,G,F}		666.9	2584	4.1	2
36 {DG,F}		639.1	2585		
37 {D,G,F}		636.4	2582	2.7	3
38 {EG,F}		669.6	2586		
39 {E,G,F}		668.3	2584	1.3	2
controlling for the individual fertility career					
41 {A,C,D,F}		624.0	2582		
42 {AC,D,F}		616.1	2578	7.9	4
43 {B,C,D,F}		630.5	2581		
44 {BC,D,F}		616.9	2575	13.6	6

*: conditional p < 0.01

In summary, educational level, work and study play no substantive role in the process of union dissolution. The previous chapter showed that better educated women enter into cohabitation at a relatively high rate. Educational level might be seen as attaching a higher value to independence. Because they value independence more, these better educated women prefer cohabitation to marriage. And because they are more individualistic in attitude, they choose a union with a lower level of commitment at the outset. Because better educated women cohabit more often, they have a higher disruption rate. Similar conclusions can be drawn both for students and working women.

7.4 Empirical findings: past and current life course experiences influencing movement out of a first union

The former procedure eliminated a number of determinants. Of all the time dimensions studied, only age at union and union cohort play a significant role in union dissolution. Neither birth cohort, calendar year, duration, nor the individual's age have any significant impact on union dissolution. Of all past life course determinants, only religion has a significant impact. Neither family size, home town, parental divorce, nor youthful age of the mother influence union disruption to a significant level. Work and education do not significantly influence the risk of a disruption either. Of all the current life course determinants, fertility is the only important factor influencing union dissolution. Although duration has no significant impact either, it is included in the final model, together with union cohort and age at union. The main reason for including duration is to examine whether there is any empirical evidence that supports the life course hypothesis for the remaining determinants.

The final multivariate model that has been estimated includes, besides union duration, all the significant determinants: *union cohort (the historical time dimension), age at union (the personal time dimension), religion, fertility and the union status*

Table 10 Parameter estimates of the model of dissolution of first unions

mean		-6.36	0.0017	
		PARAMETER	RELATIVE RISKS AVERAGE	CATEGORY=1
union status	cohabiting	1.06*	2.88	5.64
	married after cohabitation	-0.38*	0.68	1.33
	married directly	-0.67*	0.51	1.00
duration	0-48	-0.17*	0.84	1.00
	49-84	-0.07	0.93	1.11
	85+	0.25*	1.28	1.52
religion	no	0.11*	1.11	1.24
	yes	-0.11*	0.90	1.00
Age at union	< 19	0.51*	1.67	1.00
	19-20	-0.16*	0.85	0.51
	21+	-0.35*	0.70	0.42
Union cohort	< 1980	0.06	1.06	1.12
	1980-88	-0.06	0.94	1.00
Children	no child	0.30*	1.34	2.40
	1st child born within union	-0.05	0.95	1.69
	2nd child born within union	-0.58*	0.56	1.00
child/pregnant before union formation		0.33*	1.40	2.49
no religion, cohabiting		-0.05	0.95	1.23
no religion, married after cohabitation		-0.21*	0.81	1.05
no religion, married directly		0.26*	1.29	1.67
a religion, cohabiting		0.05	1.05	1.36
a religion, married after cohabitation		0.21*	1.23	1.59
a religion, married directly		-0.26*	0.77	1.00
cohabiting, union cohort <1980		-0.29*	0.75	1.00
married after coh, union cohort <1980		0.27*	1.31	1.75
married directly, union cohort <1980		0.01	1.01	1.35
cohabiting, union cohort 1980-88		0.29*	1.33	1.77
married after coh, union cohort 1980-88		-0.27*	0.76	1.01
married directly, union cohort 1980-88		-0.01	0.99	1.31

*: b/se(b) > 1.96   L2 = 330   df: 416

Table 10 presents the parameter estimates of the model. The first column shows the parameter estimates, the second column the risks relative to the average hazard rate. The third column shows risks relative to one category set equal to 1. It was expected that, if cohabitation were a means of gradual entry into a union, and if cohabitation were indeed a union with a lower commitment relative to marriage, dissolution rates should be much higher among cohabiting than among married women. It was also expected that a transition into marriage, after a period of cohabitation, should lead to greater stability. Both hypotheses are confirmed. After controlling for duration, religion, age at union, union cohort and individual developments in the fertility career, cohabiting women still have a much higher dissolution risk than married women.

Cohabiting women have a union dissolution rate 2.88 times higher than average (column 2) and 5.64 times higher than women who married without a period of cohabitation and a four times higher rate than that of married women who married after a period of cohabitation (5.64/1.33). There is thus a huge difference between cohabiting couples and married couples, in addition to any differences in other relevant determinants of union disruption. The risk for married women previously cohabiting is only 1.33 times higher than that of those directly married. The differential is not large. It is much smaller than that found in a more conventional study in which the divorce process was studied from the moment of marriage (with the same data set: Manting, 1993). In that study it was found that, after controlling for similar determinants, married women who cohabited before marriage had a 2.1 times higher risk of divorce than married women who did not cohabit before marriage. Here we see that, if the process is examined from the moment a union is formed, the differences are much smaller.

More than half the Dutch population believes that the longer a marriage has lasted, the more the couple respect and value each other (SCP, 1992), so that the expectation is that stability rises with union duration. But disruption risks rise with duration of the union. The disruption risk is 1.5 times higher after seven years of the union compared with the early years. This finding does not support Diekmann and Klein's 'sickle' model (1991), Trussell's 'theory of growing acceptance' (1992) or Becker's (1981) economic interpretation.

Disruption rates vary significantly with duration in this multivariate model due to the inclusion of the covariate measuring changes in the fertility career. If there is no control for the individual fertility career, union duration rates are stable with respect to union duration. The conclusion to be drawn from these results is that, after controlling for stabilizing factors such as childbirth, it is the mechanism of 'accumulated irritations' proposed by Trussell and colleagues (1991) that presumably is measured. Partners' becoming increasingly frustrated with each other's shortcomings and behaviour increases union instability with duration. Or perhaps it is an indication of the fact that the longer a union endures, the more likely it is that couples grow apart, and that this explanation provides a more satisfactory account of these duration-specific variations of disruption.

The only past life course determinant exerting a significant impact on union dissolution is religion. Religious women have a considerably lower likelihood of disruption than non-religious ones, and this statement accords with the hypothesis. The impact of religion on disruption differs for each union status. The combination of both religion and cohabitation prior to marriage is associated with a relatively high divorce rate.

The universal finding that a lower age at marriage leads to a higher risk of divorce is also observable from the process of dissolution of all first unions. Women who began to live together before age 19 have a risk twice as high as women who married between age 19 and 20, and a three times higher risk than women who married at ages 21 and above. By age 19, only one tenth of all women in the sample had entered into a union. By age 21, almost half the women had entered into a first union. These women run a much higher risk of disruption than those who formed a union after age 21. An early timing of union formation does not affect disruption rates of cohabiting women differently from married women. In summary, the timing of former events is likely to affect later life course behaviour.

Children stabilize a union. Childless women are at much greater risk of union disruption than those with children. Women with at least two children have a particularly low likelihood of union disruption. Childless women and women who were pregnant or who had already had children at the moment a union was formed have similar rates of disruption.

The period at which a union was formed does not lead to any significant variation in the rate of disruption. Women who entered into a union during the seventies have a somewhat, although insignificantly, higher risk of disruption than women who entered into a union in the eighties.

It was hypothesised that the effect of a determinant should not differ between the union status. Having children has however a similar effect both on married and cohabiting couples, given that there is no significant interaction effect between fertility and union status. Cohabiting couples with children have a much lower likelihood of disruption than cohabiting couples without children. Married couples with children have a much lower disruption rate too. Irrespective whether or not cohabiting couples have children, they have a much higher disruption rate than married couples. Furthermore, age at union has also the same impact on cohabiting couples as on married ones. A young age at union, irrespective of whether it is a marital or nonmarital, leads to a higher rate of disruption. Religion and union cohort, however, have a differential impact on union disruption across the union status.

The *historical change* hypothesis postulates that determinants may affect the process of breaking up differently across historical time. It was expected that, if cohabitation increasingly represents a means of gradual entry into a union, then it is likely that disruption rates are higher among current cohabiting couples than for those of the past. There is indeed a significant interaction between union status and union cohort. Cohabiting couples who entered into their union in the eighties, have a 1.8 times higher risk than cohabiting couples who did so in the seventies. On the other hand, the risk of marital break-up among women who cohabited prior to marriage is much higher among those who entered into a cohabitation in the seventies. Furthermore, a changing influence of a 'disordered' life course was expected. Having a child or being pregnant before (married) co-residence used to lead to forced marriage, and to higher instability of the unions thereafter. Today, the incidence of 'accidental' pregnancies is low and forced marriages are rare. It was expected that the impact of pregnancy on union disruption might have weakened over time.

Moreover, it was believed that, since the social significance of childlessness has changed over the years from an involuntary to a voluntary phenomenon, its negative effect should weaken across time. However, no significant interactions of the fertility career with birth cohort or union cohort were found. Childless couples, as well as women who were pregnant at the time the

union was entered or had children at the moment of union formation, used to be at greater risk of union disruption and that is still the case.
Finally, the effects of religion and age at union do not change over historical time: these determinants have remained important for union dissolution.

The *life course change hypothesis* postulates that determinants may weaken in impact the longer a union endures. If the past is overruled by the present, one of the consequences may be that determinants diminish in impact with the duration of the union. It was therefore expected that age at union and having a child before entry into a union would have short term effects only. The idea that determinants weaken in strength with increased union duration is not supported, however. Union formation at a relatively low age or pregnancy at the moment of entry into a union leads to a higher risk of disruption, both for shorter and longer years of the union.
Union status does not vary significantly with union duration either. The commitment of cohabiting couples remains lower, even when the partners stay together for seven years or more. The differences in disruption rates between cohabiting and married couples do not diminish with union duration, given that there is no significant interaction between duration and union status. Cohabiting couples have a much higher rate of disruption than married couples, and this remains so for later years of the union.

7.5 Summary

This chapter focused on union disruption and on the determinants expected to influence the process. First, the impact of several time dimension on union disruption was examined. The scheme below summarizes the findings.

Scheme 5 Summary of findings: Time influencing moving out of a first union

	General expected effect		General effect: findings
Recent birth cohort	coh	++	0
	coh -> mar	+	0
	mar	+	0
Recent union cohort	coh	++	+ / -
	coh -> mar	+	
	mar	+	
Recent calender year	coh	++	0
	coh -> mar	+	0
	mar	+	0
Short duration		?	+
Young age at union formation		+	+
Young age		+	0

Explanation: See scheme 3 (chapter 7).

Birth cohort membership did not significantly influence the process, although it was expected that later birth cohorts would have higher disruption rates than earlier ones. In a way, they do have a higher disruption rate, because later cohorts cohabit more often than earlier cohorts, and they then have an increased likelihood of break-up. After controlling for this compositional shift from marriage to cohabitation, later cohorts no longer have a significantly higher rate of disruption. The same tendency holds good for observations based on calendar year. Disruption rates are higher the more recent the period observed: but this results mainly from a shift from stable unions (marriage) to unstable unions (cohabitation). Disruption rates vary with union cohort, but only when diverging trends between the types of union status are considered. Three personal time dimensions were examined: age, age at union and union duration. Age at union was seen to determine union stability more than the age of a woman during the union.

It was expected that past life course determinants would influence union disruption. However, some of these determinants (family size and age of mother) do not influence the process at all, whereas the impact of some other determinants (parental divorce and home town) disappeared after controlling for more recent experiences. The only past life course determinant to exert an important influence on union disruption is religion, which affects union disruption in the expected direction.

Scheme 6 Summary of findings: Past life course experiences influencing movement out of a first union

	general expected effect	general effect: findings	historical change hypothesis	historical change: findings	life course change hypothesis	life course change: findings
Parental divorce	+	0	+ -> 0	0 -> 0	+ -> 0	0 -> 0
A religious affiliation	-	-	- -> 0	- -> -	- -> 0	- -> -
Being brought up in a small family	+	0	+ -> 0	0 -> 0	+ -> 0	0 -> 0
Having a young mother	+	0	+ -> 0	0 -> 0	+ -> 0	0 -> 0
Growing up in a small town	-	0	- -> 0	0 -> 0	- -> 0	0 -> 0

Explanation: See scheme 3 (chapter 7).

Contrary to expectation, there are no signs of any change in meaning attaching to these determinants over historical or personal time. Most past life course determinants did and do not differentiate union stability. The historical change hypothesis is thus not supported. Past life course determinants do not influence union stability in different ways at either early or later years of the union. The life course hypothesis, postulating that the impact of past life course determinants is higher at short union duration and lower at long union duration, is thus not supported by these empirical findings either. Religion proves to be an exception. There is support for the belief that religion 'forbids' divorce: religious women have a much lower risk of disruption than women with no religious affiliation. This was so and it remains so, given that the impact of religious belief does not change over historical time.

It was also expected that work, education and fertility influence union disruption. Neither work nor education influence union disruption. Neither do they vary in impact across historical or personal time (in the case of work: after controlling for the individual fertility career). Only the fertility career influenced union disruption in the hypothesised way. The findings are summarized below.

Scheme 7 Summary of findings: current life course experiences influencing movement out of a first union

	general expected effect	general effect: findings	historical change hypothesis	historical change: findings	life course change hypothesis	life course change: findings
Employed	+	0	+ -> 0	0 -> 0	+ -> 0	0 -> 0
Studying	+	0	+ -> 0	0 -> 0	+ -> 0	0 -> 0
High educational level	+	0	+ -> 0	0 -> 0	+ -> 0	0 -> 0
Childlessness	++	++	++ -> 0	++ -> ++	++ -> 0	++ -> ++
One child	+	+	+ -> 0	+ -> +	++ -> 0	+ -> +
Pregnant before entry into a union	++	++	++ -> 0	++ -> ++	++ -> 0	++ -> ++

Explanation: See scheme 3 (chapter 7).

Work, educational level and fertility did not vary in impact over historical or personal time.

7.6 Conclusion

The study of the process of union break-up while taking into account the legal status of different types of union is indeed of paramount importance for gaining insight into the break-up process. The evidence emerges in three different ways.

First, union stability varies with union status. Cohabiting women have a much higher likelihood of union disruption than married couples. Married couples who cohabited prior to marriage have a slightly higher rate of disruption than married couples who did not cohabit before marriage. This finding supports the concept of cohabitation as a way of gradual entry into a union, and legal status as an indicator for commitment to a union, not only at its beginning, but also during its course.

Second, variation of union stability with union status does not disappear after controlling for other relevant forces of union stability. The type of union entered and transition into marriage at a later time are thus very important for the individual's later life course.

Third, union status is far more important for union stability than several of the time dimensions, past and current life course determinants. Basically, the differentials in composition of union status afford an explanation of why:
- women with a relatively young mother have a higher rate of disruption than women with a relatively older mother
- women born in the sixties have a higher rate of disruption than women born in the fifties;
- the level of disruption was much higher in the eighties than in the seventies;
- women who entered into their union in the eighties are much more likely to experience a break-up than those entering into a union in the seventies.

The more recent the historical period (be it calendar year, birth cohort or union cohort) the higher the risk of a dissolution. This increase in disruption risk can, however, be interpreted totally in terms of a shift from unions with a higher stability (marriage) to unions with a lower stability (cohabitation). Because women born in the sixties cohabit more often than women born in the fifties, they have a much higher rate of disruption. After controlling for this compositional shift of married to unmarried unions, disruption rates are not significantly higher among the later birth cohorts. Because cohabitation is more often entered into in recent times than was earlier the case by women in this sample, disruption rates increase across the calendar years.

Furthermore, differentials in composition of union status also afford an explanation of why:
- more highly educated women have a higher rate of disruption than less well educated women;
- working women have a higher rate of disruption than unemployed women;
- students have a higher rate of disruption than non-students.

Because better educated women prefer cohabitation to marriage, they have a higher rate of disruption. Because working women are more often found among the cohabiting than among the married couples, they have a higher rate of disruption. After controlling for the compositional effects of union status, work and education no longer significantly influence the break-up process.

The fact that more and more women cohabit is a reflection of an underlying change in the way relationships are valued and positioned within the life course. The words of Roussel (1989), translated into the case of models of unions, might be cited here: people who take a possible dissolution into account, cohabit. The fact that members of later birth cohorts cohabit more often than members of earlier birth cohorts reflects this attitudinal change. This fact does not thus challenge the assertion that birth cohorts differ on account of their growing up in some other historical era. On the contrary, the fact that members of later birth cohorts were socialized in a period during which traditional perceptions of marriage were seriously challenged is reflected in the shift in union status and the associated higher risks of disruption of these unions.
On the other hand, these results show that it is more the historical period in which a union is formed (union cohort) which influences women's lives than the period in which they were born. While the divorce risk of married women was lower for those who married in the eighties, the

risk of a disruption was higher for those who began to cohabit in the eighties. A similar conclusion can be drawn for education or work. Because working women cohabit more often at later years of the union than unemployed women, they run a higher risk of break-up.

The assumption underpinning the life course approach is that the timing and occurrence of one event affects future events; this assumption is certainly supported. First, type of union entered has repercussions for the later life course. Further, the timing of entry into a union is important for the later stability of the unions. A young age at entry leads to a higher rate of disruption. The order of marriage relative to childbirth is also important for the later life course. Having or expecting a child at the moment of entry into a union raises union instability substantially. In general, the conclusion can be drawn that *point-in-time determinants are more important than time-varying temporal* determinants. Union duration, calendar year and age are examples of time-varying determinants, whereas age at union, birth cohort and union cohort are constant determinants. Point-in-time events (union cohort and age at union) are thus of greater importance in union dissolution than these time-varying determinants (calendar year, age and union duration). The moment at which a union is formed is thus more crucial than the current moment at which a union is observed. The timing of a first union (age at union), studied in chapter 5, is thus a crucial determinant of union stability.

It was expected that the determinants would have a diminishing impact on the level of union dissolution, but no support was found for any changing meaning of the determinants over historical time (either with birth cohort or with union cohort). Perhaps more specific results would be found if women could be traced for a longer period of time and more disruptions had occurred. Although the technique used controls for censoring, there is a possibility that interaction effects are non-significant because relatively few women have (yet) experienced a disruption. Union disruption was examined for nearly 4500 women who entered into a first union. About 600 of these women had experienced a union disruption. On the other hand, other event history analyses, in other countries and of other events, showed a number of interaction effects although these analyses were based on smaller samples than that used here.

The historical change hypothesis is only supported for union status. The interaction effect between union status and union cohort supports the notion that cohabitation is increasingly a process of gradual moving in. It was expected that, if this were so, the disruption of cohabitation would become increasingly higher. Cohabiting couples who entered into their union in the eighties have indeed a higher rate of disruption than cohabiting couples who did so in the seventies.

Finally, all these determinants have a constant effect during the union. There is clearly no evidence at all for the life course hypothesis. This conclusion can only be drawn for relatively short unions. Religious women have at all times a lower rate of union dissolution. A young age at union, a child born before entry into a union and childlessness produce a higher rate of disruption, even after couples have survived the first six years of shared life.

8 SUMMARY AND CONCLUSION

8.1 Introduction

In the Netherlands, as in many other Western countries, revolutionary changes have occurred in the life courses of women. Women's education has been prolonged, women stay for a longer period in the labour market, the age at which women marry and give birth has been delayed, marriages increasingly break down. The order in which transitions in several life domains take place has also been altered. Historically, entry into marriage marked the moment a woman left the parental home, the start of an intimate sexual relationship, the onset of family formation and the end of participation in the labour market. Since the end of the sixties, these links have weakened in strength. An alternative form of life with a partner emerged: non-married cohabitation.

The *goal* of this study was to gain insight into the process of union formation and dissolution of women, giving explicit attention to both cohabitation and marriage. This chapter provides a summary of the research and draws conclusions.

8.2 Theoretical background

The literature on marriage and divorce reveals the long-term social processes put forward as explanations of the decline in marriage, its delay, rising divorce rates and the emergence of cohabitation. These processes form a complex structure of social, economic and cultural forces operating simultaneously. Long-term macro-level developments (secularization, individualization, emancipation) have created a continuously evolving shift in individual preferences (towards individuality, freedom and independence), in constraints (towards fewer rigid norms and reduced affirmation to the institutional regulations of the state, church and family) and in opportunities (women's economic independence through labour market participation and through the individualization of social security).

The literature summarized in chapter 2 made it clear that the meaning of both marriage and cohabitation has changed with time. Cohabitation started as an alternative way of living, developed into a temporary phase before marriage and finally became a strategy for moving into a union gradually. For women, the perception of marriage as a means of gaining economic security and independence from parents has weakened. Marriage has lost its place as a prerequisite for an intimate sexual relationship, for the bearing and rearing children, or for living with a partner.

The assumption that cohabitation and marriage have changed in social meaning over historical time influences the way in which the process of union formation and dissolution should be examined. This study widens the usual scope of demographic studies on marriage and divorce to the formation and dissolution of both married and non-married unions. In this study, the entry into a union is marked by the onset of shared living and not (as in conventional studies) by the start of marriage. To gain insight into the circumstances causing women to enter cohabitation or marriage, this study gives explicit attention to the legal status of the union at the moment of entry.

Union formation is increasingly marked by two transitions; cohabitation, followed by marriage. Cohabiting couples may or may not have any intention to marry. They may, or may not, marry eventually because individual circumstances affecting the transition from cohabitation to marriage change. This research project also studied entry into subsequent marriage to gain insight into the different patterns from which women move into a union.

The assumption that cohabitation and marriage have changed in meaning over historical time influences not only the way the processes of first union formation are examined, but also the way in which the processes of union disruption should be studied. Here union disruption has been studied from the moment of co-residence. This does not imply that the time-varying element of legal status is ignored. On the contrary, union disruption is studied while giving explicit attention to the union status during the union. The following processes of union formation and dissolution have been studied: the selection process into marriage and cohabitation, the transition from cohabitation to marriage, and union disruption.

The assumption that cohabitation and marriage have changed in meaning over historical time implies that women today are confronted with advantages and disadvantages of cohabitation, marriage and union disruption that differ from those for women who grew up in earlier times. One way of analysing the impact of (varying) contextual circumstances on individual behaviour is to follow a group of women, born in a similar historical period, as they grow up. Women born in different periods face different historical conditions, alternatives and norms, not only with regard to primary relationships, but also with regard to education, work and fertility. The shift in attitude to both marriage and cohabitation, for instance, indicates that women born earlier are confronted with different advantages and disadvantages with regard to union formation and dissolution than women born more recently. For women born in the beginning of the fifties, cohabitation was not an option to be taken on lightly. Women born in the early sixties were confronted with negative attitudes towards divorce. As a result, they might have preferred to enter into a union more gradually. For women born at the end of the sixties, cohabitation was almost 'a matter of course'. This study focused on patterns in union formation and dissolution for women born in the fifties and the sixties.

Of course, being born in a certain period is not the only factor determining union formation and dissolution. Intra-cohort differentials, caused by an individual's past experiences (such as the family in which one is brought up) and an individual's current experiences (such as education or work), also affect union formation and dissolution. Women are exposed to family circumstances which affect their later union formation and disruption. When women grow up, their individual circumstances, which might affect their inclination to move into or out of a union, change. Work, fertility and education are examples of changing individual circumstances.

Because cohabitation and marriage have changed in meaning over historical time, the forces underlying the formation and dissolution of unions might also have varied with historical time. Through studying union formation and dissolution over historical time, more insight can be gained into the impact of past and current life course determinants leading to union, as well as into the varying impact over time. If these determinants have a decreasing impact on aspects of union formation or dissolution, the union career of more recent birth cohorts will be less influenced by these past and current life course experiences. Alternatively, if these factors grow in strength, then there will be more differentiation among more recent birth cohorts. In short, between-cohort comparisons reveal the importance of growing up in different historical periods, while within-cohort comparisons reveal the importance of an individual's characteristics for the process of union formation and dissolution. The combination of both of these reveals possible changes in the links between the determinants and union formation and dissolution.

Women decide upon entry into or exit from a union not only in a certain historical period, but also at a certain moment in their lives and a at a certain moment during their relationship. Past and current life course determinants may vary in impact with individual time: with the age of a woman, or the duration of a union. This study approached the process of union formation and dissolution from a life course perspective, because this approach gives explicit attention to temporal dimensions in daily life; to the fact that a woman's position changes with personal time, and to the varying impact this may have over personal and historical time.

All these assumptions were set down in a conceptual framework that guided the empirical analysis (chapter 2).

Four research questions were formulated:

1. How have the life course patterns in formation and dissolution of first unions changed across birth cohorts?

2. How have past and current individual life course experiences influenced first union formation?
   - How have they influenced the (timing and type of) entry into a first union?
   - Are there signs of a change in the impact of these determinants over personal and historical time, and if so, how does the impact change?

3. How have past and current individual life course experiences influenced the entry into marriage of cohabiting women?
   - How have they influenced the (timing of) entry into marriage?
   - Are there signs of a change in the impact of these determinants over personal and historical time, and if so, how does the impact change?

4. How have (past and current) individual life course experiences influenced first union dissolution over time?
   - How have they influenced the (timing of) union dissolution?
   - Are there signs of a change in the impact of these determinants over personal and historical time, and if so, how does the impact change?

The study of union formation and dissolution was carried out with a multivariate event history technique. This technique is very well suited to life course analysis, since it has the advantage that many explanatory variables can be examined for their impact on the occurrence and the timing of events (for instance entry into a union) simultaneously, that it uses information from people who have and have not experienced the behaviour under study, and that it can handle time-varying situations through the life course.

The hazard rate (of events such as union formation, subsequent marriage or union disruption) is the dependent variable in the analyses. The hazard is the risk of an event occurring in a given duration interval, provided that the event had not already occurred before that interval. Multivariate hazard analyses were performed with a loglinear hazard model to examine the impact of the determinants on the hazard rate simultaneously. The log rate model is preferred to other techniques of hazard analysis for several reasons. First, the model does not require an *a priori* assumption of how the hazard varies with time. Second, this model relaxes the assumption of proportionality. Third, it can cope with time-varying covariates in a straightforward way. Fourth, competing risks (in this case, cohabitation and marriage) can be considered in the same analysis.

Multivariate analyses have been carried out on individual data from the Netherlands Fertility and Family Survey 1988 of Statistics Netherlands. This data set contains information on union formation and dissolution and on several past and current life course experiences of nearly 6000 women born between 1950 and 1969. Although this data set offers a large amount of formation needed for life course analysis, it also has limitations. Information about previous partners is unknown so it was almost impossible to investigate the influence of the partner. Some determinants were measured at the time of interview instead of at the moment of union formation or dissolution. And finally, some assumptions had to be made with regard to filling the gap of information of some life careers studied.

8.3 Empirical findings

The role of the legal status of the union
When studying the process of union formation, taking the legal status into consideration is of the utmost importance. Some determinants do not influence entry into a union overall, because of their differential impact on cohabitation and marriage. Other determinants influence entry into cohabitation in dissimilar ways from entry into marriage. Insight into how past and current life course determinants influence union formation can only be gained by examining the selection process underlying marriage and cohabitation. That selection process is highly differentiated among women: and there is no sign that this distinction has become less important over time. Moreover, the influence of certain past and current life course determinants is different for the transition from single status to cohabitation relative to the influence on the transition from single status to marriage.

Legal status is even more important for the study of union disruption. Evidence emerges in three different ways. Cohabiting couples have a much higher risk of disruption than married couples. Married couples who cohabited prior to marriage have a slightly higher rate of disruption than married couples who did not cohabit before marriage. These findings support the concept of legal status as proxy for commitment to a union, not only at the start of a union, but also during it. Second, variation of union stability with union status does not disappear after controlling for other relevant forces of union stability. The type of union entered in addition to transition into marriage at a later time is thus very important for gaining insight into the process of union disruption. Third, union status is far more important for union stability than a number of time dimensions, past and current life course determinants.

The influence of past life course determinants
The past life course determinants studied for their impact on union formation and dissolution were living at home (for the case of union formation only), parental divorce, religion, family size, age of the mother and home town.

First union formation
The impact of the past life course experiences varies with the type of union. If the impact on entry into direct marriage is positive, then the significance on entry into cohabitation is generally negative. This is the case regarding religious affiliation, growing up in a small town, and being brought up in a large family. Because of the differential impact of these past life course determinants on cohabitation and marriage, they do not always influence entry into a union overall. Other past life course experiences do not show this opposing influence. In cases where the mothers of women were relatively young, generally implying early marriage of the mother, then daughters of these women are more likely to enter into marriage and cohabitation themselves. If women live at home, they are less likely to move into a union, either cohabitation or marriage, than women who live independently from their parents.

Subsequent marriage

The expectation was that cohabiting women brought up in the following circumstances would marry less frequently: those who experienced a parental divorce, had no religious background, a relatively young mother, were brought up in a small family, or grew up in a large city. These factors do not, however, influence subsequent marriage after a period of cohabitation. Past life course experiences do not play a substantial role in the process of marriage, once cohabitation has been entered. Religious affiliation stands out as the only past life course determinant to influence movement into subsequent marriage. Even after controlling for current activity and life course statuses, such as work and pregnancy, religious affiliation influences the transition from cohabitation to marriage in a positive way.

Disruption

Although it was expected that past life course determinants influence union disruption, it transpired that they did not. A few past life course determinants (family size and age of mother) do not influence the process at all, whereas the impact of some other determinants (parental divorce and home town) disappears after controlling for more recent life course experiences. The only past life course determinant to exert an important influence on union disruption is religion. Even after controlling for more current life course experiences, women with religious affiliation have a lower rate of disruption.

Birth cohort membership

Union formation and dissolution was observed for women born between 1950 and 1969. Entry into a first union is progressively lower across the cohorts, at least at younger ages. Women born in the sixties have a lower rate of union formation than women born in the fifties. During the period in which these women grew up, a shift occurred within the process of union formation. Entry into a union by marriage became less common, via cohabitation more usual practice.

It was expected that later birth cohorts would encounter less conformist pressure to marry soon after entry into cohabitation. Moreover, since cohabitation and marriage have become more equal in terms of rights and obligations, the need to move into marriage should have declined across the cohorts. Recent birth cohorts do indeed have a much lower rate of subsequent marriage than earlier birth cohorts. This might also be seen as an indication of a more gradual entry into a union for increasing numbers of women who do not really consider marriage at the start of cohabitation. The effect of cohort membership remains significant after controlling for other important determinants.

Birth cohort membership does not significantly influence the process of disruption, although it was expected that later birth cohorts would have higher disruption rates than earlier cohorts. The fact that cohort membership does not significantly influence the process of union disruption does not, however, disturb the view that differences between the birth cohorts arise from distinct historical circumstances. On the contrary, the fact that members of younger birth cohorts were socialized in a period during which attitudes towards marriage changed is reflected in the shift from entry into more stable unions (marriage) to entry into more unstable ones (cohabitation).

Historical changes in the influence of past life course determinants
Factors affecting the process of union formation vary in impact across the cohorts. The expectation was that past life course determinants would increasingly affect entry into direct marriage and decreasingly affect entry into cohabitation. This is indeed so for the covariates measuring whether or not a women lives at home and for religion and to a certain extent for family size.
The impact of age of the mother on *union formation* remained fairly stable across the cohorts; the effect of growing up in a small town did not change linearly. As a result of these changes, conclusions drawn with regard to the relationships between the determinants and union formation are highly time-specific. A study of these processes for women born in the early sixties would have led to the conclusion that, for instance, religion does not affect union formation, only the type of union entered. A study of women born in the fifties would have led to the conclusion that religious women have a much lower risk of union formation than women without a religious affiliation. As a result of these countervailing tendencies of the effects on marriage and cohabitation, the effects of determinants on union formation across cohorts do not always vary or change in direction. These findings support the view, stemming from life course theory, that an individual life course is embedded in a historical context.

Cohort-varying effects of past life course determinants on subsequent marriage or on union disruption were not found, however. Past life course experience were and are of no importance for entry into subsequent marriage and union disruption. Only religion has been important for explaining differentiation in marriage risks of cohabiting women and the risk of union disruption.

Life course variations in the influence of past life course determinants
The expectation was that past life course experiences weaken in impact over personal time. Empirical evidence supports this view; living at home, having a young mother, being brought up in a small family (not for the case of cohabitation), size of home town and religion (both for entry into cohabitation only) weaken in their effects with the age of a woman.

Past life course determinants do not influence subsequent marriage and union disruption at all. This is further evidence that the impact of past life course experiences on the later life course disappears. Once a union is formed, past life course experiences no longer influence a woman's behaviour. Religion is an exception. The impact of religion on union formation and marriage does not weaken with age. In addition to its impact on union formation, it affects both entry into subsequent marriage and union disruption. There is no sign whatsoever that religion weakens in impact over personal time with regard to subsequent marriage and union disruption.

In short, an important finding is that women's past life course experiences influence their *early*, but not their *later,* life courses. Moreover, these relationships are highly time-dependent: they vary with age and with cohorts. Past life course experiences are, first of all, highly important for entry into a union, be it direct marriage or entry into cohabitation. Apart from this selection effect they do not, however, influence the transition from cohabitation to marriage. Nor do they influence the process of union disruption. Religion proves to be an exception. Religious affiliation not only influences movement into a union, but also the transition from cohabitation to marriage and union disruption.

Current life course experiences
The current life course experiences studied were: work, educational achievement, and the fertility career.

First union formation
As described earlier, several past life course determinants affect entry into marriage positively, but entry into cohabitation negatively. For current life course experiences, however, a positive impact on marriage also means a positive impact on cohabitation and hence, a positive impact on union formation, too. Pregnant women have a much higher rate of marriage or cohabitation. Students are not only less likely to marry, they are also less likely to enter into cohabitation. By comparison with unemployed women, working women have a slightly higher rate of marriage, but also a slightly higher rate of cohabitation. Educational achievement proves to be an exception. A higher level of education stimulates entry into cohabitation and hampers entry into marriage. Because its effect on marriage is much higher than its impact on cohabitation, higher education leads to a much lower rate of union formation.

Subsequent marriage
The dynamics in the fertility career are of paramount importance for entry into subsequent marriage. Once a woman is pregnant, she soon marries. But, if she does not marry during the period of pregnancy, the rate of subsequent marriage drops to a level as low as that for childless couples. Other life course experiences (although not all) also influence movement into subsequent marriage. Working women have a slightly higher subsequent marriage risk relative to unemployed women. Educational enrolment was found to influence the process of marriage in the expected, negative, way. However, educational achievement does not affect subsequent marriage.

Union disruption
It was expected that work and educational achievement would influence union disruption; but it transpired that they do not. Only the fertility career influenced union disruption in the manner hypothesised. That is, childless women have a much higher rate of disruption than women who have children. The more children there are, the lower is the rate of disruption.

Historical changes in the influence of current life course determinants
Some relationships between current life course experiences and union formation vary with historical time. In contrast, the expectation that determinants would increasingly affect entry into direct marriage but decreasingly affect entry into cohabitation, is not supported. However,

relationships do vary across time. The negative impact for students on marriage, cohabitation and union formation increases across the cohorts. The changing effect of educational level supports the historical change hypothesis for cohabitation: across the cohorts, its effect on cohabitation decreases. The impact of work remains stable across the cohorts. The influences of current life course experiences do not, however, vary with historical time on subsequent marriage and on union disruption.

Life course changes in the influence of current life course experiences?
It was expected that current life course experiences hampering entry into a union at lower ages would stimulate a union formation at later ages. Results show that this view is supported in so far as work hampers marriage, cohabitation and union formation at younger ages, but stimulates it later ages. Highly educated women, or women enrolled on higher education courses, do not catch up later in life since the effect remains negative at later ages. On the other hand, the differences between the subgroups decrease over time since the negative impact of educational enrolment and achievement becomes smaller with age.

Current life course determinants do not vary with the duration of cohabitation, nor do current life course determinants vary with union duration in their impact on union dissolution.

In short, later life course experiences play an important role in the entry into direct marriage and entry into cohabitation. The influence of some of these experiences varies with personal and historical time. Furthermore, some of the current life course experiences influence the transition from cohabitation to marriage as well. They have, however, no significant impact on union disruption. The only exception is the individual fertility career. This not only affects entry into a union and the transition from cohabitation to marriage, but also has an important impact on the process of union disruption.

Timing and order of past life course events
Life course theorists assume that the timing and order of past life course events influence the later life course. The age at which cohabitation was entered does not, however, significantly influence the risk of a subsequent marriage. The expectation that women who entered into cohabitation at a relatively young age would postpone marriage more than women who entered into it at a relatively higher age was not confirmed.
The assumption that the timing and occurrence of one event affects future events is certainly supported for the case of union disruption. First, the timing of entry into a union is important for the later stability of the unions. A young age at entry leads to a higher rate of disruption. The order of marriage relative to childbirth is also important for the later life course. Having or expecting a child at the moment of entry into a union raises union instability substantially. For the women studied, point-in-time events (union cohort and age at union) matter more for union dissolution than time-varying determinants (calendar year, age and union duration). The moment at which a union is formed is thus more crucial than the point in time at which a union

is observed. The timing of a first union (age at union) studied in chapter 5, is thus more crucial for union stability than the age of a woman during the union.

General result

In short, it has become clear that past life course determinants are of primary importance for transitions in the early life course, but much less so in the later life course. Once a union has been formed, past life course determinants, with the exception of religious affiliation, no longer influence next transitions in the life course. The impact of these past life course experiences not only diminishes after such an important life event, but also loses ground anyway as a woman grows older.

Current life course experiences are important in explaining union formation at all ages and in explaining the transition from cohabitation to marriage. The most important factor in this regard is fertility. Once a woman is pregnant she is likely to marry, while once she has a child, she is not. The timing of union formation proves to be highly important for union dissolution. Current life course experiences, with the exception of fertility, must give way when considering union dissolution. Demographic variables such as the type of union, the timing of the first union, and the timing of the children are the most important variables when considering union dissolution.

This principle of new experiences replacing older experiences is the same for women born in the fifties and the sixties. However, when past life course experiences do exert an influence, the impact of these variables changes over historical time (e.g. on union formation) and there is a different effect on the different types of union. The only exception is religious affiliation. Although one generally assumes that, through secularization, the impact of the church on daily life is on the wane, it remains important for understanding the differentials in union formation and dissolution.

Life course patterns differ enormously across the birth cohorts, for several reasons. First, they develop in a different historical setting. Because they are situated in different economic, social and cultural conditions, women differ in their union formation and dissolution patterns. Second, there are compositional differentials in determinants influencing union formation and dissolution. Because members of more recent birth cohorts have, for instance, more often been brought up in smaller families, have more often experienced a parental divorce, stay longer at school, have a higher level of education or participate in the labour market for a longer period than female members of earlier cohorts, they also reveal different union formation and dissolution patterns. Finally, cohort change emerges because the relationships between the different individual aspects of life change with historical time.

A general assumption in demographic studies is that the increasing economic independence of women is most important for understanding the decline in marriage and the rise in divorce rates. This study shows, however, that employment does not influence union formation and dissolution in the hypothesised way. The (minor) impact of labour force participation on union formation, marriage and cohabitation alike is positive rather than negative. Working women also have a higher risk of subsequent marriage. Employment was not found to influence union disruption at all. More important than labour force participation was prolonged enrolment in education, which brought about a delay of marriage and cohabitation.

This study shows that it is impossible to study marriage without taking cohabitation into account. It makes quite a difference whether marriage occurs "directly", or follows a period of cohabitation. The same observation holds good for disruption. In estimating disruption levels, it is important to know the varying legal status of the union. On the other hand, this study also shows that many underlying forces do not influence entry into or exit from cohabitation differently from entry into or exit from marriage. Most current life course determinants, for instance, have a similar effect on entry into both marriage and cohabitation. With the exception of religion, the few past and current determinants that matter for union disruption do not influence the union disruption of cohabiting couples any differently from that of married couples. Having children, for instance, raises the stability of both married and cohabiting couples.

Past and present life course experiences are only of minor importance in the disruption process. The individual demographic history (the timing and type of a union, the order of fertility and union formation) is, however, most important in explaining the different patterns in union disruption. Since past and current life course determinants influence the fundamentally important timing and type of first union, researchers cannot ignore them.

8.4   Conclusions

In the past two decades, there have been dramatic changes in union formation and dissolution patterns in the Netherlands. A very important change is the emergence of cohabitation. Although cohabitation is generally a short-lived phenomenon, this study shows that the role of cohabitation is very important for understanding changes in union formation and dissolution.

Gaining insight into and forecasting the process of (first) union formation and dissolution is important in respect to many areas of social life such as housing, social security, the labour-force and mobility. Until now, most studies have focused on the consequences of marriage and divorce. Many studies have examined the consequences of divorce at the individual level: the psychological, economic, social, legal and financial consequences for a couple and their children. Other studies have examined the consequences of marriage and divorce at the aggregate level: how developments in the numbers of divorces affect the demand for social, economic and housing services.

These studies have ignored the consequences of the dynamics in cohabitation. Since there are currently more disruptions of cohabiting couples than of married couples, and since new cohorts will, in the future, more often experience the disruption of cohabitation rather than of marital union, it is time to investigate the causes and consequences of the dynamics of cohabitation.

This study makes clear, as is summarized above, that there are indeed important differences between those who marry and those who cohabit.

This study shows that, when cohabitation and marriage are studied, it is important not to overlook two important preconditions in which behaviour is studied; the historic-specific setting, and the life course specific-setting.

Although it is important to take account of the historic-specific setting in which individual behaviour emerges, many researchers assume that the role of the determinants remains constant over historical time. This study shows, however, that the relationships vary with historical time. The examination of historical changes in life course patterns demands a cohort analysis which shows how individual life courses unfold in dissimilar ways in different periods.

Studying cohort developments in individual behaviour from a life course perspective has many advantages. In contrast with cross-sectional studies, this strategy addresses the complexity of time in the study of social behaviour. First, it points to the historic-specific setting in which individual behaviour emerges. All studies should take into account the time-frame in which individual behaviour is studied, since many relationships between underlying forces and individual outcomes vary with historical time. Second, many individual changes closely linked with each other occur with the unfolding of the life course. Several areas of life, such as education, housing, fertility, union, and occupational career are in competition with each other. Because of this mutual competition, it is impossible to gain full insight into one life domain without taking the others into account. Further, by following the life course from start to finish, temporal sequences and their impact on the future life course are revealed. These have proved to be of the utmost importance. Such a strategy can show not only the degree to which past life course experiences influence the later life course, but also the degree to which past life course experiences are mediated by more immediate life course experiences.

The relatively new multivariate event history techniques are extremely useful in the investigation of the complexity of the individual life course. They overcome many problems of cross-sectional methods. They can handle censoring (the fact that not all people have, or have not yet experienced the event of interest), they can deal with developments in the individual life, and they can deal with a simultaneous investigation of many relevant (time-varying) individual characteristics. Event history techniques which allow for non-proportionality are particularly useful, since the technique permits researchers to study explicitly varying relationships between several factors with historical or with personal time.

Studies of life course patterns at the micro level require individual life history data. The data set used in this study, the Netherlands Fertility and Family Survey 1988, largely covers the entire history of relevant demographic and non-demographic careers. It afforded a certain degree of insight, into the complexity of the inter-connecting links between the different individual life domains and union formation and dissolution. In the past few years, an increasing number of surveys designed to obtain individual life history data have been carried out. Through these surveys, more knowledge of the dynamics of individual behaviour can be acquired; of the influence of individual life domains at different moments in individual and historical time and of the influence of individual's past on the future life course.

Cohabitation started as an protest against the bourgeois marriage pattern, but changed into a means of gradual movement into a union, whereas direct entry into marriage changed from normal to deviant behaviour. The shift from marriage to cohabitation may reflect a decreasing level of commitment, at least at the start of cohabitation. At the first years of a union, a break up of cohabiting couples may therefore involve fewer legal, social, economic consequences than the break-up of married couples. However, this does not necessarily imply that the psychological consequences of break-up are invariably less serious for cohabiting than for married couples. Since many individual and couple-related circumstances change during the union, the consequences of disruption of both cohabiting and married couples might change with time. Perhaps future research can gain more insight into the time-varying developments of the consequences of the break up of both cohabiting and married couples.

The shift from marriage to cohabitation indicates a change in the stability of primary relationships. Although the desire to form a union has not declined over the years, and although the number of women who entered a union has not declined dramatically, more men and women will be confronted with a period of living alone. The stability of cohabitation, even after controlling for other relevant factors influencing the stability of a union, is much lower than that of marital unions. This implies that more people will experience at least one break up during their life course and that increasingly more people will live alone after a period of shared co-residence. Since this has many repercussions for other life domains, such as housing and the fertility career, and for society as a whole, gaining insight into the causes and consequences of dynamics in union formation and dissolution is of the utmost importance.

SAMENVATTING EN CONCLUSIES

1 De aanleiding van het onderzoek

In Nederland zijn in de afgelopen jaren grote veranderingen opgetreden in de levenslopen van vrouwen. Vrouwen gaan langer naar school, ze blijven langer werken, het huwelijk en de geboorte van kinderen word uitgesteld, en er doen zich steeds meer (echt) scheidingen voor. De volgorde waarin zich deze overgangen voordoen is ook sterk gewijzigd. Vroeger markeerde het huwelijk voor vrouwen het moment waarop ze het ouderlijk huis verlieten als mede het begin van een intieme seksuele relatie, van de gezinsvorming en van het samenleven met een partner. Sinds het einde van de jaren zestig zijn al deze overgangen wat minder sterk met elkaar verbonden.

Samenwonen met een vriend of vriendin, zonder dat men daarmee gehuwd is, is in korte tijd heel gewoon geworden. Hoewel niet-gehuwd samenwonen tegenwoordig veelvuldig voorkomt, is er relatief weinig bekend over de achtergronden van de vorming van niet-gehuwd samenwonenden. Ook is er weinig onderzoek gedaan naar de achtergronden van het uit elkaar gaan van relaties, terwijl het aantal samenwonenden dat op jaarbasis uit elkaar gaat veel groter is dan het aantal huwelijken dat jaarlijks ontbonden wordt. Veel demografisch en niet-demografisch onderzoek richt zich op de ontwikkelingen, achtergronden en consequenties van (ontwikkelingen in) burgerlijke staat en negeert tot op zekere hoogte de ontwikkelingen, achtergronden en gevolgen van veranderingen in het samenwonen. Dit komt onder meer doordat er veel meer gegevens beschikbaar zijn over huwelijkssluiting en echtscheiding, dan over de vorming en ontbinding (in deze studie wordt met ontbinding niet zozeer het overlijden van de partner bedoeld als wel het uit elkaar gaan door (echt) scheiding) van niet gehuwde samenwoonrelaties. Gevolgen of oorzaken van, alsmede ontwikkelingen in niet-gehuwd samenwonen kunnen alleen via steekproefonderzoek verkregen worden. Een andere reden is dat het huwelijk veelal als een serieuzere verbintenis wordt beschouwd dan het niet-gehuwd samenwonen. Dat komt vooral tot uiting in onderzoek naar de achtergronden van de echtscheiding. Recent onderzoek met betrekking tot echtscheiding richt zich vooral op de relatie tussen het niet-gehuwd samenwonen en de stabiliteit van het huwelijk dat daarop volgt maar besteedt geen aandacht aan de scheiding van samenwonenden als zodanig.

Dit onderzoek had als doel inzicht te vergroten in de achtergronden van de relatievorming en -ontbinding (voor de eerste keer) van vrouwen, waarbij expliciet een onderscheid werd gemaakt in niet-gehuwd en gehuwd samenwonen.

De onderzoeksvragen van deze studie zijn als volgt:

1. Hoe zijn patronen in eerste relatievorming en -ontbinding tussen de geboortecohorten veranderd?
2. Hoe beïnvloeden factoren uit de eerdere en latere levensloop de (eerste) relatievorming van vrouwen?
   - Hoe beïnvloeden deze factoren de (leeftijd bij aanvang van en het type relatie van) de eerste relatievorming?
   - Zijn er aanwijzingen voor een veranderende invloed van deze factoren met het verloop van de historische en/of individuele tijd, en als dat zo is, hoe verandert de invloed?
3. Hoe beïnvloeden factoren uit de eerdere en latere levensloop de huwelijkssluiting tijdens het samenwonen?
   - Hoe beïnvloeden deze factoren (het tijdstip van) de huwelijkssluiting tijdens het samenwonen?
   - Zijn er aanwijzingen voor een veranderende invloed van deze factoren met het verloop van de historische en/of individuele tijd, en als dat zo is, hoe verandert de invloed?
4. Hoe beïnvloeden factoren uit de eerdere en latere levensloop de relatie-ontbinding van vrouwen?
   - Hoe beïnvloeden deze factoren (het tijdstip van) de relatie-ontbinding?
   - Zijn er aanwijzingen voor een veranderende invloed van deze factoren met het verloop van de historische en/of individuele tijd, en als dat zo is, hoe verandert de invloed?

De data die geanalyseerd zijn voor de beantwoording van deze onderzoeksvragen zijn afkomstig uit het Onderzoek Gezinsvorming 1988 van het Centraal Bureau van de Statistiek. Dit steekproefonderzoek bevat levensloopgegevens van zesduizend vrouwen in de leeftijd van 18 tot en met 37 jaar, geboren tussen 1950 en 1969.

2 Theoretische achtergrond

Uit de literatuur over huwelijk en echtscheiding blijkt dat lange termijn ontwikkelingen in de samenleving als verklaringen genoemd worden voor de daling in en het uitstellen van de huwelijkssluiting, de stijging in de echtscheiding alsmede de opkomst van het niet-gehuwd samenwonen. Secularisering, individualisering en emancipatie veroorzaken een continue veranderingen in individuele preferenties, mogelijkheden en beperkingen. Door processen van secularisering en individualisering zijn individuen steeds minder belang gaan hechten aan de rol van instituties, zoals de familie en de kerk. Er wordt meer belang gehecht aan vrijheid en onafhankelijkheid. Ook speelt de economische verzelfstandiging van vrouwen een belangrijke rol in de ontwikkelingen in huwelijkssluiting en echtscheiding. De economische visie op de achtergronden van demografische ontwikkelingen, legt de nadruk op de emancipatorische ontwikkelingen in de samenleving, met name vertaald in de toegenomen scholing en arbeidspar-

Samenvatting en conclusies

ticipatie van vrouwen. Deze heeft de zogenoemde 'opbrengsten' van het huwelijk en de financiële drempel om tot een echtscheiding over te gaan verlaagd.

In de loop der tijd is, onder invloed van deze veranderingen, de betekenis van het huwelijk en het niet-gehuwd samenwonen veranderd. Het huwelijk markeert tegenwoordig steeds minder vaak het moment waarop men gaat samenwonen met een partner. Vaak volgt het huwelijk een paar jaar nadat men is gaan samenwonen. Ook is de betekenis van het niet-gehuwd samenwonen sterk gewijzigd. In het begin van de jaren zeventig was niet-gehuwd samenwonen (of hokken, zoals het in die tijd genoemd werd) een alternatieve wijze van samenleven met een partner en een reactie op het 'burgerlijke' huwelijk. Tegenwoordig is niet-gehuwd samenwonen, met of zonder kinderen, heel gewoon. Het revolutionaire karakter ervan is geheel en al verdwenen. Samenwonen voltrekt zich nu vaak als een geleidelijk proces: via het blijven overnachten, via het overbrengen van persoonlijke eigendommen van de ene naar de andere woning en uiteindelijk, via het opzeggen van één of beide vorige woonadressen.

De aanname dat zowel het huwelijk als het niet-gehuwd samenwonen in de loop der jaren van betekenis veranderd is, heeft consequenties voor de manier waarop relatievorming en -ontbinding bestudeerd zou moeten worden. Deze studie heeft geprobeerd om het traditionele demografische onderzoek te verbreden door niet alleen de achtergronden en ontwikkelingen in de huwelijkssluiting en echtscheiding te analyseren, maar de achtergronden van relatievorming en -ontbinding in het algemeen. In deze studie wordt het begin van de relatievorming gemarkeerd door het moment waarop men, al dan niet gehuwd, is gaan samenwonen en niet, zoals gebruikelijk is, door het moment van de huwelijkssluiting. Veel samenwonenden trouwen in een later stadium. Over de achtergronden van de overgang van niet-gehuwd samenwonen naar trouwen is weinig bekend. Dit onderzoek heeft geprobeerd daarin inzicht te verkrijgen. De stabiliteit van relaties wordt bestudeerd vanaf het moment van de samenwoning in plaats vanaf het moment van de huwelijkssluiting, zoals in de meer traditionele studies gebruikelijk is. Dat betekent niet, dat het type relatie niet van belang wordt geacht voor de stabiliteit van relaties. Integendeel, het onderzoek richtte zich ook op de mate waarin het type relatie als mede een verandering daarin (van samenwonend naar gehuwd) een rol speelt voor de verklaring van verschillen in scheidingskans.

Samenvattend zijn de volgende processen bestudeerd: het selectieproces dat tot een eerste gehuwde of een ongehuwde samenwoonrelatie leidt, de overgang van samenwonend naar gehuwd, en de scheiding van een eerste (gehuwde en ongehuwde) samenwoonrelatie.

De veronderstelling dat de betekenis van het samenwonen en het huwelijk in de loop der tijd veranderd is, houdt in dat vrouwen tegenwoordig met andere voor- en nadelen van samenwoning, huwelijk of (echt)scheiding geconfronteerd worden dan vrouwen die in een eerdere periode opgroeiden. Een manier om de invloed van de zich wijzigende historische context op de relatievorming en -ontbinding zichtbaar te maken, is door de bestudering en vergelijking van geboortecohorten. Een geboortecohort is een groep mensen, die in een bepaald jaar of in een bepaalde periode zijn geboren. Tijdens het ouder worden, worden de leden van een geboortecohort beïnvloed door gemeenschappelijke omgevingsfactoren op hetzelfde moment in de levensloop. Als er nieuwe opties ontstaan in de samenleving, zoals het niet-gehuwd samenwonen, kan dat alleen gekozen worden door diegenen, die nog niet gehuwd zijn. Zo was het niet-gehuwd samenwonen een weinig gebruikelijke optie voor vrouwen die geboren werden in het begin van de jaren vijftig, terwijl samenwonen, eventueel gevolgd door een huwelijk, voor vrouwen geboren in de tweede helft van de jaren zestig veel vanzelfsprekender is geworden dan trouwen zonder te hebben samengewoond. Het feit dat geboortecohorten opgroeien in een andere historische periode leidt niet alleen tot andere relatiepatronen, maar ook tot verschillen in andere loopbanen, zoals de opleiding en arbeidsloopbaan. Zo ontstaan er compositionele verschillen tussen geboortecohorten in het aandeel werkende, studerende, kerkelijke vrouwen. Dit leidt op zijn beurt weer tot verschillen in de relatievorming en -ontbinding, er van uitgaande dat werk, studie of kerkelijke gezindte de relatievorming en -ontbinding beïnvloeden.

Omdat voor- en nadelen van het samenwonen, het huwelijk en een (echt)scheiding in de loop der tijd aan verandering onderhevig zijn, werd verwacht dat de betekenis van factoren die van oudsher tot de relatievorming en -ontbinding stimuleerden of tegenwerkten, in de loop der tijd veranderd zouden kunnen zijn. Door te bestuderen of het effect van bepaalde determinanten tussen de geboortecohorten in kracht toe of juist afgenomen is, wordt onderzocht in hoeverre er zich inderdaad wijzigingen hebben voorgedaan.

Naast de periode waarin men geboren is spelen allerlei andere omstandigheden een rol in de relatievorming en -ontbinding. Verschillen tussen leden van een geboortecohort worden veroorzaakt door jeugdervaringen of door omstandigheden die men in het verdere verloop van het leven meemaakt. Studeren, werken of de aanwezigheid van kinderen hebben invloed op de relatievorming en -ontbinding.

Een beslissing om te gaan samenwonen, om te trouwen, of om uit elkaar te gaan, hangt ook af van de levensfase waarin deze beslissing overwogen wordt. Zo is het denkbaar dat de invloed van factoren die in de beginjaren van een (huwelijks)relatie een rol spelen in de stabiliteit van zo'n relatie, verdwijnen naarmate de relatie langer voortduurt.
Omdat persoonlijke omstandigheden met het ouder worden kunnen veranderen, is levensloopanalyse een geschikte manier om de invloed van wijzigingen in persoonlijke omstandigheden op de relatievorming en -ontbinding te bestuderen. Een van de belangrijke elementen van de levensloopbenadering is de expliciete aandacht voor de verschillende tijdsdimensies die een rol kunnen spelen in de verklaring van gedrag.

Om inzicht te verkrijgen in hoeverre individuele demografische en niet-demografische veranderingen van invloed zijn op de individuele relatievorming en -ontbinding zijn longitudinale analyses nodig. De techniek die gebruikt is voor deze longitudinale analyse is het multivariate discrete loglineare hazard model. Een hazard is een kans dat een persoon in een bepaald tijdsinterval (in dit onderzoek: een maand) een gebeurtenis meemaakt (in deze studie een relatievorming of een -ontbinding), gegeven dat deze persoon die gebeurtenis nog niet eerder meegemaakt heeft. Hazardmodellen hebben het voordeel dat ze informatie van de geschiedenis van alle vrouwen, ook van diegenen die de betreffende gebeurtenis (nog) niet hebben meegemaakt, gebruiken. Het discrete loglineare hazard model werd gebruikt om de (simultane) invloed van verschillende factoren op de kans op een relatievorming of -ontbinding te schatten. Deze techniek werd om verschillende redenen uitverkoren. Ten eerste omdat het model geen parametrische functie van de kansen op een relatievorming en/of een scheiding met het verloop van de persoonlijk tijd oplegt. Dit werd van belang geacht vanwege tegenstrijdige verwachtingen over het verloop van de kans op een scheiding met de duur van de relatie, en vanwege het feit dat weinig bekend is over het tijdsverloop van de kans op een vorming of ontbinding van een samenwoonrelatie. Ook heeft deze techniek het voordeel dat het op een eenvoudige wijze kan toetsen of determinanten in de loop van de tijd van invloed veranderen. Een ander voordeel is het gemak waarmee het model de invloed van tijdsvariërende factoren (zoals de vruchtbaarheids- of de arbeidsloopbaan) op de relatievorming en -ontbinding kan schatten.

3   De bevindingen

Het criterium van niet-gehuwd versus gehuwd

Uit het onderzoek blijkt dat een onderscheid in gehuwd of niet gehuwd voor de relatievorming (nog steeds) van groot belang is voor een beter begrip van de relatievorming en ontbinding. Ten eerste is er duidelijk sprake van een selectieproces met betrekking tot het type relatie dat wordt aangegaan; en de factoren die dat selectieproces beïnvloeden, worden zeker niet minder belangrijk, in de loop der tijd. Op gedrag dat in de loop der tijd steeds vanzelfsprekender is geworden - het niet-gehuwd samenwonen - is de invloed van een aantal individuele kenmerken weliswaar steeds minder belangrijk, maar op gedrag dat in toenemende mate afwijkend is - het direct trouwen -hebben kenmerken steeds meer invloed. Als gevolg van het tegenovergestelde effect op samenwonen of trouwen heeft een aantal factoren bovendien geen invloed op de relatievorming als geheel.

Het belang van het criterium van een gehuwde of niet-gehuwde relatie komt echter nog duidelijker tot uiting in het onderzoek naar de scheiding. Samenwonenden gaan veel sneller uiteen dan gehuwden. Ook hebben samenwonenden die na verloop van tijd trouwen, een iets hogere echtscheidingskans dan gehuwden die voor het huwelijk niet met elkaar samengewoond hebben. Ook nadat gecontroleerd is voor allerlei andere verschillen, die in het algemeen tussen samenwonenden en gehuwden bestaan en die belangrijk zijn voor de verschillen in scheidingskansen, zoals de aanwezigheid van kinderen of de leeftijd bij het begin van de samenwoning, hebben gehuwden nog steeds een kleinere kans om uit elkaar te gaan dan niet-gehuwd samenwonenden. Het is zelfs zo, dat het type relatie belangrijker is voor de verklaring van de differentiatie in scheiding dan een aantal andere, individuele, kenmerken. Dit is bijvoorbeeld het geval voor het opleidingsniveau of de arbeidsmarktparticipatie van vrouwen. Hoger opgeleide vrouwen hebben een hogere scheidingskans dan lager opgeleide vrouwen, maar dit wordt alleen veroorzaakt door het feit dat hoger opgeleide vrouwen relatief vaker samenwonen dan lager opgeleide vrouwen. Controleert men voor de type relatie, dan vallen de verschillen tussen werkenden en niet werkenden, tussen hoger opgeleiden en lager opgeleiden zelfs helemaal weg. Het type relatie is daarom een criterium dat niet genegeerd kan worden in de studie van relatievorming en -ontbinding.

3.1 De invloed van factoren uit het verleden van de vrouw

Een aanname in dit onderzoek is dat de invloed van omstandigheden gedurende de jeugd op gedrag dat steeds normaler en steeds meer geaccepteerd is en steeds veelvuldiger voorkomt (samenwonen, trouwen nadat men is gaan samenwonen, relatie-ontbinding), in de loop der tijd gedaald zal zijn, maar dat deze invloed op gedrag dat steeds uitzonderlijker geworden is (trouwen zonder te hebben samengewoond), toegenomen is. De factoren uit het verleden van vrouwen die in deze studie bestudeerd zijn voor hun invloed op de relatievorming en -ontbinding zijn: het meemaken van een echtscheiding van de ouders, of men bij de ouders woont of niet, de godsdienst, het aantal zussen en broers met wie men is opgegroeid, of men een relatief jonge of oude moeder heeft, en de grootte van de plaats waarin men is opgegroeid.

Relatievorming
De invloed van het verleden van vrouwen is verschillend voor samenwonen en voor (direct) trouwen. Als determinanten een positieve invloed op de huwelijkssluiting hebben, hebben ze het in het algemeen een negatieve invloed op de samenwoning. Dit geldt voor de godsdienst, het aantal broers of zussen en de gemeentegrootte. Als gevolg van het tegenovergestelde effect op samenwoning en huwelijk, hebben niet alle determinanten een invloed op de relatievorming als zodanig.
Vrouwen die bij de ouders wonen hebben echter niet alleen een kleinere kans om te gaan samenwonen, ze hebben ook een kleinere kans om te gaan trouwen dan vrouwen die niet langer thuis wonen. Vrouwen van wie de moeder op jonge leeftijd kinderen heeft gekregen (en dus meestal op jonge leeftijd getrouwd is) hebben een hogere kans om te trouwen én om te gaan samenwonen dan vrouwen van wie de moeder wat ouder is.

Huwelijkssluiting van samenwonenden
Sinds de opkomst van het niet-gehuwd samenwonen in het begin van de jaren zeventig is het in snel tempo heel normaal geworden om een tijdje met een partner samen te wonen zonder dat men getrouwd is. Meestal volgt een huwelijk een paar jaar later. Verwacht werd dat de bovengenoemde indicatoren uit de jeugd van vrouwen van invloed zouden zijn op de huwelijkssluiting van samenwonende vrouwen. Met uitzondering van godsdienst, hebben de determinanten uit het verleden echter geen invloed op deze overgang.

Scheiding

Net als voor de huwelijkssluiting van samenwonenden, geldt dat de bestudeerde indicatoren van het verleden van vrouwen geen invloed hebben op de scheidingskans. Sommige determinanten beïnvloeden het proces helemaal niet, de invloed van andere factoren (echtscheiding van de ouders en grootte van de woonplaats waarin men is opgegroeid) verdwijnt nadat gecontroleerd wordt voor individuele omstandigheden die zich later in het leven, gedurende de samenwoning, hebben voorgedaan. Ook hier geldt dat religie echter wel invloed heeft. Religieuze vrouwen hebben een lagere kans op een scheiding dan onkerkelijke vrouwen.

Historische veranderingen in de samenhang van achtergrond variabelen en relatievorming en -ontbinding

Een aantal van de indicatoren uit het verleden van vrouwen verandert van invloed tussen de geboortecohorten. Verwacht werd dat deze factoren steeds minder belangrijk zouden worden voor de kans op een samenwoning en steeds belangrijker voor de kans op een huwelijkssluiting. Voor een aantal factoren (godsdienst en of men al dan niet thuiswoont) is dit inderdaad het geval. Zo blijkt dat de relatie tussen kerkelijke gezindte en direct huwen tussen de geboortecohorten steeds hechter wordt, terwijl de divergentie met betrekking tot de samenwoning steeds kleiner wordt.

Als gevolg van de veranderende invloed van factoren op samenwonen en trouwen, wijzigt de invloed van een aantal factoren op de totale relatievorming (ongeacht het type relatie). De invloed van godsdienst en gemeentegrootte op de relatievorming verandert van positief via geen tot een negatief effect tussen de cohorten. Zo gingen niet-religieuze vrouwen, geboren in de jaren vijftig vaker een relatie aan dan religieuze leden van dat geboortecohort, maar gingen niet-religieuze vrouwen geboren in de tweede helft van de jaren zestig juist minder vaak een relatie aan dan religieuze vrouwen van dat geboortecohort. Deze analyses tonen aan dat de conclusie over de samenhang van bepaalde factoren sterk afhankelijk is van de groep vrouwen die men bestudeert. Had men bijvoorbeeld alleen de relatievorming van vrouwen onderzocht die in het begin van de jaren zestig waren geboren, dan had men geconcludeerd dat godsdienst geen rol speelt in het vormen van een relatie (ongeacht de formele status), had men de relatievorming van vrouwen geboren in de jaren vijftig onderzocht, dan had men bijvoorbeeld geconcludeerd dat godsdienst samenhangt met een lagere kans op een relatievorming.

Hoewel verwacht werd dat er zich ook een cohortsgewijze verandering zou voordoen in de invloed die deze factoren op de huwelijkssluiting van samenwonenden en op de scheidingskans van gehuwd en niet-gehuwd samenwonenden, bleek dit niet het geval te zijn. De variabelen die aspecten uit het verleden van vrouwen indiceerden, blijken zoals hierboven werd beschreven geen invloed te hebben op deze overgangen, ongeacht of vrouwen geboren zijn in de jaren vijftig of in de jaren zestig.

Veranderingen in de invloed van factoren uit het verleden van vrouwen gedurende de levensloop
De verwachting was dat de invloed van deze factoren uit het verleden van vrouwen leeftijdsafhankelijk zouden zijn. Verondersteld werd dat deze determinanten vooral op jonge leeftijd van invloed zijn, maar het effect wegebt met het ouder worden. Dit werd inderdaad gevonden: of men al dan niet bij de ouders woont, of men is opgegroeid in een relatief klein gezin, of men een relatief jonge moeder heeft, de grootte van de woonplaats waarin men de jeugd heeft doorgebracht alsmede de godsdienst van vrouwen (de laatste twee alleen voor de samenwoning) heeft minder invloed op de huwelijkssluiting, samenwoning of relatievorming als geheel naarmate vrouwen ouder worden.

Daarnaast is voor de huwelijkssluiting van samenwonenden en voor de relatie-ontbinding bestudeerd of het effect van deze variabelen groter is gedurende de eerste jaren van de relatie en kleiner gedurende de latere jaren van een relatie. De effecten van de determinanten veranderen echter niet naarmate de relatie langer duurt. Dit geldt zowel voor de effecten op de huwelijkskans van samenwonenden als op de scheidingskans.

In het kort betekent het vorige dat het verleden van vrouwen vooral de eerdere fasen van de levensloop beïnvloedt en dat de invloed van deze factoren zich tussen de cohorten wijzigt. Er is echter geen samenhang tussen het verleden van vrouwen en de latere fasen van de levensloop. Uit deze studie blijkt immers dat deze factoren weliswaar van groot belang zijn voor de vorming van een relatie, maar als een relatie gevormd is, dan hebben deze factoren geen invloed meer op het vervolg. Met uitzondering van religie, wordt de kans om te gaan trouwen na een periode van samenwonen of de kans op een scheiding niet beïnvloedt door factoren uit het verleden van vrouwen.

3.2 Latere individuele levensloopkenmerken

Naast de invloed van het verleden van vrouwen, is ook bestudeerd in hoeverre opleiding, werk en het hebben en krijgen van kinderen de relatievorming en -ontbinding beïnvloeden. Het effect van opleiding op relatievorming en -ontbinding is op twee manieren bestudeerd. Ten eerste is geanalyseerd of het opleidingsniveau van invloed is, ten tweede is het effect van studeren of naar school gaan bestudeerd.

Relatievorming
Hierboven werd beschreven dat een positief effect van factoren uit het verleden op de huwelijkssluiting vaak samengaat met een negatief effect van deze factoren op de samenwoning. Voor de latere levensloopskenmerken geldt dit echter niet: een positief effect op de huwelijkssluiting gaat samen met een positief effect op de samenwoning. Vrouwen die zwanger zijn hebben een veel grotere kans om te trouwen én om te gaan samenwonen (en dus ook om te gaan samenleven ongeacht de burgerlijke staat). Vrouwen die studeren of op school zitten hebben een veel lagere kans om te trouwen en om te gaan samenwonen (en dus ook om te gaan

Samenvatting en conclusies

samenleven). Werkende vrouwen hebben, in vergelijking met vrouwen die geen betaalde baan hebben, niet alleen een iets hogere kans om te gaan samenwonen maar ook om te trouwen. Een uitzondering op deze regel is de invloed van opleidingsniveau. Hoger opgeleide vrouwen gaan vaker niet-gehuwd samenwonen maar minder vaak trouwen.

Huwelijkssluiting van samenwonenden

In het algemeen wordt aangenomen dat de geboorte van kinderen voor samenwonenden een belangrijke motivatie is om te trouwen. Dat blijkt inderdaad het geval te zijn. Echter, er treedt een verschil op tussen zwangere vrouwen die daarna snel trouwen, en vrouwen die niet tijdens de zwangerschapsperiode trouwen. Als een vrouw niet met haar partner trouwt op het moment dat zij zwanger is, dan is de kans om te trouwen nadat het kind geboren is voor deze vrouwen net zo laag als voor vrouwen die nog geen kinderen hebben en nog niet zwanger zijn. Werkende vrouwen hebben een iets hogere huwelijkskans na een periode van samenwonen dan niet werkende vrouwen. Studerende, samenwonende, vrouwen hebben een heel lage kans om te trouwen. Het opleidingsniveau van vrouwen heeft echter geen invloed op de huwelijkskans van samenwonenden.

Scheiding

In het algemeen wordt verondersteld dat emancipatie van de vrouw tot een hogere instabiliteit van (huwelijks) relaties geleid heeft. Vrij onverwacht hebben werk en opleidingsniveau van de vrouw geen effect op de relatie-ontbinding. Zoals hierboven al beschreven werd, hebben deze factoren geen invloed op de scheidingskans nadat gecontroleerd wordt voor het type relatie. De aanwezigheid van kinderen leidt tot een veel lagere echtscheidingskans. De kans op een scheiding neemt af naarmate het aantal kinderen toeneemt. Of het nu samenwonende of gehuwde vrouwen betreft, voor beiden geldt dat de kans op een scheiding het hoogst is bij vrouwen die (nog) geen kinderen hebben.

Historische veranderingen in de samenhang van achtergrond variabelen en relatievorming en -ontbinding

Net als voor de invloed van determinanten uit het verleden van vrouwen werd verwacht, werd verondersteld dat deze latere levensloopfactoren steeds minder belangrijk zouden worden voor de kans op een samenwoning en steeds belangrijker voor de kans op een huwelijkssluiting. Dit mechanisme is alleen gedeeltelijk zichtbaar met betrekking tot het opleidingsniveau. Het verschil in samenwoonkans tussen hoger en lager opgeleide vrouwen nam tussen de geboortecohorten af. De kans onder studerende vrouwen varieerde ook tussen de geboortecohorten, zij het op een andere manier. Zowel de kans op een samenwoning als op een huwelijk neemt onder studerende vrouwen af naarmate vrouwen later geboren zijn.

Hoewel verwacht werd dat determinanten steeds minder invloed zouden uitoefenen op de huwelijkskans van samenwonenden naarmate vrouwen later geboren zijn, leverde de analyse van de huwelijkssluiting van samenwonenden geen indicaties op dat verbanden tussen determinanten en de huwelijkskans van samenwonenden zich in de loop der tijd gewijzigd hebben. Dat

houdt in dat de kenmerken die samengaan met een hoge huwelijkskans onder samenwonenden, onveranderd zijn gebleven over de geboortecohorten.
De analyse van relatie-ontbinding leverde ook geen indicaties op voor wijzigingen in de verbanden tussen de kans op een relatie-ontbinding en de diverse determinanten. Dat houdt in dat er geen aanwijzingen zijn, dat de kenmerken die samengaan met een relatief hoog scheidingsniveau, in de loop der tijd veranderd zijn.

Veranderingen in de invloed van de latere levensloopfactoren gedurende de levensloop
Terwijl de invloed van de variabelen uit het verleden van vrouwen verminderde naarmate de vrouwen ouder werden, is dit niet het geval voor de latere levensloopfactoren. Verwacht werd dat werk en opleiding vooral op jonge leeftijd de kans op een relatievorming zou verminderen, maar dat werk en opleiding de kans op oudere leeftijd zouden verhogen. Het is inderdaad zo dat de arbeidsparticipatie van vrouwen de kans op een relatievorming op jonge leeftijd verlaagt, maar op oudere leeftijd verhoogt. Uitstel van relatievorming wordt dus op latere leeftijd ingehaald. Voor vrouwen met een hoog opleidingsniveau en voor schoolgaande vrouwen geldt dat de kleinere kans op een relatievorming weliswaar afneemt naarmate ze ouder zijn, maar het is niet zo dat ze op oudere leeftijd een hogere kans op een relatievorming hebben.
De invloed van deze factoren op de huwelijkskans van samenwonenden en op de echtscheidingskans blijkt niet te variëren met de duur van de relatie.

Samenvattend blijken al deze factoren (werk, opleiding en het hebben en krijgen van kinderen) een belangrijke rol spelen in de kans om te gaan trouwen of te gaan samenwonen. De invloed van een aantal van deze factoren verschilt tussen de geboortecohorten. Een deel van deze factoren beïnvloedt bovendien de huwelijkssluiting van samenwonenden. Er heeft zich geen cohortsgewijze verandering voorgedaan in de samenhang van deze factoren met de huwelijkskans van samenwonenden. Geen van de factoren speelt echter een rol in de scheiding, met uitzondering van het krijgen van kinderen alsmede de aanwezigheid van kinderen, die alle overgangen beïnvloeden.
Met uitzondering van de vruchtbaarheidsloopbaan, hebben de latere levensloopfactoren weliswaar invloed op alle bestudeerde processen van relatievorming, maar niet op de relatie-ontbinding. Omdat werkende vrouwen vaker samenwonen hebben ze een hogere kans op een scheiding dan niet werkende vrouwen. Maar de scheidingskans voor niet-gehuwde samenwonende werkende vrouwen is gelijk aan die van niet-gehuwde samenwonende vrouwen die niet werken. Een zelfde conclusie kan voor opleidingsniveau getrokken worden.

3.3 De invloed van tijdstip en volgorde van demografische gebeurtenissen

Levenslooponderzoekers veronderstellen dat het tijdstip en de volgorde waarin gebeurtenissen zich in het verleden van mensen hebben voorgedaan van invloed is op de latere levensloop. In dit onderzoek is bestudeerd in hoeverre vrouwen die op jonge leeftijd zijn gaan samenwonen

Samenvatting en conclusies 191

minder snel zullen trouwen dan vrouwen die op latere leeftijd zijn gaan samenwonen. Uit de analyse bleek dat dit geen significante invloed heeft op de huwelijkskans.

Uit onderzoek in een groot aantal landen blijkt dat hoe ouder men is op het moment van huwelijkssluiting, hoe lager de kans op een echtscheiding. Uit dit onderzoek blijkt dat dit ook geldt voor de scheidingskans van samenwonenden. Zowel vrouwen die op jonge leeftijd zijn gaan samenwonen als vrouwen die op jonge leeftijd gehuwd zijn, hebben een hogere (echt)scheidingskans. Naarmate de relatie voortduurt, worden vrouwen ouder. Om het effect van het ouder worden van vrouwen op de echtscheidingskans apart te bestuderen van het effect van de leeftijd bij aanvang van de samenwonen, is ook geanalyseerd in hoeverre de leeftijd tijdens de relatie van invloed is op de echtscheidingskans. Het bleek dat de kans op een relatie-ontbinding afnam naarmate vrouwen ouder werden. Dit effect verdween echter nadat gecontroleerd werd voor de leeftijd bij aanvang. Dit betekent dat de leeftijd waarop vrouwen een relatie aangaan een grotere invloed op de echtscheidingskans heeft dan de leeftijd die ze tijdens de relatie hebben.

De volgorde van gebeurtenissen is ook van belang. Vrouwen die zwanger waren of kinderen hadden op het moment dat ze, al dan niet gehuwd, gingen samenwonen, hebben een veel hogere kans op een relatie-ontbinding dan vrouwen die dat niet waren.

De effecten van deze variabelen blijven onveranderd tussen de geboortecohorten. Ook verandert de invloed van deze variabelen niet naarmate de relatie langer duurt.

3.4 Het nut van multivariate 'event history' technieken

De multivariate 'event history' techniek is bijzonder geschikt gebleken voor de bestudering van de complexiteit van levensloopatronen. Ten eerste gebruikt het zowel de informatie van diegenen die de gebeurtenis (nog) niet en van diegenen die de gebeurtenis al wel al hebben meegemaakt. Ten tweede kan deze methode de invloed van in de tijd veranderende kenmerken schatten op dat gedrag dat men wenst te onderzoeken. De niet-proportionele 'event-history' techniek die in deze studie gebruikt werd is van niet te onderschatten belang gebleken. Omdat de samenhang van factoren verandert gedurende het leven en tussen cohorten, is deze methode die het mogelijk maakt om deze veranderingen in het niveau van de hazard te schatten, een vereiste.

4 Conclusie

In de laatste twee decennia zijn er grote veranderingen opgetreden in de relatievorming en -ontbinding in Nederland. Een heel belangrijke wijziging is de opkomst van het samenwonen. Hoewel samenwonen meestal slechts een paar jaar duurt, is de rol van samenwonen in de ontwikkelingen van relatievorming en -ontbinding groot.

Inzicht in de ontwikkelingen van relatievorming en -ontbinding is noodzakelijk voor allerlei aspecten in de samenleving. De dynamiek in relaties alsmede de verdere gelijkstelling van gehuwde en samenwonende paren heeft invloed op de vraag en aanbod in de woningmarkt, op de vraag naar sociale voorzieningen, pensioenen, het sociale zekerheidsstelsel of op de ontwikkelingen in de arbeidsmarkt. Het meeste onderzoek dat tot op heden verricht is richt zich vooral op de (micro- en macro-) gevolgen van huwelijkssluiting en echtscheiding. Meestal worden vormingen van samenwoonrelaties in deze studies tot op zekere hoogte genegeerd. Aangezien er zich op het moment van de huwelijkssluiting zich tegenwoordig minder veranderingen in het dagelijkse leven van individuen voordoen dan op het moment van de samenwoning, wordt het tijd de consequenties van relatievorming van samenwonenden te bestuderen. Ook naar de gevolgen en oorzaken van relatie-ontbinding van samenwonenden wordt weinig onderzoek verricht, hoewel zich tegenwoordig meer ontbindingen van samenwoonrelaties dan van huwelijksrelaties voordoen.

Indien men onderzoek doet naar relatievorming en -ontbinding, dan zal men aandacht moeten schenken aan een tweetal zaken: gedrag is specifiek voor een bepaalde historische periode en voor een bepaalde periode in de levensloop.
Een manier om deze twee verschillende aspecten te verenigen in één analyse is door de levenslooppatronen van verschillende cohorten met elkaar te vergelijken. De levensloopanalyse van cohorten heeft vele voordelen. In vergelijking met cross-sectionele studies, biedt het meer mogelijkheden om de complexiteit van de verschillende tijdsdimensies die van belang zijn in de bestudering van individueel gedrag enigszins te ontrafelen. Door een vergelijking van opeenvolgende geboortecohorten krijgt men meer inzicht in de historische context waarin individueel gedrag zich afspeelt. Aangezien deze studie heeft laten zien dat de samenhang tussen bepaalde factoren en de relatievorming en -ontbinding tussen de cohorten aan verandering onderhevig is, betekent dat dat conclusies over geconstateerde samenhangen sterk tijdsafhankelijk zijn.
Verder is de wisselwerking tussen allerlei individuele wijzigingen die zich gedurende het leven voordoen, van belang voor een goed begrip van de individuele relatievorming en -ontbinding. Schoolgaande vrouwen hebben een veel lagere kans om te gaan samenwonen of om te gaan trouwen, maar dat betekent niet dat dat uitstel niet op een later tijdstip zal worden ingehaald. Ten eerste blijkt dat het verschil in de trouw- en samenwoonkans tussen schoolgaande en niet-schoolgaande vrouwen verminderd naarmate men ouder wordt, en ten tweede blijkt dat, als men eenmaal van school af is, een veel hogere kans op een samenwoning of huwelijk loopt. De competitie tussen verschillende loopbanen kan het best vanuit een longitudinaal perspectief bestudeerd worden. Een ander voordeel van levensloopanalyse is dat men het leven van mensen kan volgen van het begin tot het 'eind', waardoor het duidelijk wordt of en wanneer bepaalde factoren uit het verleden geen invloed meer hebben op de latere levensloop. Uit deze studie bleek dat de invloed van eerdere levensloopervaringen verdwijnt door de cumulatie van latere levensloopervaringen.

Samenvatting en conclusies

In de loop der jaren is de betekenis van samenwonen gewijzigd. Het begon als een reactie op het burgerlijk huwelijk en veranderde in een tijdelijke fase voor het huwelijk. Tegenwoordig voltrekt het samenwonen zich steeds geleidelijker: via het blijven overnachten, en dat steeds vaker, gevolgd door het overbrengen van persoonlijke eigendommen van de ene naar de andere woning, en uiteindelijk, via het opzeggen van één of beider vorige woonadressen. Deze verschuiving gaat hoogstwaarschijnlijk gepaard met een lagere niveau van commitment tijdens het begin van de samenwoning. Dat houdt in dat een verbreking in de eerste jaren van de samenwonen waarschijnlijk wat minder financiële, sociale of economische gevolgen heeft dan de verbreking van een huwelijksrelatie. Dat hoeft echter niet in te houden dat een verbreking van een samenwoonrelatie minder psychologische gevolgen heeft dan de verbreking van een huwelijksrelatie. Omdat allerlei omstandigheden zich wijzigen naarmate de relatie langer voortduurt, zullen ook de gevolgen van een relatieverbreking van samenwonenden en gehuwden met het verstrijken van de tijd veranderen.

Met de verschuiving van het gehuwde naar het ongehuwde samenwonen is de stabiliteit van relaties verminderd. Hoewel de wens om samen te wonen in de loop der tijd niet gedaald is, zullen mensen steeds vaker geconfronteerd worden met het feit dat ze (een tijdje) alleen zullen wonen als gevolg van een relatie-ontbinding. Er is tot op heden weinig onderzoek verricht naar de gevolgen van een relatieverbreking van samenwonenden. Toekomstig onderzoek kan wellicht meer inzicht bieden in de, zich tijdens de relatie wijzigende, gevolgen van een relatieverbreking.

LITERATURE

Allaart, P.C., R. Kunnen, H.A. van Stiphout (1989). *Trendrapport Arbeidsmarkt 1989*, OSA-voorstudie nr. V32, The Hague.
Allison, P.D. (1982). Discrete-time Methods for the Analysis of Event Histories, in: S. Leinhardt (ed), *Sociological Methodology*, San Francisco, Jossey-Bass Publishers, 61-98.
Allison, P.D. (1984). Event history Analysis, Regression for Longitudinal Event Data, *Sage University Paper Series on Quantitative Applications in the Social Science*, Sage, Beverly Hills.
Alwin, D.F. (1991). Attitude Development in Adulthood: The Role of Generational and Life-Cycle Factors, in D. Krebs & P. Schmidt (eds.), *The relevance of Attitude Measurement in Sociology*, Frankfurt & New York: Springer, 57-89.
Axinn, W.G. & A. Thornton (1992). The relationship between cohabitation and divorce: selectivity or causal influence?, in: *Demography*, vol. 29, no. 3, August, 343-388.
Balakrishnan, T.R., Rao, V.K., E. Lapierre-Adamcyk and K.J. Krotki (1987). A hazard model analysis of the covariates of marriage dissolution in Canada, in: *Demography*, vol 24., no. 3, august, 395-406.
Becker, H.A. (1990). Dynamics of life histories and generation research, chapter 1, in: *Life histories and Generations, volume I and II*, Proceedings of a Symposium held on 22 and 23 June 1989 at the Netherlands Institute for Advanced Study in the Humanities and Social Sciences, at Wassenaar, H.A. Becker (ed), ISOR/Faculty of Social Sciences, University of Utrecht, 1-55.
Becker, H.A. (1992), (ed) Dynamics of Cohort and Generations Research. Proceedings of a Symposium held on 12, 13 and 14 December 1991 at the University of Utrecht, The Netherlands, Amsterdam, Thesis.
Becker, H.A. en Sanders, K. (1993). Overgang van onderwijs naar arbeid. Een beschrijving en verklaring van het verblijf in het onderwijsbestel voor vrouwen en mannen geboren tussen 1940 en 1965, in: *Tijdschrift voor Arbeidsvraagstukken*, jrg. 9, 230-240.
Becker, G.S. (1974). A theory of marriage, in: *Economics of the Family. Marriage, Children and Human Capital*, T.W. Schultz, ed., Chigaco, University of Chigaco Press, 299-344.
Becker, G.S. (1981). *A treatise on the family*. Cambridge, MA: Harvard University Press.
Becker, G.S. & E.M. Landes & R.T. Michael (1977). An Economic Analysis of Marital Instability, in: *Journal of Political Economy*, vol. 85, no. 61, 1141-1187.
Beekes, A. (1990). The Development of Cohort Analysis, in: *Life Histories and Generations, volume I and II*, Proceedings of a Symposium held on 22 and 23 June 1989 at the Netherlands Institute for Advanced Study in the Humanities and Social Sciences, at Wassenaar, H.A. Becker (ed), ISOR/Faculty of Social Sciences, University of Utrecht, 547-562.
Beets, G.C.N and Cruijsen, H. (1987). Huwelijkssluitingen in Nederland, 1950-1986 (Marriages in the Netherlands, 1950-1986), in *Maandstatistiek van de Bevolking*, (CBS), 87/8, 34-43.
Beets, G.C.N. (1989a). Toenemend aantal ongehuwd samenwonenden met kinderen (Increasing numbers of cohabitors with children), in: *Maandstatistiek van de Bevolking*, (CBS), 89/2, 8-9.
Beets, G.C.N (1989b). Relatie-ontbinding groter dan ooit tevoren (Higher frequencies of relationship dissolution than ever before), in: *Maandstatistiek van de Bevolking*, (CBS), 89/9, 10.
Beets, G.C.N. (1990). Samenwonen: werkt het proefhuwelijk?, in: *Demos*, jrg 6 no. 9, 65-67.
Beets, G.C.N. (1991). Cohabitants and marrieds in the Netherlands. Facts, knowlegde and opinions. Paper presented at the *European Population Conference 1991*, EAPS/IUSSP/INED, Paris, October 21-25.
Bennett, N.G, Blanc, A.K. & D.E. Bloom (1988). Commitment and the modern union: assessing the link between premarital cohabitation and subsequent marital stability, in: *American Sociological Review*, vol. 53, February, 127-138.
Bernhardt, E. & Hoem, B. (1985). Cohabitation and social background: Trends observed for Swedish women born between 1936 and 1960, in: *European Journal of Population* I, 375-396.
Birg, H. (1987). *A biography Approach to Theoretical Demography*, IBS-Materialien Nr. 23, University of Bielefeld.

Birg, H., E.J. Flöthmann, I. Reiter (1990). Biographic Analysis of the Demographci Characteristics of the Life Histories of Men and Women in Regional Labour Market Cohorts as Clusters of Birth Cohorts, in: *Life Histories and Generations, volume I and II*, Proceedings of a Symposium held on 22 and 23 June 1989 at the Netherlands Institute for Advanced Study in the Humanities and Social Sciences, at Wassenaar, H.A. Becker (ed), ISOR/Faculty of Social Sciences, University of Utrecht, 148-182.

Blom, S. (1992). Entry into first marriage or cohabitation by Norwegian Men and Women born 1945 and 1960, in: *Papers from Central Bureau of Statistics*, Part 1, presented at 10th Scandinavian Demographic Lund, Sweden, August 12-14, 5-35.

Bloom, D.E. (1988). Commitment and the Modern Union: Assessing the Link between Premarital Cohabitation and Subsequent Marital Stability, in: *American Sociological Review*, vol. 53 (February), 127-138.

Blossfeld, H.-P, A. Hamerle & K.U Mayer (1989). Event History Analysis, Statistical Theory and Application in the Social Sciences, Lawrence Erlbaum, Associates, Publ., Hillsdale, New Yersey.

Blossfeld, H.-P., R. Nuthmann (1990). Transition from Youth to Adulthood as a Cohort Process in the Federal Republic of Germany, in: *Life Histories and Generations, volume I and II*, Proceedings of a Symposium held on 22 and 23 June 1989 at the Netherlands Institute for Advanced Study in the Humanities and Social Sciences, at Wassenaar, H.A. Becker (ed), ISOR/Faculty of Social Sciences, University of Utrecht, 183-217.

Blossfeld, H.-P. & J. Huinink (1991). Human capital investments or norms of role transition? How women's schooling and career affect the process of family formation. *American Journal of Sociology*, 97, 143-68.

Blossfeld, H.-P., Manting D. & Rohwer G. (1993a). Patterns of Change in Family Formation in the Federal Republic of Germany and the Netherlands: some Consequences for Solidarity between Generations, paper prepared for the Conference on *Solidarity of Generations, Demographic, Economic, and Social Change, and its Consequences*, Utrecht, 7-8 april.

Blossfeld, H.-P., A. De Rose, J.M. Hoem, & G. Rowher (1993b). Education, modernization, and the risk of marriage disruption: Differences in the effect of women's educational attainment in Sweden, West-Germany, and Italy. *Stockholm Research Reports in Demography*, 76. Stockholm University.

Blossfeld, H.-P. & G. Rohwer (forthcoming). New developments in family formation and women's improvement in educational attainment in the Federal Republic of Germany. in: H.-P. Blossfeld (ed.): *Family formation in modern societies and the new role of women*: A cross-national comparative study of ten countries, Boulder.

Booth, A., D.R. Johnson & L.K. White (1987). Divorce and Marital Instability over the Life Course, in: *Journal of Family Issues*, vol. 7. no. 4, December, 421-442.

Booth, A. & D. Johnson (1988). Premarital Cohabitation and Marital Success, in: *Journal of Family Issues*, Vol. 9, No. 2, June, Sage Publication, Inc., 255-272.

Bracher, M. & G. Santow & S.P. Morgan & J. Trussell (1993). Marital dissolution in Australia: Models and Explanations, in: *Population Studies*, 47, 403-425.

Bumpass, L.L. & Sweet, J.A. (1989). National estimates of cohabitation, in: *Demography*, vol. 26, no. 4, november, 615-625.

Bumpass, L.L. (1990). What's Happening to the Family?, in: *Demography*, vol. 27, no 4, November, 483-498.

Bumpass, L.L. & Sweet, J.A. (1991). The Role of Cohabitation in declining Rates of Marriage, *Journal of Marriage and the Family 53*, November, 913-927.

Bumpass, L.L. & T. Castro Martin & J.A. Sweet (1991). The Impact of Family Background and Early Marital Factors on Marital Disruption, in: *Journal of Family Issues*, vol. 12, no. 1, March, 22-42.

Burkart, G & M. Kohli (1989). Ehe und Elternschaft im Individualisierungsprozeß Bedeutungswandel und Milieudifferenzierung, in: *Zeitschrift für Bevölkerungswissenschaft*, 405-426.

Buunk, B.P. & B. van Driel (1989). Variant Lifestyles and Relationships. *Family studies*, Text Series no. 11. Sage Publications, Inc., California.

Caldwell, J.C., P. Caldwell, M.D. Bracher, & G. Santow (1988). The contemporary marriage and fertility revolutions in the West. *Working Paper No. 3 of the Australian Family Project*. Research School of Social Sciences. The Australian National University, Canberra, ACT 2601.

Carlson, E. (1979). Divorce rate fluctuation as a cohort phenomenon, *Population Studies*, Vol 33, 529-536.

Castro Martin, T. & Bumpass, L.L. (1989). Recent Trends in Marital Disruption, in: *Demography*, vol.26, no. 1, February, 37-51.

Cherlin, A.J. (1981). *Marriage, Divorce, Remarriage*. Harvard University Press, Cambridge, England.

Coale, A. (1977). The development of new models of Nuptiality and Fertility, *Population*, numero special, 131-150.

Literature

Corijn, M. & F. Deven (1991). *Keuze of evidentie?* De leefvorm, het relatiepatroon en het seksueel gedrag van Vlaamse jongvolwassenen in 1990, C.B.G.S. Monografie 2, Brussel.
Cox, D.R. (1972). Regression Models and Life-Tables, in: *Journal of the Royal Statistical Society*, Series B, 34, pp. 187-202.
Crommentuijn, L. (1993). Analysis and Modelling of a Regional Household Projection: the use of a log-linear method with rates, in: W.F. Sleegers & Goethals A L J (eds). *Quantitative Geographical Methods, Applied in Demographic and Urban Planning Research*, Amsterdam: SISWO, 53-86.
De Beer, J.A.A. (1989). Jaren tachtig: ombuiging of voortzetting van demografische trends? (The eighties: change or continuity in demographic trends?) in: *Maandstatistiek van de Bevolking*, (CBS), 89/12, 16-37.
De Bruijn, B. (1993). *Interdisciplinary Backgrounds of Fertility Theory*. Amsterdam, PDOD (PDOD-paper no. 16).
De Feijter, H (1991). *Voorlopers Bij Demografische Veranderingen*, NIDI, rapport nr. 22, 's-Gravenhage.
De Graaf, A. (1990). Waarom trouwen samenwoners? (Why most cohabitators marry?), in: *Maandstatistiek van de Bevolking*, August 1990, 12-13.
De Graaf, A., (1991). De invloed van echtscheiding van de ouders op demografisch gedrag van de vrouw (The influence of parental divorce on children's demographic behaviour), in: *Maandstatistiek van de Bevolking*, CBS, 91/8, 3-38.
De Jong Gierveld, J. & A.C. Liefbroer (1991). Exploring the impact of educational attainment and labour market participation on the demographic behaviour of women in the Netherlands, paper presented at the conference on "Recent Changes in the Process of Family Formation in Europe and the New Role of Women", Fiesole, November 8-9.
De Jong Gierveld, J. & A.C. Liefbroer (1992). Een verkenning van de invloed van veranderingen in opleidingsdeelname en arbeidsparticipatie op het demografisch gedrag van vrouwen, in: *Emancipatie en Bevolkingsontwikkeling. Hechte partners?* Nederlandse Vereniging voor Demografie, 's-Gravenhage, 1-18.
De Jong Gierveld, J. & A.C. Liefbroer (1993). Veranderingen in de leefvormen van volwassenen: De samenhang met attitudes en sociale herkomst. In C. Bouw & B. Kruithof (red), *De kern van het verschil: Culturen en Identiteiten*, amsterdam: Amsterdam University Press, 191-216.
DeMaris, A. & Rao, K.V. (1992). Premarital Cohabitation and Subsequent Marital Stability in the United States: A Reassesment, in: *Journal of Marriage and the Family*, 54 (February), 178-190.
Demographic Change (1990). Demographic change, Household Evolution, The Housing and Labour Market. Research Program of the Northern Center of the NWO Priority Program on Population Studies.
Diekmann, A. & P. Mitter (1984). A comparison of the "Sickle Function" with Alternative Stochastic Models of Divorce Rates, in: *Stochastic Modelling of Social Processes*, Diekmann, A. & P. Mitter (eds), IASA, Vienna, Austria, Academic Press, inc, 123-153.
Diekmann, A. (1990). Diffusion and Survival Models for the Process of Entry into Marriage, in: Mayer, K.U. & N.B. Tuma (eds). *Event History Analysis in Life Course Research*, The University of Wisconsin Press, 171-181.
Diekmann, A. & T. Klein, (1991). Bestimmungsgrunde des Ehescheidungsrisikos. Eine empirische Untersuchung mit den Daten des sozio-ökonomischen Panels, *Kölner Zeitschrift fur Soziologie und Sozialpsychologie*, Jg. 43, Heft 2, 271-290.
Dieleman, F.M. & R.J. Schouw (1989). Divorce, mobility and housing demand. in: *European Journal of Population*, 235-252.
Easterlin, R.A. (1980). *Birth and Fortune*, the impact of numbers on personal welfare, New York.
Elchardus, M. (1984). Life Cycle And Life Course: The Scheduling and Temporal Integration of Life, in: S.Feld & R. Lesthaeghe (eds), *Population and societal Outlook*. Brussels, Koning Boudewijnstichting, 251-267.
Elder, G. (1981). History and the life course, in: D. Bertaux, ed., *Biography and Society. The Life History Approach in the Social Sciences*, Sage Studies, Intern. Sociology 23, ISA, 77-115.
Eldridge, S. & Kiernan, K. (1985). Declining First-marriage rates in England and Wales, a Change in Timing or a Rejection of Marriage?, in: *European Journal of Population*, 327-345.
Espenshade, T.J. (1985). Marriage Trends in America: Estimates, Implications and Underlying Causes, in: *Population and Development Review*, 11, no 2., June, 193-245.
Fergusson, D.M. & L.J. Horwood & F.T. Shannon (1984). A Proportional Hazards Model of Family Breakdown, in: *Journal of Marriage and the Family*, August, 539-549.

Goldscheider F K & Waite L J (1987). Nest-Leaving Patterns and the Transition to Marriage for Young Men and Women, *Journal of Marriage and the Family*, 49, 507-516.
Guttentag, M. & Secord, P.F. (1983). *Too Many Women? The Sex Ratio Question*, Sage Publications, London.

Hachen, D.S. (1988). The competing risk model: A method for analyzing processes with multiple types of events, *Sociological Methods and Research*, 17, 21-54.
Hagenaars, J.A. (1990). *Categorical Longitudinal Data*. Log-linear Panel, Trend, and Cohort Analysis, Sage Publications, Inc. London.
Halman, L. (1991). *Waarden in de Westerse Wereld*. Tilburg University Press.
Haskey, J. (1991). Formation and Dissolution of Unions in the Different Countries of Europe, in: Blum, A. & J-L Rallu (eds), *European Population II. Demographic dynamics*, Éditions John Libbey Eurotext, Paris, 211-229.
Haurin, R. (1992). Patterns of Childhood residence and the Relationship to Young Adults Outcomes, in: *Journal of Marriage and the Family*, 54(4), November.
Heaton, T.B. (1991). Time-Related Determinants of Marital Dissolution, in: *Journal of Marriage and The Family*, may, 285-295.
Hoem, J. & B. Rennermalm (1985). Modern family initiation in Sweden: experience of women born between 1936 and 1960. *European Journal of Population* 1, 81-112.
Hoem, J.M. (1986). The impact of education on modern family-union initiation, in: *European Journal of Population*, 2, 113-133.
Hoem, B. & J. M. Hoem (1988). Dissolution in Sweden: The break-up of conjugal unions to Swedish women born in 1936-60, *Stockholm Research Reports in Demography*, No. 45, University of Stockholm.
Hoem, B. & J.M. Hoem (1992). The Disruption of Marital and Non-Marital Unions in Contemporary Sweden, in: *Demographic applications of event history analysis*, J. Trussell, R. Hankinson and J. Tilton (eds), Clarendon Press, Oxford, 61-93.
Hoem, J.M. (1991). To Marry, Just in Case...: the Swedish Widow's-Pension Reform and the Peak in Marriages in December 1989, in: *Scandinavian Sociological Association*, 34, 127-135.
Hoem, J.M. (1993). Classical demographic methods of analysis and modern event-history techniques: introduction comments by the organizer of Session 35 on event-history analysis, in: *Demography*, presented at 14SSP 22nd General Conference, Montreal, august-september.
Hoffman-Nowotny, H-J (1988). Structural and cultural Determinants of Europe's second Demographic Transition, in: *Bevolking en Gezin*, 1988, 1, 73-89.
Hogan, D.P. (1981). Transitions and Social Change. The early lives of American Men. Academic Press Inc., New York (Studies in Population).
Hooghiemstra, B.T.J. & M. Niphuis-Nell (1993). *Sociale Atlas van de Vrouw*. Deel 2. Arbeid, inkomen en faciliteiten om werken en de zorg vaoor kinderen te combineren. Sociaal en Cultureel Planbureau, Rijswijk, januari.
Höpflinger, F. (1990). The future of household and family structures in Europe, *Seminar on present demographic trends and lifestyles in Europe*, Strasbourg, 18-20 September, 5th sitting.
Keilman, N. (1993). Emerging issues in demographic methodology, in: Blum, A. & J-L Rallu (eds), *European Population II. Demographic dynamics*, Éditions John Libbey Eurotext, Paris, 483-508.
Kiernan, K. & P.L. Chase-Lansdale (1993). Children and marital breakdown: short and long-term consequences, in: Blum, A. & J-L Rallu (eds), *European Population II. Demographic dynamics*, Éditions John Libbey Eurotext, Paris, 295-307.
Klaus, J. & Hooimeijer, P. (1993) Inkomen en ouderschap: een longitudinale analyse (Income and parenthood: a longitudinal analysis), in supplement Sociaal-Economisch Maandstatistiek, (CBS), 93/4, 15-24.
Klijzing, F.K.H. (1989). Relatievorming en sociaal-economische positie, in: Relatievorming in Nederland. Resultaten van een survey-onderzoek, NIDI, rapport nr. 8, Den Haag, 1989, 91-109.
Klijzing, F.K.H. (1992). 'Weeding' in the Netherlands: First-Union Disruption among Men and Women Born between 1928 and 1965, in: *European Sociological Review*, Vol. 8, No. 1, May, 53-70.
Kobrin, F.E. & L.J. Waite (1984). Effects of Childhood Family Structure on the Transition to Marriage, in: *Journal of Marriage and the Family*, 807-816.

Kooy, G.A. (1983). *Sex in Nederland.* Het meest recente onderzoek naar houding en gedrag van de Nederlandse bevolking. Het Spectrum, Utrecht/Antwerpen.

Kravdal, O. (1988). The Impact of first-birth timing on divorce: new evidence from a longitudinal analysis based on the central population register of Norway, in: *European Journal of Population,* 247-269.

Kuijsten, A.C. & E. Klijzing (1990). Domestic histories in the Netherlands: a comparison of generations, in: *Life histories and Generations, volume I and II,* Proceedings of a Symposium held on 22 and 23 June 1989 at the Netherlands Institute for Advanced Study in the Humanities and Social Sciences, at Wassenaar, H.A. Becker (ed), ISOR/Faculty of Social Sciences, University of Utrecht, 308-340.

Kuijsten, A.C. (1986). *Advances in Family Demography,* 's-Gravenhage, NIDI/CBGS.

Laird, N. & D. Oliver (1981). Covariance analysis of censored survival data using log-linear analysis techniques. *Journal of the American Statistical Association,* 76:231-40.

Langeveld, H.M. (1985). Binding in vrijheid. Een studie naar toekomstige gezinnen, relaties en hulpverlening. *Sociaal en Culturele Studies - 6.,* Sociaal en Cultureel Planbureau, Staatsuitgeverij, 's-Gravenhage.

Larson, M.G. (1984). Covariate Analysis of Competing-Risks Data with Log-Linear Models, in: *Biometrics* 40, 459-469.

Latten, J.J. (1992). Trouwen zonder te hebben samengewoond. Van gewoon naar bijzonder? (Married without having cohabited. From normal to exceptional?), in: *Maandstatistiek van de Bevolking,* juni 1992, 24-30.

Lee, H.Y, Rajulton, F., Wijewickrema, S. & Lesthaeghe, R. (1987). Gezinsvorming in Vlaanderen: Nieuwe vormen, andere timing, in: *Tijdschrift voor Sociologie,* jrg. 8, nr II/III, 35-103.

Leridon H. (1989). Cohabitation, Marriage, Separation: an analysis of life histories of French cohorts from 1968 to 1985. *Population Studies,* 44:127-144.

Leridon, H. & Villeneuve-Gokalp, C. (1989). The new couples: number, characteristics and attitudes, in: *Population,* 1, 203-235.

Lesthaeghe R. (1983). A Century of Demographic and Cultural Change in Western Europe: an Exploration of Underlying Dimensions, *Population and Development Review,* 9, no. 3, 411-435.

Lesthaeghe, R. (1991). The Second Demographic Transition in Western Countries: an interpretation. *IPD-working paper,* Brussels, 2.

Lesthaeghe, R. & G. Moors (1992). De gezinsrelaties: De ontwikkeling en stabilisatie van patronen, in: J. Kerkhofs et al., *De versnelde ommekeer,* Lannoo, Tielt, 19-68.

Lesthaeghe, R., G. Moors, & L. Halman (1992). Living arrangements and values among young adults in the Netherlands, Belgium, France and Germany, 1990. *IPD-Working Paper,* 3, Vrije Universiteit Brussel.

Lesthaeghe, R. & D. Meekers (1987). Demografische verschuivingen en de evolutie van waardenpatronen in de Europese gemeenschap, in *Tijdschrift voor Sociologie,* Jrg.8, nr 2/3, 131-200.

Lesthaeghe, R. & J. Surkyn (1988). Cultural dynamics and economic Theories of Fertility Change, in: *Population and Development Review,* vol 14, no. 1, March, 1-46.

Lesthaeghe, R. & D.J. Van de Kaa (1986), Twee demografische Transities? in: *Mens en Maatschappij,* boekafl, jrg. 61, 9-24.

Lesthaeghe, R. & G. Verleye (1992). De tweede demografische transitie: Conceptuele basis en recente evolutie, in: *De Demografische Uitdaging: Nederland in Europa op weg naar de 21ste eeuw* (Van Nimwegen, J. & J. De Jong Gierveld, Bohn Stafleu van Loghum, 's-Gravenhage, 15-49.

Liefbroer, A.C. (1991a). *Kiezen tussen ongehuwd samenwonen en trouwen,* Centrale Huisdrukkery Vrije Universiteit, Amsterdam.

Liefbroer, A.C. (1991b). The choice between a married or unmarried first union by young adults; A competing risks analysis. *European Journal of Population,* 7:273-98.

Liefbroer, A.C. (1991c). Ongehuwd samenwonen voor steeds meer jongeren een vanzelfsprekendheid in *Demos,* jaargang 7 nummer 5, 36-39.

Liefbroer, A.C. & J. De Jong Gierveld (1992). Social Background and life course influences on patterns of union formation among young adults in the Netherlands, in: Becker, H.A. (eds). *Dynamics of cohort and generations research,* Thesis, Amsterdam, 481-514.

Liefbroer, A.C. & J. De Jong Gierveld (1993). The Impact of Rational Considerations and Perceived Opinions on Young Adults' Union Formation Intentions, in: *Journal of Family Issues,* Vol. 14 No. 2, June 1993, Sage Publications, Inc, 213-235.

Liefbroer, A.C. & L. Gerritsen & J. de Jong Gierveld (1993). Bouwbestek of luchtkasteel? De invloed van plannen en levensloopfactoren op relatievormingsgedrag, in: *Sociologische Gids*, jrg XL, 111-125.
Lindenberg, S. & Frey, B.S. (1993). Alternatives, Frames and Relative Prices: A braoder view of Rational Choice Theory, in: *Acta Sociologica*, 36, 191-205.
Lutz, W., Wils, A.B. & M. Nieminen (1991). The Demographic Dimensions of Divorce: The Case of Finland, in: *Population Studies*, 45, 437-453.
Manting, D. (1991). First Union Formation in the Netherlands, paper presented at the *European Population Conference 1991*, EAPS/IUSSP/INED, Paris, October 21-25 1991, PDOD-paper no. 5, Amsterdam.
Manting, D. & J. Helleman & A.C. Kuijsten (1993). From Youth to Adulthood; Transitions of Female Birth Cohorts in The Netherlands, in: *Population and Family in the Low Countries 1992*: Family and Labour, G.C.N. Beets, R.L. Cliquet, G. Dooghe & J. de Jong Gierveld (eds), Swets and Zeitlinger, Amsterdam/Lisse, 55-76.
Manting, D. (1993a). Welke vrouwen maken een echtscheiding mee? (Which women experience divorce?), in: *Maandstatistiek van de Bevolking*, (CBS), 93/2, 18-29.
Manting, D. (1993b). Niet-gehuwd samenwonen: vaker wel dan niet (Cohabitation: from exception to common behaviour), in: *Maandstatistiek van de Bevolking*, CBS, 93/12, 9-10.
Manting, D. (1993c). Cohabiting Women in the Netherlands and their Timing of Marriage, in: W.F. Sleegers & Goethals A L J (eds). *Quantitative Geographical Methods, Applied in Demographic and Urban Planning Research*, Amsterdam: SISWO, 85-92.
Manting, D. (1994a). Meer scheidingen dan echtscheidingen (More separations than divorces), in: *Maandstatistiek van de Bevolking*, april 1994, 6-8.
Manting, D. (1994b). Verscheidenheid in partnerrelaties (Diversity of couple relationships), in: Maandstatistiek van de Bevolking, mei 1994, 23-29.
Marini, M.M. (1985). Determinants of the Timing of Adult Role Entry, in: *Social Science Research*, volume 14, Academic Press, Inc., 303-350.
Mayer, K.U. & N.B. Tuma (1990). Life Course Research and Event History Analysis: An Overview, in: Mayer, K.U. & N.B. Tuma (eds). *Event History Analysis in Life Course Research*, The University of Wisconsin Press, 3-20.
McLanahan, S. & L. Bumpass (1988). Intergenerational Consequences of Family Disruption, in: *American Journal of Sociology*, vol 94, no 1, July, 130-152.
Menken, J., Trussel, J., Stempel & Babakol, O. (1981). Proportional hazards life table models: an Illustrative Analysis on Marriage Dissolution in the United States, in: *Demography*, vol. 18, no. 2, May, 181-200.
Michael, R.T. & Tuma, N.B. (1985). Entry into marriage and parenthood by young men and women: The influence of family background, in: *Demography*, vol. XXII, no. 4., november, 515-544.
Moors, H.G. & van Nimwegen, N. (1990). Social and demographic effects of changing household structures on children and young people. In: *Seminar on Present Demographic Trends and Lifestyles in Europe*. Strasbourg, 116-158.
Morgan, P.S. & Rindfuss, R.R. (1985). Marital Disruption: Structural and Temporal Dimensions, in: *American Journal of Sociology*, vol. 90, no. 5, 1055-1076.
Mueller, C.W. & H. Pope (1977). Marital Instability: A Study of Its Transmission Between Generations, in: *Journal of Marriage and the Family*, 83-92.
Mulder, C.H. & D. Manting (1993a). "Strategies of Nest-leavers: 'Settling down' versus Flexibility", paper prepared for Session 20 "Women's and men's life strategies in developed societies" of the IUSSP XXIInd *General Population Conference*, Montreal.
Mulder, E.H. & D. Manting (1993b). Strategieën van uithuisgangers: vastigheid of flexibiliteit, in: *Volwassen worden. Generaties toen en nu: transities in de levensloop*, du Bois-Reymond, M. & J. de Jong Gierveld (eds), Bohn Stafleu van Loghum, Houten, 54-72.
Mulder, C.H. & M. Wagner (1993). Migration and Marriage in the Life Course: a Method for Studying Synchronized Events, in: *European Journal of Population* 9, Kluwer Academic Publishers, 55-76.
Mulder, C.H. (1993). *Migration dynamics: A life course Approach*, PDOD publications series A (doctoral dissertation), Thesis, Amsterdam.
Namboodiri, K. & Suchindran, C.M. (1987). Life table techniques and their applications. Orlando. FL: Academic Press.

Newcomb, M.D. (1987). Cohabitation and Marriage: A Quest for Independence and Relatedness, in: *Social Psychological Aspects*, Sage Publications, Inc, 128-156.
Oppenheimer, V.K. (1988). A Theory of Marriage Timing, in: *American Journal of Sociology*, vol. 94, no. 3. (November), 563-91.
Papastefanou, G. (1990). *Familiengründung im Lebensverlauf, Eine empirische Anayse socialstruktureller Bedingungen der Familiengründung bei den Kohorten 1929-31, 1939-41 und 1949-51*, Studien und Berichte 50, Max-Planck-Institut fur Bildungsforschung, Berlin.
Peters, E. & Du Bois-Reymond, M. (1990) Levensontwerpen van jonge vrouwen en mannen. Resultaten uit een actuele jeugdstudie en een intergenerationele vergelijking. *Mens en Maatschappij*, 4, 396-417.
Prins, C.J.M. (1990). Fractie buitenechtelijke geborenen stijgt op alle leeftijden (Proportion of non-marital births up for all ages, *Maandstatistiek van de Bevolking*, CBS, 90/7, 8-9.
Rindfuss, R.R. & Vandenheuvel, A.(1990). Cohabitation: A precursor to marriage or an alternative to being Single, in: *Population and Development Review*, 16, no 4. december, 703-726.
Rindfuss, R.R., R.A. Rosenfeld, C.G. Swicegood (1987). Disorder in the life course: how common and does it matter? in: *American Sociological Review*, Vol. 52, December, 785-801.
Rindfuss, R.R. & Parnell, A.M. (1989). The Varying Connection between Marital Status and childbearing in the Untied States, in: *Population and Development Review 15*, no. 3 (september), 447-470.
Rodgers, W.L. & Thornton, A.(1985). Changing Patters of First Marriage in the United States, Vol. 22, No. 2., *Demography*, Vol. 22, No. 2, May, 265-279.
Rogers, A. (1986). Parameterized Multistate Population Dynamics and Projections, in: *Journal of American Statistical Association*, March, Vol. 82, No. 393, 48-61.
Roussel, L. & Festy, P. (1979). Recent trends in attitudes and behaviour affecting the family in council of Europe member states, Council of Europe, Strasbourg, *Population Studies*, 4.
Roussel, L. (1989). Types of Marriage and Frequency of Divorce, in: E. Grebenik, C. Höhn & R. Mackensen (eds), *Later Phases of the Family Cycle and Demographic Aspects*, Clarendon Press, Oxford, 19-36.
Runyan, W.M. (1984). The Life course as a theoretical orientation, in: W.M. Runyan, *Life Histories and Psychobiography. Explorations in theory and method*, New York, Oxford up, 81-99.
Ryder, N.B. (1965). The Cohort as a Concept in the Study of Social Change, in: *American Sociological Review*, vol. 30, 843-861.
Ryder, N.B. (1985). The cohort as a concept in the study of social change, in: M. Mason & S.E. Fienberg (eds.) *Cohort analysis in Social Research*, New York, Springer, 9-44.
Sanders, K. en Becker, H.A. (1993). De overgang van onderwijs naar arbeidsmarkt. Een vergelijking tussen Nederland, West-Duitsland, Groot Britannië en de Verenigde Staten in de beroepsbevolking tussen 15 en 25 jaar voor de cohorten 1945-1965, paper gepresenteerd tijdens de bijeenkomst *NWO-Prioriteitenprogramma Bevolkingsvraagstukken CEPOP*, 23 oktober, Utrecht.
Santow, G. & M. Bracher (1993). Change and Continuity: an analysis of the formation of first marital unions in Australia. Paper presented at Session 34, *the XXII General Conference of the International Union for the Scientific Study of Population*, Montreal, 25 august-1 september.
Schoen, R. (1992). First Unions and the Stability of First Marriages, in: *Journal of Marriage and the Family 54*, May, 281-284.
Schoen, R. & Baj, J. (1984). Twentieth-Century Cohort Marriage and Divorce in England and Wales, in: *Population studies*, 38, 439-449.
Schumacher, J. & R. Vollmer (1981). Partnerwahl und Partnerbeziehung, in: *Zeitschrift für Bevölkerungswissenschaft*, jg 7, 4, 499-518.
SCP (1992), Sociaal en Cultureel Planbureau, *Sociaal en Cultureel Rapport 1992*. Rijswijk, september 1992.
Singer, J.D. & J.B. Willett (1991). Modeling the Days of Our Lives: Using Survival Analysis When Designing and Analyzing Longitudinal Studies of Duration and the Timing of Events, in: Psychological Bulletin, 1991, Vol. 110, No. 2, *American Psychological Association*, Inc, 268-290.
South, S.J. & G. Spitze (1986). Determinants of Divorce over the Marital Life Course, in: *American Sociological Review*, vol. 51, aug, 583-590.
Statistics Netherlands, (1985). Special Data. Demographic key-figures, in: *Maandstatistiek van de Bevolking*, CBS, 85/7, 15-17.

Statistics Netherlands, (1990a). Door huwelijkssluiting gewettigde kinderen, 1981-1988. (Children legitimized by marriage, 1981-1988, in: *Maandstatistiek van de Bevolking* (CBS), 90/1, 39-41.
Statistics Netherlands, (1990b). Annual Statistics. Demographic key-figures, 1980-1989, in: *Maandstatistiek van de Bevolking*, CBS, 90/5, 26-29.
Statistics Netherlands, (1990c). Size & Population Dynamics, 1946-1990, in: *Maandstatistiek van de Bevolking*, CBS, 90/4, 26-29.
Statistics Netherlands, (1990d). *Onderzoek Gezinsvorming 1988: samenwonen, trouwen, geboorteregeling, werken en kinderen krijgen*. Staatsuitgeverij, 's-Gravenhage.
Statistics Netherlands, (1991a). Population trends, October 1990. Non-marital birth up again. in: *Maandstatistiek van de Bevolking*, (CBS), 91/2, 5.
Statistics Netherlands, (1992). Statistical yearbook 1992.
Statistics Netherlands, (1993). Children legitimized by marriage, 1987-1991, (CBS), 93/1 page 42-43.
Statistics Netherlands, (1994). Relatie- en gezinsvorming in de jaren negentig.
Tas, R.F.J. (1989). Echtscheidingen in Nederland (Divorces in The Netherlands, 1950-1987), in: *Maandstatistiek van de Bevolking*, (CBS), 89/3, 17-27.
Teachman, J.D. (1982). Methodological issues in the analysis of family formation and dissolution, in: *Journal of Marriage and the Family*, november, 1037-1053.
Teachman, J.D., Thomas, J. & K. Paasch (1991). Legal Status and the Stability of Coresidential Unions, in: *Demography*, vol. 28, no. 4, November, 571-585.
Thornton, A. & W.L. Rodgers (1987). The Influence of Individual and Historical time on Marital Dissolution, in: *Demography*, vol. 24, no.1, February, 1-22.
Thornton, A. (1988). Cohabitation and marriage in the 1980s, in: *Demography*, vol. 25, no. 4, November, 497-508.
Thornton, A. (1991). Influence of the marital history of parents on the marital and Cohabitational experiences of children, *American Journal of Sociology*, vol 96, no 4., jan. 91, 868-894.
Thornton, A. & W.G. Axinn, D.H. Hill (1992). Reciprocal effects of Religiosity, Cohabitation and Marriage, in: *Americal Journal of Sociology*, vol 98, no. 3, november, 628-651.
Trost, J. (1979a). *Unmarried cohabitation*. International Library.
Trost, J. (1979b). Dissolution of Cohabitation and Marriage in Sweden, in: *Journal of Divorce*, Vol, 2(4), Summer, Haworth Press, 415-421.
Trost, J. (1981). Cohabitation in the Nordic Countries. From Deviant Phenomenon to Social Institution, in: *Alternative Lifestyles*, vol. 4., November 1981, Sage publications, Inc., 401-427.
Trost, J. (1986). What holds Marriages Together? in: *Acta Sociologica 1986* (29), 4, 303-310.
Trost, J. (1988). Cohabitation and marriage: transitional pattern, different lifestyle, or just another legal form, in: *Lifestyles, contraception and parenthood*, H. Moors & J. Schoorl (eds), NIDI, The Hague/Brussels, 3-14.
Trussell, J. (1992). Introduction, in: *Demographic applications of event history analysis*, J. Trussell, R. Hankinson & J. Tilton (eds), Clarendon Press, Oxford, 1991, 1-7.
Trussell, J., G. Rodríguez & B. Vaughan (1992). Union Dissolution in Sweden, in: *Demographic applications of event history analysis*, J. Trussell, R. Hankinson & J. Tilton (eds), Clarendon Press, Oxford, 38-60.
Tuma, N.B. & M.T. Hannan (1984). Dynamic Analysis of Event Histories, in: *American Journal of Sociology*, vol 84, no. 4, 821-854.
Van Delft, M. & Niphuis-Nell (1988). *Eenoudergezinnen: ontstaan, leefsituatie en voorzieningengebruik*, Sociale en Culturele Studies - 9, Sociaal en Cultureel Planbureau, Alphen aan den Rijn.
Van de Giessen, G.J. (1988). Marriage and cohabitation, 1988, Netherlands Fertility Survey, in: *Maandstatistiek van de Bevolking*, 88/11, 7-8.
Van de Kaa, D.J. & Kuijsten, A.C. (1988). Onderzoekvoorstel: 'Levenslooppatronen van in Nederlandse geboortegeneraties: *Relatie- en Gezinsvorming*.
Van de Kaa, D.J. (1987). Europe's Second Demographic Transition, *Population Bulletin*, vol. 42, No. 1, Population reference Bureau, March.
Van de Kaa, D.J. (1988). Europe's Second Demographic Transition revisited: Theories and Expectations, *Werkstukken Planologisch en Demografisch Instituut*, no. 109, December.
Van den Akker, P.A.M. (1982). *Huwelijk in de verzorgingsstaat*. (Een sociaal-demografische studie naar aanleiding van een analyse van de hertrouw in Nederland), IVA, Tilburg, oktober.

Van den Akker, P.A.M. (1988). Mannen, vrouwen en kinderen in verschuivend perspectief, in: *Het kind als keuze*, Demografische ontwikkelingen in Nederland, G.A.B. Frinking & J.H.M. Nelissen (eds.), Den Haag, SDU Uitgeverij, 1-33.

Van den Akker, P. & T. Mandemaker (1991). *Geborgenheid en zelfontplooiing*. Een verkennend sociologisch en sociaal-psychologisch onderzoek naar de betekenis en de realisatie van twee waardencomplexen in primaire leefvormen, IVA, Tilburg, juni.

Van der Avort, A.J.P.M. (1987). *De gulzige vrijblijvendheid van expliciete relaties*. Tilburg University Press.

Van Leeuwen, L.Th. (1989). Nieuwe patronen in de individuele levensloop, in: *Relatievormen in Nederland*, NIDI, rapport nr. 8, 's-Gravenhage, 48-63.

Van Leeuwen, L.Th. & M.J.H. Ploegmakers (1990). *Patronen in de individuele levensloop. Een verkennende studie*. Nederlandse Gezinsraad, Den Haag, juli.

Van Poppel, F. & de Beer, J. (1991). Het effect van veranderingen in de echtscheidingswetgeving op het echtscheidingscijfer: een toepassing van interventie-analyse (The effect of changes in divorce laws on the divorce rate: an application of intervention analysis), in: *Maandstatistiek van de Bevolking*, (CBS), 6/91, 27-35.

Van Poppel, F. (1992). *Trouwen in Nederland*. Een historisch-demografische studie van de 19e en vroeg-20e eeuw, Nidi, Rapport nr. 31, 's-Gravenhage.

Vermunt, J.K. (1991). Een multivariaat model voor de geboorte van het eerste kind (A multivariate model of first childbirth), in: *Maandstatistiek van de Bevolking*, (CBS), 91/5, 22-33.

Voets, S.Y & A.C. Kuijsten, (1989). Echtscheiding en leefsituatieveranderingen van kinderen: een overzicht van benaderingen, in: *Bevolking en Gezin*, nr 2, november, 73-101.

Wagner, M. (1991). Sozialstruktur und Ehestabilität, in: *Vom Regen in die Traufe: Frauen zwischen Beruf und Familie*, K.U. Mayer, J. Allmendinger & J. Huinink (eds), Frankfurt, 359-384.

Waite, L.J. & Spitze, G.D. (1981). Young women's transition to marriage, in: *Demography*, vol. 18, no. 4, november, 681-694.

Weeda, I. (1991). *Echtscheiding. Een regenboog van ervaringen*. Uitgeverij bosch & Keuning/Sesam, Baarn.

Wiersma, G.E. (1983). *Cohabitation, an alternative to marriage? A cross-national study*. A NIDI CBGS publication, The Hague.

Willekens, F.J. (1991). Understanding the Interdependence between Parallel Careers, in: *Female Labour Market Behaviour and Fertility, A Rational-Choice Approach*, J.J. Siegers, J. de Jong-Gierveld, E. van Imhoff (Eds.), 2-31.

Yamaguchi K (1991). *Event History Analysis*, Newbury Park: Sage (Applied Social Research Methods Series 28).

APPENDIX CHAPTER 3

Appendix A Parameter estimates of several models of first union formation

			based on unweighted data	based on weighted data	censoring at age 27	censoring at age 25
		L2:	152	150	148	150
		df:	138	138	138	138
		p:	0.22	0.23	0.26	0.23
	mean		-5.72	-5.85	-5.69	-5.72
	marriage		-0.14	-0.22	-0.13	-0.12
age	16-18		-1.15	-1.08	-1.18	-1.15
	19-21		0.27	0.30	0.25	0.28
birth cohort	1950-54		-0.04	0.10	0.01	-0.04
	1955-59		0.18	0.23	0.19	0.17
	1960-64		-0.08	-0.06	-0.11	-0.07
occupational status	unemployed		0.33	0.30	0.37	0.32
	at school		-0.73	-0.70	-0.78	-0.72
educational level	low		0.43	0.46	0.42	0.43
	medium		-0.16	-0.17	-0.16	-0.15

second-order-effects						
marriage*	16-18		-0.07	-0.05	-0.08	-0.09
	19-21		0.05	0.07	0.04	0.04
marriage*	1950-54		0.46	0.53	0.48	0.48
	1955-59		0.12	0.13	0.12	0.12
	1960-64		-0.27	-0.26	-0.28	-0.27
age 16-18*	1950-54		-0.12	-0.07	-0.15	-0.12
	1955-59		0.13	0.18	0.12	0.13
	1960-64		0.09	0.08	0.11	0.10
age 19-21*	1950-54		0.16	0.13	0.13	0.17
	1955-59		0.11	0.10	0.09	0.11
	1960-64		-0.01	0.00	0.02	0.00
marriage	unemployed		0.17	0.14	0.18	0.19
	at school		-0.33	-0.31	-0.33	-0.35
age 16-18*	unemployed		0.39	0.40	0.35	0.40
	at school		-0.32	-0.31	-0.28	-0.33
age 19-21*	unemployed		0.02	0.03	-0.02	0.03
	at school		-0.11	-0.13	-0.07	-0.12
cohort 1950-54*	unemployed		-0.11	-0.08	-0.05	-0.12
	at school		0.25	0.26	0.20	0.26
cohort 1955-59*	unemployed		0.01	0.02	0.00	-0.01
	at school		0.01	0.00	0.00	0.01
cohort 1960-64*	unemployed		-0.04	-0.06	-0.08	-0.03
	at school		-0.03	-0.01	0.01	-0.04
marriage*	low		0.38	0.43	0.37	0.37
	medium		-0.08	-0.07	-0.08	-0.08
age 16-18*	low		0.32	0.33	0.33	0.32
	medium		-0.07	-0.08	-0.06	-0.07
age 19-21*	low		-0.10	-0.09	-0.10	-0.10
	medium		0.07	0.06	0.07	0.06
cohort 1950-54*	low		-0.23	-0.26	-0.24	-0.22
	medium		0.05	0.05	0.03	0.03
cohort 1955-59	low		-0.12	-0.13	-0.12	-0.13
	medium		0.03	0.01	0.03	0.03
cohort 1960-64	low		0.17	0.16	0.18	0.17
	medium		0.13	0.14	0.13	0.13
unemployed*	low		-0.01	-0.04	0.00	-0.01
	medium		0.12	0.14	0.11	0.12

student*	low		0.11	0.13	0.09	0.11
	medium		-0.22	-0.25	-0.20	-0.22

Third-order-effects marriage*						
age 16-18*	1950-54		0.07	0.08	0.05	0.06
	1955-59		0.03	0.04	0.03	0.02
	1960-64		-0.04	-0.07	-0.03	-0.04
age 19-21*	1950-54		0.14	0.12	0.12	0.12
	1955-59		0.07	0.04	0.07	0.07
	1960-64		0.00	0.00	0.02	0.01

marriage*						
cohort 1950-54*	unemployed		0.24	0.24	0.24	0.23
	at school		0.04	0.01	0.04	0.06
cohort 1955-59*	unemployed		0.07	0.07	0.07	0.08
	at school		0.03	0.05	0.03	0.02
cohort 1960-64*	unemployed		-0.04	-0.04	-0.04	-0.04
	at school		0.00	-0.01	0.00	0.00

age 16-18*						
cohort 1950-54*	low		-0.08	-0.15	-0.09	-0.08
	medium		-0.04	-0.08	-0.03	-0.03
cohort 1955-59*	low		-0.03	-0.09	-0.04	-0.03
	medium		-0.07	-0.14	-0.07	-0.07
cohort 1960-64*	low		0.09	0.08	0.10	0.09
	medium		-0.04	-0.02	-0.05	-0.04
age 19-21*						
cohort 1950-54*	low		-0.11	-0.09	-0.10	-0.10
	medium		-0.08	-0.06	-0.07	-0.07
cohort 1955-59*	low		0.01	0.03	0.00	0.01
	medium		-0.10	-0.07	-0.10	-0.10
cohort 1960-64*	low		0.05	0.02	0.04	0.04
	medium		0.04	0.04	0.03	0.03
marriage						
unemployed*	low		-0.05	-0.03	-0.06	-0.06
	medium		0.08	0.09	0.07	0.07
work*	low		0.23	0.24	0.24	0.24
	medium		-0.23	-0.25	-0.22	-0.22

baseline categories omitted
baseline category can be estimated by minus the sum of the other categories
L2 = log likelihood ratio, df = degree of freedom

Appendix B

Coding of educational attainment (measured at time of interview)

Low educational level:
primary education
secondary education; first level
secondary grammar school (first three years)
senior secondary school (first three years)
junior secondary school (first four years)
junior vocational training (first four years)

Middle educational level:
secondary education; second level
secondary grammar school (fourth to sixth year)
senior secondary school (fourth and fifth year)
senior vocational training (two to four years)

High educational level:
vocational colleges (higher level)
university education

APPENDIX CHAPTER 5

Table 1 Results of conditional log likelihood ratio tests of a model of first union formation, including past life course determinants, type of union, birth cohort and age

	L2	df	ΔL2	Δdf
{}	6908	1728		
{A} type	6835	1726	72	2*
{B} age	4462	1725	2445	3*
{C} birth cohort	6663	1724	245	4*
{D} parental home	4615	1726	2292	2*
{E} religion	6897	1725	10	3
{F} parental family size	6892	1726	15	2*
{G} age difference with mother	6886	1726	22	2*
{H} home town	6904	1725	3	3
{A,B,C,D,E,F,G,H} (all first-order-effects)	3371	1714		
{ B,C,D,E,F,G,H}	3443	1715	72	1*
{A, C,D,E,F,G,H}	4411	1716	1040	2*
{A,B, D,E,F,G,H}	3397	1717	26	3*
{A,B,C, E,F,G,H}	4240	1715	869	1*
{A,B,C,D, F,G,H}	3374	1716	3	2
{A,B,C,D,E, G,H}	3374	1715	3	1
{A,B,C,D,E,F, H}	3454	1715	84	1*
{A,B,C,D,E,F,G, }	3371	1716	0	2
{A,B,C,D,E,F,G,H,AE}	2936	1712	435	2*
{A,B,C,D,E,F,G,H,AF}	3313	1713	58	1*
{A,B,C,D,E,F,G,H,AH}	3267	1712	103	2*
{AB,AC,AD,AE,AF,AG,AH}	2190	1702		
{ B,AC,AD,AE,AF,AG,AH}	2232	1704	42	2*
{AB, C,AD,AE,AF,AG,AH}	2644	1705	454	3*
{AB,AC, D,AE,AF,AG,AH}	2407	1703	217	1*
{AB,AC,AD, E,AF,AG,AH}	2493	1704	303	2*
{AB,AC,AD,AE, F,AG,AH}	2200	1703	10	1*
{AB,AC,AD,AE,AF, G,AH}	2196	1703	6	1
{AB,AC,AD,AE,AF,AG, H}	2244	1704	54	2*
{AB,AC,AD,AE,AF,AH,BC,CD,CE,CF,CG,CH}	2069	1676		
{AB,AC,AD,AE,AF,AH, CD,CE,CF,CG,CH}	2080	1682	11	6
{AB,AC,AD,AE,AF,AH,BC, CE,CF,CG,CH}	2105	1679	36	3*
{AB,AC,AD,AE,AF,AH,BC,CD, CF,CG,CH}	2099	1682	30	6*
{AB,AC,AD,AE,AF,AH,BC,CD,CE, CG,CH}	2084	1679	15	3*
{AB,AC,AD,AE,AF,AH,BC,CD,CE,CF, G,CH}	2080	1679	11	3
{AB,AC,AD,AE,AF,AH,BC,CD,CE,CF,CG}	2094	1682	25	6*
{AB,AC,AD,AE,AF,AH,CD,CE,CF,CH,BD,BE,BF,BG,BH}	1701	1671		
{AB,AC,AD,AE,AF,AH,CD,CE,CF,CH, BE,BF,BG,BH}	1957	1673	256	2*
{AB,AC,AD,AE,AF,AH,CD,CE,CF,CH,BD, BF,BG,BH}	1737	1675	36	4*
{AB,AC,AD,AE,AF,AH,CD,CE,CF,CH,BD,BE, BG,BH}	1708	1673	7	2
{AB,AC,AD,AE,AF,AH,CD,CE,CF,CH,BD,BE,BF, BH}	1714	1673	13	2*
{AB,AC,AD,AE,AF,AH,CD,CE,CF,CH,BD,BE,BF,BG }	1744	1675	43	4*
{AB,AC,AD,AE,AF,AH,CD,CE,CF,CH,BD,BE,BG,BH,DE,DF,DG,DH}	1657	1667		
{AB,AC,AD,AE,AF,AH,CD,CE,CF,CH,BD,BE,BG,BH, DF,DG,DH}	1702	1669	45	2*
{AB,AC,AD,AE,AF,AH,CD,CE,CF,CH,BD,BE,BG,BH,DE, DG,DH}	1658	1668	0	1
{AB,AC,AD,AE,AF,AH,CD,CE,CF,CH,BD,BE,BG,BH,DE,DF, DH}	1657	1668	0	1
{AB,AC,AD,AE,AF,AH,CD,CE,CF,CH,BD,BE,BG,BH,DE,DF,DG }	1659	1669	2	2
{AB,AC,AD,AE,AF,AH,CD,CE,CF,CH,BD,BE,BG,BH,DE,ABC,ACD,ACE,ACF,ACG,ACH}	1525	1634		
{AB,AC,AD,AE,AF,AH,CD,CE,CF,CH,BD,BE,BG,BH,DE, ACD,ACE,ACF,ACG,ACH}	1558	1646	32	12*
{AB,AC,AD,AE,AF,AH,CD,CE,CF,CH,BD,BE,BG,BH,DE,ABC, ACE,ACF,ACG,ACH}	1547	1637	22	3*
{AB,AC,AD,AE,AF,AH,CD,CE,CF,CH,BD,BE,BG,BH,DE,ABC,ACD, ACF,ACG,ACH}	1561	1640	36	6*
{AB,AC,AD,AE,AF,AH,CD,CE,CF,CH,BD,BE,BG,BH,DE,ABC,ACD,ACE, ACG,ACH}	1528	1637	2	3
{AB,AC,AD,AE,AF,AH,CD,CE,CF,CH,BD,BE,BG,BH,DE,ABC,ACD,ACE,ACF, ACH}	1538	1641	13	7
{AB,AC,AD,AE,AF,AH,CD,CE,CF,CH,BD,BE,BG,BH,DE,ABC,ACD,ACE,ACF,ACG }	1541	1640	15	6

{AB,AC,AD,AE,AF,AH,CD,CE,CF,CH,BD,BE,BG,BH,DE,ABC,ACD,ACE,ABD,ABE,ABF,ABG,ABH}	1525	1633		
{AB,AC,AD,AE,AF,AH,CD,CE,CF,CH,BD,BE,BG,BH,DE,ABC,ACD,ACE, ABE,ABF,ABG,ABH}	1529	1635	4	2
{AB,AC,AD,AE,AF,AH,CD,CE,CF,CH,BD,BE,BG,BH,DE,ABC,ACD,ACE,ABD, ABF,ABG,ABH}	1530	1637	5	4
{AB,AC,AD,AE,AF,AH,CD,CE,CF,CH,BD,BE,BG,BH,DE,ABC,ACD,ACE,ABD,ABE, ABG,ABH}	1539	1637	14	4*
{AB,AC,AD,AE,AF,AH,CD,CE,CF,CH,BD,BE,BG,BH,DE,ABC,ACD,ACE,ABD,ABE,ABF, ABH}	1533	1636	8	3
{AB,AC,AD,AE,AF,AH,CD,CE,CF,CH,BD,BE,BG,BH,DE,ABC,ACD,ACE,ABD,ABE,ABF,ABG }	1526	1637	1	4
{AB,AC,AD,AE,AF,AH,CD,CE,CF,CH,BD,BE,BG,BH,DE,ABC,ACD,ACE,ABF,BCD,BCE,BCF,BCG,BCH}	1485	1601		
{AB,AC,AD,AE,AF,AH,CD,CE,CF,CH,BD,BE,BG,BH,DE,ABC,ACD,ACE,ABF, BCE,BCF,BCG,BCH}	1505	1607	19	6*
{AB,AC,AD,AE,AF,AH,CD,CE,CF,CH,BD,BE,BG,BH,DE,ABC,ACD,ACE,ABF,BCD, BCF,BCG,BCH}	1516	1617	31	16
{AB,AC,AD,AE,AF,AH,CD,CE,CF,CH,BD,BE,BG,BH,DE,ABC,ACD,ACE,ABF,BCD,BCE, BCG,BCH}	1487	1607	2	6
{AB,AC,AD,AE,AF,AH,CD,CE,CF,CH,BD,BE,BG,BH,DE,ABC,ACD,ACE,ABF,BCD,BCE,BCF, BCH}	1499	1610	13	9
{AB,AC,AD,AE,AF,AH,CD,CE,CF,CH,BD,BE,BG,BH,DE,ABC,ACD,ACE,ABF,BCD,BCE,BCF,BCG }	1500	1613	14	12
{AB,AC,AD,AE,AF,AH,CD,CE,CF,CH,BD,BE,BG,BH,DE,ABC,ACD,ACE,ABF,BCD}	1522	1640		
{AB,AC,AD,AE,AF,AH,CD,CE,CF,CH,BD,BE,BG,BH,DE,ABC,ACD,ACE, BF,BCD}	1527	1642	5	2
{AB,AC,AD,AE, AH,CD,CE,CF,CH,BD,BE,BG,BH,DE,ABC,ACD,ACE, BF,BCD}	1537	1643	10	1*
{AB,AC,AD,AE,AF,AH,CD,CE,CF,CH,BD,BE,BG,BH,DE,ABC,ACD,ACE, BCD}	1537	1644	10	2*
{AB,AC,AD,AE,AF,AH,CD,CE,CF,CH,BD,BE,BF,BG,BH,DE,ABC,ACD,ACE,BCD}	1527	1642		
{AB,AC,AD,AE,AF,AH,CD,CE,CF,CH,BD,BE,BF,BG,BH,DE, ACD,ACE,BCD}	1551	1648	24	6*
{AB,AC,AD,AE,AF,AH,CD,CE,CF,CH,BD,BE,BF,BG,BH,DE,ABC, ACE,BCD}	1552	1645	25	3*
{AB,AC,AD,AE,AF,AH,CD,CE,CF,CH,BD,BE,BF,BG,BH,DE,ABC,ACD, BCD}	1564	1648	37	6*
{AB,AC,AD,AE,AF,AH,CD,CE,CF,CH,BD,BE,BF,BG,BH,DE,ABC,ACD,ACE, }	1547	1648	20	6*

* indicates conditional p < 0.01

{}	indicates nul model
{A}	indicates a model including first-order-effect of determinant A only
{ B,C,D,E,F,G,H}	indicates a model including all first-order-effects with the exception of covariate A
{A,B,C,D,E,F,G,H,AB}	indicates a model including all first-order-effects and a second-order- effect of covariate A with covariate B

Table 2 Results of conditional log likelihood ratio tests of a model of first union formation, including past life course determinants, type, age, birth cohort, occupational status and education

	L2	df	ΔL2	Δdf
1. The influence of parental home and home town				
1. with all determinants	2828	1282		
2. without parental home	4011	1283	1183	1*
3. without home town	2829	1284	1	2
4. with type*home town	2725	1280	103	2*
2. The influence of religion				
1. with all determinants	4310	420		
2. without religion	4411	422	102	2*
3. The influence of parental family size and age difference with mother				
1. with all determinants	648	277		
2. without fam.size	671	278	23	1*
3. without age mother	662	278	14	1*

* indicates conditional p < 0.01

Appendix chapter 5

Table 3 Parameter estimates of past life course determinants, type of union, birth cohort and age for the process of first union formation

(ABC,ACD,ACE,DE, BH, BG, BF, BE, BCD)		b	exp(b)		
mean		-5.30	0.01		
risk	marriage	-0.09	0.92		
	cohabitation	0.09	1.09		
age	16-18	-0.71	0.49		
	19-21	0.27	1.31		
	22 or more	0.44	1.56		
birth cohort	1950-54	-0.01	0.99		
	1955-59	0.20	1.22		
	1960-64	0.01	1.01		
	1965-69	-0.20	0.82		
parental home	at home	-0.71	0.49		
	not at home	0.71	2.03		
religion	none	-0.02	0.98		
	rk	-0.00	1.00		
	other	0.03	1.03		
parental family size	0-1 children	-0.08	0.92		
	2 or more	0.08	1.08		
age difference with mother					
	<= 25	0.19	1.20		
	25 or more	-0.19	0.83		
home town	>=400,000	0.07	1.07		
	>=100,000	-0.04	0.96		
	< 100,000	-0.03	0.97		

		marriage		cohabitation	
		b	exp(b)	b	exp(b)
age	16-18	-0.02	0.99	0.02	1.02
	19-21	0.06	1.06	-0.06	0.95
	22 or more	-0.04	0.96	0.04	1.04

		marriage		cohabitation	
birth cohort	1950-54	0.65	1.92	-0.65	0.52
	1955-59	0.25	1.29	-0.25	0.78
	1960-64	-0.27	0.76	0.27	1.31
	1965-69	-0.63	0.53	0.63	1.88

		marriage		cohabitation	
parental home	at home	0.22	1.25	-0.22	0.80
	not at home	-0.22	0.80	0.22	1.25

		marriage		cohabitation	
religion	none	-0.54	0.58	0.54	1.72
	rk	0.15	1.16	-0.15	0.86
	other	0.39	1.48	-0.39	0.67

parental family size	0-1 children	-0.06	0.94	0.06	1.06
	2 or more	0.06	1.06	-0.06	0.94

		marriage		cohabitation	
home town	>=400,000	-0.15	0.86	0.15	1.16
	>=100,000	-0.07	0.93	0.07	1.07
	< 100,000	0.22	1.24	-0.22	0.80

		age 16-18		19-21		22 or more	
		b	(exp)b	b	(exp)b	b	(exp)b
birth cohort	1950-54	-0.20	0.82	0.11	1.12	0.09	1.09
	1955-59	0.01	1.01	0.08	1.08	-0.09	0.92
	1960-64	0.10	1.10	-0.00	1.00	-0.10	0.91
	1965-69	0.09	1.09	-0.19	0.83	0.10	1.10
		age 16-18		19-21		22 or more	
parental home	at home	-0.55	0.58	0.05	1.05	0.49	1.64
	not at home	0.55	1.72	-0.05	0.95	-0.49	0.61
		age 16-18		19-21		22 or more	
religion	none	0.11	1.12	0.04	1.04	-0.15	0.86
	rk	-0.11	0.89	-0.01	0.99	0.12	1.13
	other	-0.00	1.00	-0.03	0.97	0.03	1.03
		age 16-18		19-21		22 or more	
family size	0-1	-0.11	0.90	0.03	1.03	0.08	1.08
	2 or more	0.11	1.11	-0.03	0.97	-0.08	0.92
		age 16-18		19-21		22 or more	
age mother	<= 25	0.11	1.11	-0.04	0.96	-0.07	0.93
	25 or more	-0.11	0.90	0.04	1.04	0.07	1.07
home town		age 16-18		19-21		22 or more	
	>=400,000	0.30	1.34	-0.10	0.90	-0.20	0.82
	>=100,000	-0.10	0.90	0.07	1.07	0.04	1.04
	< 100,000	-0.19	0.83	0.04	1.04	0.16	1.17
		birth cohort						b	(exp)b
parental home	at home	-0.01	0.99	0.00	1.00	0.08	1.08	-0.07	0.93
	not at home	0.01	1.01	-0.00	1.00	-0.08	0.93	0.07	1.08
		birth cohort							
religion	none	0.29	1.33	0.19	1.21	0.01	1.01	-0.49	0.61
	rk	-0.07	0.93	-0.08	0.92	0.02	1.02	0.13	1.14
	other	-0.22	0.80	-0.11	0.89	-0.03	0.97	0.36	1.43
		birth cohort							
parental family size	0-1 children	-0.01	0.99	0.09	1.10	0.01	1.01	-0.09	0.91
	2 or more	0.01	1.01	-0.09	0.91	-0.01	0.99	0.09	1.10
home town		birth cohort							
	>=400,000	-0.23	0.80	-0.12	0.88	0.17	1.19	0.18	1.20
	>=100,000	0.05	1.05	0.03	1.03	0.13	1.14	-0.20	0.82
	< 100,00	0.18	1.20	0.10	1.10	-0.30	0.74	0.02	1.02
		at home		not at home			
religion	none	0.17	1.18	-0.17	0.85		
	rk	-0.07	0.94	0.07	1.07		
	other	-0.10	0.90	0.10	1.11		
risk*age*cohort		marriage		cohabitation			
	16-18						
	1950-54	0.12	1.12	-0.12	0.89		
	1955-59	0.02	1.02	-0.02	0.98		
	1960-64	-0.05	0.96	0.05	1.05		
	1965-69	-0.09	0.92	0.09	1.09		
	19-21						
	1950-54	0.11	1.12	-0.11	0.89		
	1955-59	0.07	1.07	-0.07	0.94		
	1960-64	0.03	1.03	-0.03	0.97		
	1965-69	-0.20	0.82	0.20	1.23		
	22 or more						
	1950-54	-0.23	0.80	0.23	1.25		
	1955-59	-0.09	0.92	0.09	1.09		
	1960-64	0.02	1.02	-0.02	0.98		
	1965-69	0.29	1.34	-0.29	0.75		

Appendix chapter 5

risk*cohort*par. home		marriage		cohabitation	
	at home	b	(exp)b	b	(exp)b
	1950-54	0.13	1.13	-0.13	1.13
	1955-59	0.07	1.08	-0.07	1.13
	1960-64	-0.06	0.95	0.06	1.13
	1965-69	-0.14	0.87	0.14	1.13
	not at home				
	1950-54	-0.13	1.13	0.13	1.13
	1955-59	-0.07	1.08	0.07	1.13
	1960-64	0.06	0.95	-0.06	1.13
	1965-69	0.14	1.16	-0.14	1.13

age*cohort*par. home		at home		not at home	
	16-18				
	1950-54	0.02	1.02	-0.02	1.02
	1955-59	0.10	1.10	-0.10	1.02
	1960-64	0.10	1.11	-0.10	1.02
	1965-69	-0.22	0.81	0.22	1.02
	19-21				
	1950-54	-0.03	0.97	0.03	1.02
	1955-59	0.08	1.08	-0.08	1.02
	1960-64	0.01	1.01	-0.01	1.02
	1965-69	-0.05	0.95	0.05	1.02
	22 or more				
	1950-54	0.01	1.01	-0.01	1.02
	1955-59	-0.17	0.84	0.17	1.02
	1960-64	-0.11	0.90	0.11	1.02
	1965-69	0.27	1.31	-0.27	1.02

risk*cohort*religion		marriage 1950-54		1955-59		1960-64		1965-69	
						b	(exp)b	b	(exp)b
	none	0.10	1.11	0.08	1.08	0.08	1.08	-0.26	0.77
	rk	0.04	1.04	0.12	1.12	-0.02	0.98	-0.14	0.87
	other	-0.14	1.13	-0.19	0.83	-0.06	0.95	0.40	1.49
	cohabitation								
	none	-0.10	0.90	-0.08	0.93	-0.08	0.92	0.26	1.30
	rk	-0.04	0.96	-0.12	0.89	0.02	1.02	0.14	1.15
	other	0.14	1.16	0.19	1.21	0.06	1.06	-0.40	0.67

L2 = 1527
df = 1642

Table 4 Results of conditional log likelihood ratio tests of a model of union formation, including current life course determinants, type, age and birth cohort

	L2	df	ΔL2	Δdf
{}	4596	216		
{A} type	4524	214	72	2*
{B} age	2151	213	2445	3*
{C} birth cohort	4352	212	245	4*
{D} occupational status	2723	213	1874	3*
{E} educational level	1263	205	3333	11*
{A,B,C,D,E}	1263	205		
{ B,C,D,E}	1336	206	72	1*
{A, C,D,E}	2577	207	1314	2*
{A,B, D,E}	1284	208	21	3*
{A,B,C, E}	1704	207	441	2*
{A,B,C,D, }	1381	207	118	2*
{AB,AC,AD,AE}	537	196		
{ B,AC,AD,AE}	566	198	29	2*
{AB, C,AD,AE}	940	199	403	3*
{AB,AC, D,AE}	595	198	58	2*
{AB,AC,AD, E}	682	198	145	2*
{AB,AC,AD,AE,BC,CD,CE}	401	178		
{AB,AC,AD,AE, CD,CE}	424	184	23	6*
{AB,AC,AD,AE,BC, CE}	441	184	40	6*
{AB,AC,AD,AE,BC,CD }	454	184	53	6*
{AB,AC,AD,AE,BC,CD,CE,BD,BE}	260	170		
{AB,AC,AD,AE,BC,CD,CE, BE}	330	174	70	4*
{AB,AC,AD,AE,BC,CD,CE,BD }	309	174	49	4*
{AB,AC,AD,AE,BC,CD,CE,BD,BE}	260	170		
{AB,AC,AD,AE,BC,CD,CE,BD,BE,DE}	254	166	5	4
{AB,AC,AD,AE,BC,CD,CE,BD,BE,DE,ABC,ACD,ACE}	198	148		
{AB,AC,AD,AE,BC,CD,CE,BD,BE,DE, ACD,ACE}	217	154	19	6*
{AB,AC,AD,AE,BC,CD,CE,BD,BE,DE,ABC, ACE}	202	154	4	6
{AB,AC,AD,AE,BC,CD,CE,BD,BE,DE,ABC,ACD }	222	154	24	6*
{AB,AC,AD,AE,BC,CD,CE,BD,BE,DE,ABC,ACE,ABD,ABE}	184	146		
{AB,AC,AD,AE,BC,CD,CE,BD,BE,DE,ABC,ACE, ABE}	191	150	7	4
{AB,AC,AD,AE,BC,CD,CE,BD,BE,DE,ABC,ACE,ABD }	194	150	10	4
{AB,AC,AD,AE,BC,CD,CE,BD,BE,DE,ABC,ACE}	207	158		
{AB,AC,AD,AE,BC,CD,CE,BD,BE,DE,ABC,ACE,ADE}	179	150	28	8*
{AB,AC,AD,AE,BC,CD,CE,BD,BE,DE,ABC,ACE,ADE,CDE}	173	138	6	12
{AB,AC,AD,AE,BC,CD,CE,BD,BE,DE,ABC,ACE,ADE,BDE}	164	142	15	8
{AB,AC,AD,AE,BC,CD,CE,BD,BE,DE,ABC,ACE,ADE,BCD}	153	138	26	12
{AB,AC,AD,AE,BC,CD,CE,BD,BE,DE,ABC,ACE,ADE,BCE}	151	138	28	12*

* indicates conditional $p < 0.01$

Appendix chapter 5

Table 5 Parameter estimates of current life course determinants for the process of first union formation

{ABC,ACE,ADE,BCE,BD,CD}		b	exp(b)				
mean		-5.72	0.00				
risk	marriage	-0.14	0.87				
	cohabitation	0.14	1.15				
age	16-18	-1.15	0.32				
	19-21	0.27	1.31				
	22 or more	0.88	2.41				
birth cohort	1950-54	-0.04	0.96				
	1955-59	0.18	1.19				
	1960-64	-0.08	0.93				
	1965-69	-0.06	0.94				
occupational status	unemployed	0.33	1.39				
	at school	-0.73	0.48				
	at work	0.41	1.50				
education	low	0.43	1.54				
	medium	-0.16	0.86				
	high	-0.28	0.76				

		marriage		cohabitation			
		b	(exp)b	b	(exp)b		
age	16-18	-0.07	0.93	0.07	1.08		
	19-21	0.05	1.05	-0.05	0.95		
	22 or more	0.02	1.02	-0.02	0.98		
		marriage		cohabitation			
birth cohort	1950-54	0.46	1.59	-0.46	0.63		
	1955-59	0.12	1.12	-0.12	0.89		
	1960-64	-0.27	0.76	0.27	1.31		
	1965-69	-0.31	0.73	0.31	1.36		
		marriage		cohabitation			
occupational status	unemployed	0.17	1.18	-0.17	0.84		
	at school	-0.33	0.72	0.33	1.39		
	at work	0.16	1.18	-0.16	0.85		
		marriage		cohabitation			
education	low	0.38	1.46	-0.38	0.69		
	medium	-0.08	0.92	0.08	1.08		
	high	-0.30	0.74	0.30	1.35		

		age 16-18		19-21		22 or more	
						b	(exp)b
birth cohort	1950-54	-0.12	0.89	0.16	1.18	-0.05	0.95
	1955-59	0.13	1.14	0.11	1.12	-0.24	0.79
	1960-64	0.09	1.10	-0.01	0.99	-0.09	0.92
	1965-69	-0.10	0.90	-0.27	0.76	0.38	1.46
		age 16-18		19-21		22 or more	
occupational status	unemployed	0.39	1.48	0.02	1.02	-0.41	0.67
	at school	-0.32	0.72	-0.11	0.90	0.43	1.54
	at work	-0.07	0.93	0.09	1.10	-0.02	0.98
		age 16-18		19-21		22 or more	
education	low	0.32	1.37	-0.10	0.90	-0.22	0.80
	medium	-0.07	0.93	0.07	1.07	0.00	1.00
	high	-0.25	0.78	0.04	1.04	0.21	1.24

		b	(exp)b	b	(exp)b	b	(exp)b	b	(exp)b
		cohort							
occupational status	unemployed	-0.11	0.90	0.01	1.01	-0.04	0.96	0.14	1.15
	at school	0.25	1.28	0.01	1.01	-0.03	0.97	-0.23	0.80
	at work	-0.14	0.87	-0.02	0.98	0.08	1.08	0.08	1.09
		cohort							
education	low	-0.23	0.80	-0.12	0.88	0.17	1.19	0.18	1.20
	medium	0.05	1.05	0.03	1.03	0.13	1.14	-0.20	0.82
	high	0.18	1.20	0.10	1.10	-0.30	0.74	0.02	1.02
		occupational status							
education	low	-0.01	0.99	0.11	1.12	-0.10	0.90		
	medium	0.12	1.13	-0.22	0.80	0.10	1.10		
	high	-0.11	0.90	0.11	1.11	0.00	1.00		

risk*age*cohort		marriage		cohabitation	
	<19				
	1950-54	0.07	1.08	-0.07	0.93
	1955-59	0.03	1.03	-0.03	0.97
	1960-64	-0.04	0.96	0.04	1.04
	1965-69	-0.06	0.94	0.06	1.06
	<21				
	1950-54	0.14	1.15	-0.14	0.87
	1955-59	0.07	1.07	-0.07	0.94
	1960-64	0.00	1.00	-0.00	1.00
	1965-69	-0.21	0.81	0.21	1.24
	21 or more				
	1950-54	-0.21	0.81	0.21	1.24
	1955-59	-0.10	0.91	0.10	1.10
	1960-64	0.03	1.04	-0.03	0.97
	1965-69	0.27	1.32	-0.27	0.76

risk*cohort*education		marriage		cohabitation	
	1950-54				
	low	0.24	1.27	-0.24	0.79
	medium	0.04	1.04	-0.04	0.96
	high	-0.28	0.75	0.28	1.33
	1955-59				
	low	0.07	1.07	-0.07	0.94
	medium	0.03	1.03	-0.03	0.97
	high	-0.09	0.91	0.09	1.10
	1960-64				
	low	-0.04	0.96	0.04	1.04
	medium	0.00	1.00	-0.00	1.00
	high	0.04	1.04	-0.04	0.96
	1965-69				
	low	-0.27	0.76	0.27	1.31
	medium	-0.07	0.93	0.07	1.08
	high	0.33	1.39	-0.33	0.72

risk*occupational status*education		marriage		cohabitation	
	unemployed				
	low	0.24	1.27	-0.24	0.79
	medium	0.04	1.04	-0.04	0.96
	high	-0.28	0.75	0.28	1.33
	studying				
	low	0.07	1.07	-0.07	0.94
	medium	0.03	1.03	-0.03	0.97
	high	-0.09	0.91	0.09	1.10
	at work				
	low	-0.31	0.74	0.31	1.36
	medium	-0.07	0.93	0.07	1.07
	high	0.38	1.46	-0.38	0.69

Appendix chapter 5

age*cohort*education		b	(exp)b	b	(exp)b	b	(exp)b	b	(exp)b
	age 16-18 cohort								
	low	-0.08	0.92	-0.03	0.97	0.09	1.10	0.02	1.02
	medium	-0.04	0.96	-0.07	0.94	-0.04	0.96	0.15	1.16
	high	0.13	1.13	0.10	1.11	-0.05	0.95	-0.17	0.84
	age 19-21								
	low	-0.11	0.90	0.01	1.01	0.05	1.05	0.05	1.05
	medium	-0.08	0.92	-0.10	0.90	0.04	1.04	0.14	1.15
	high	0.19	1.21	0.09	1.10	-0.09	0.92	-0.20	0.82
	age 22+								
	low	0.19	1.21	0.03	1.03	-0.14	0.87	-0.08	0.93
	medium	0.12	1.13	0.17	1.18	-0.00	1.00	-0.29	0.75
	high	-0.31	0.73	-0.19	0.82	0.14	1.15	0.37	1.45

$L2 = 151$
$df = 138$

APPENDIX CHAPTER 6

Table 1 Results of conditional log likelihood ratio tests of a model of subsequent marriage, including past life course determinants, duration and birth cohort

	L2	df	ΔL2	Δdf
2. all first-order-effects	322	373		
2a. without duration	335	374	13	2*
2b. without birth cohort	335	376	13	3*
2c. without parental divorce	323	374	1	1
2d. without religion	336	374	14	1*
2e. without family size	322	374	1	1
2f. without age mother	324	374	2	1
2g. without home town	326	375	4	2
2h. with birth cohort*parental divorce	322	370	0	3
2i. with birth cohort*family size	318	370	4	3
2j. with birth cohort*age mother	321	370	1	3
2k. with birth cohort*home town	310	367	12	6
2l. with duration*parental divorce	322	372	0	1
2m. with duration*family size	322	372	0	1
2n. with duration*age mother	322	372	0	1
2p. with duration*home town	318	372	4	2

Table 2 Results of conditional log likelihood ratio tests of a model of subsequent marriage, including current life course determinants, duration and birth cohort

	L2	df	ΔL2	Δdf
3. all first-order-effects	407	635		
3a. without duration	429	636	22	1*
3b. without birth cohort	426	638	19	3*
3c. without occupational status	432	637	25	2*
3d. without pregnancy	630	637	223	2*
3e. without educational level	412	637	5	2
3f. without age at cohabitation	412	637	5	2
3g. with birth cohort*education	396	629	11	6
3h. with birth cohort*age at cohabitation	403	629	4	6
3i. with duration*education	406	629	1	6
3j. with duration*age at cohabitation	397	629	10	6

Table 3 Results of conditional log likelihood ratio tests of a model of subsequent marriage, including significant past and current life course determinants, duration and birth cohort

	L2	df	ΔL2	Δdf
4. all first-order-effects	134	134		
4a. without duration	171	135	37	1*
4b. without birth cohort	155	137	21	3*
4c. without occupational status	169	136	35	2*
4d. without fertility	365	136	231	2*
4e. without religion	145	135	11	1*
4f. with duration*birth cohort	119	131	15	3*

with all first-order-effects, second-order-effect duration*birth cohort and

4g. with duration*occupational status	115	129	4	2
4h. with duration*fertility	117	129	2	2
4i. with duration*religion	113	130	6	1
4j. with b. cohort*occupational status	114	125	5	6
4k. with birth cohort*fertility	109	125	10	6
4l. with birth cohort*religion	116	128	3	3

* significant (P<.01)

APPENDIX CHAPTER 7

Table 1 Parameter estimates of several models of union disruption

a. Model without controlling for months separated before divorce
b. Model including estimation for months of separation before divorce (assuming 6 months separation before divorce if date of separation was unknown)

		model a	model b
	L2	320	354
	p	0.99	0.99
	df	416	416
		-6.36	-6.36
duration	0 - 48	-0.17	-0.30
	49 -84	-0.07	-0.09
fertility	child at/before	0.30	0.35
	no child	0.33	0.32
	1 child	-0.05	-0.05
religion	none	0.11	0.10
age at union	16-18	0.51	0.51
	19-20	-0.16	-0.16
union type	cohabiting	1.06	1.09
	married directly	-0.67	-0.68
union cohort	< 1980	0.06	0.02
no religion, cohabiting		-0.05	-0.04
no religion, direct marriage		0.26	0.25
cohort < 1980, cohabiting		-0.29	-0.27
cohort < 1980, direct marriage		0.01	0.01

baseline categories omitted
baseline categories can be estimated by minus the sum of the other categories

Table 2 Results of conditional log likelihood ratio tests of a model of first union disruption, including temporal covariates and union status

			L2	df	ΔL2	Δdf
0	{ }		925.6	2592		
1	{A}	duration	876.4	2589	49	3*
2	{B}	birth cohort	825.1	2588	100	4*
3	{C}	age	827.1	2588	98	4*
4	{D}	age at union	837.2	2589	88	3*
5	{E}	calender year	921.5	2589	4	3
6	{F}	union status	443.3	2589	482	3*
7	{G}	union cohort	874.8	2590	51	2*

controlling for union status
8	{F}	443.3	2589		
9	{A,F}	440.3	2587	3	2
10	{B,F}	434.1	2586	9	3
11	{C,F}	424.0	2586	19	3*
12	{D,F}	359.0	2587	84	2*
13	{E,F}	439.8	2587	4	2
14	{G,F}	443.3	2588	0	1

second-order-effect with union status
15	{A,F,AF}	436.2	2583	4	4.0
16	{B,F,BF}	431.3	2580	3	6.0
17	{E,F,EF}	436.4	2583	3	4.0
18	{G,F,GF}	425.3	2586	18	2.0*

second-order-effect with duration
19	{AB,F}	426.9	2578		
20	{A,B,F}	429.5	2584	3	6
21	{AC,F}	407.4	2578		
22	{A,C,F}	412.1	2584	5	6
23	{AD,F}	353.6	2581		
24	{A,D,F}	357.4	2585	4	4
25	{AE,F}	424.8	2581		
26	{A,E,F}	436.9	2585	12	4
27	{AG,F}	440.0	2584		
28	{A,G,F}	440.2	2586	0	2

second-order-effect with birth cohort
29	{BC,F}	410.1	2574		
30	{B,C,F}	421.5	2583	11	9
31	{BD,F}	346.1	2578		
32	{B,D,F}	356.6	2584	11	6
33	{BE,F}	426.6	2578		
34	{B,E,F}	430.7	2584	4	6
35	{BG,F}	429.8	2582		
36	{B,G,F}	430.6	2585	1	3

second-order-effect with union cohort
37	{CG,F}	415.3	2582		
38	{C,G,F}	424.0	2585	9	3
39	{DG,F}	354.8	2584		
40	{D,G,F}	357.1	2586	2	2
41	{EG,F}	439.7	2584		
42	{E,G,F}	439.7	2586	0	2

* $P < 0.01$

Appendix chapter 7

	L2	df	ΔL2	Δdf
age or age at union				
43 {C,F}	424.0	2586		
44 {C,D,F}	356.6	2584	68	2*
45 {D,F}	359.0	2587		
46 {C,D,F}	356.6	2584	3	3
47 {D,F,G}	357.1	2586		
48 {D,F,G,FG}	339.2	2584	18	2*
49 {D,F}	359.0	2587		
50 {B,D,F}	356.6	2584	2	3
51 {A,E,D,F}	354.5	2583		
52 {AE,D,F}	346.4	2579	8	4
53 {C,G,D,F}	354.1	2583		
54 {CG,D,F}	347.7	2580	6	3
55 {E,C,F}	420.5	2584		
56 {E,C}	424.0	2586	4	2

* P< 0.01

Table 3 Results of conditional log likelihood ratio tests of a model of first union disruption, including past life course determinants, union status, union duration and birth cohort

			L2	df	ΔL2	Δdf
0	{ }		1089.4	1152		
1	{A}	duration of union	1040.2	1149	49	3*
2	{B}	birth cohort	989.0	1148	100	4*
3	{C}	parents divorced	1055.4	1150	34	2*
4	{D}	religion	992.4	1150	97	2*
5	{E}	parental family size	1084.6	1150	5	2
6	{F}	age differences with mother	1078.1	1150	11	2*
7	{G}	union status	607.1	1149	482	3*
8	{H}	size of municipality	1063.7	1150	26	2*
	{G}		607.1	1149		
9	{A,G}		604.1	1147	3	2
10	{B,G}		598.0	1146	9	3
11	{C,G}		594.8	1148	12	1*
12	{D,G}		590.1	1148	17	1*
13	{E,G}		607.0	1148	0	1
14	{F,G}		602.8	1148	4	1
15	{G,H}		599.1	1148	8	1*

second-order-effect of union status {G} and

16	{A,G,AG}	600.1	1143	4	4
17	{B,G,BG}	595.1	1140	3	6
18	{E,G,EG}	605.1	1146	2	2
19	{F,G,FG}	600.2	1146	3	2

second-order-effect with duration {A} and (controlling for union status {G})

20	{A,B,G}	593.3	1144		
21	{AB,G}	590.7	1138	3	6
22	{A,C,G}	591.9	1146		
23	{AC,G}	586.3	1144	6	2
24	{A,D,G}	587.6	1146		
25	{AD,G}	586.7	1144	1	2
26	{A,E,G}	604.0	1146		
27	{AE,G}	602.6	1144	1	2
28	{A,F,G}	599.9	1146		
29	{AF,G}	598.5	1144	1	2
30	{A,H,G}	596.4	1146		
31	{AH,G}	595.1	1144	1	2

second-order-effect with birth cohort of women {B} and (controlling for union status {G})

32	{B,C,G}	587.3	1145		
33	{BC,G}	581.7	1142	6	3
34	{B,D,G}	579.1	1145		
35	{BD,G}	575.7	1142	4	3
36	{B,E,G}	598.0	1145		
37	{BE,G}	596.3	1142	2	3
38	{B,F,G}	594.8	1145		
39	{BF,G}	593.7	1142	1	3
40	{B,H,G}	588.9	1145		
41	{BH,G}	583.0	1142	6	3

* $P < 0.01$

Table 4 Results of conditional log likelihood ratio tests of a model of first union disruption, including past life course determinants, duration, union status and union cohort

duration {A}, parents divorced {B}, religion {C}, union cohort {D}, parental family size {E}, age differences with mother {F}, union status {G} and home town {H}

	L2	df	ΔL2	Δdf
second-order-effect of union cohort {D} and (controlling for union status {G})				
1 {A,D,G}	413.5	570		
2 {AD,G}	413.3	568	0	2
3 {B,D,G}	404.3	571		
4 {BD,G}	400.0	570	4	1
5 {C,D,G}	399.4	571		
6 {CD,G}	399.4	570	0	1
7 {D,E,G}	416.5	571		
8 {DE,G}	415.2	570	1	1
9 {D,F,G}	412.3	571		
10 {DF,G}	409.2	570	3	1
11 {D,H,G}	408.5	571		
12 {DH,G}	408.5	570	0	1
13 {D,G}	416.6	572		
14 {DG}	398.6	570	18	2*

* p < 0.01

Table 5 Results of conditional log likelihood ratio tests of a model of first union disruption, including current life course determinants, duration, union status, union cohort, religion and home town

duration {A}, children {B}, religion {C}, age at union {D}, home town {E}, union status {F}, union cohort {G}

	L2	df	ΔL2	Δdf
1 {A,B,C,D,E,F,G}	552.6	851		
2 {A,B, ,D,E,F,G}	561.2	852	9	1*
3 {A,B,C,D, ,F,G}	556.4	852	4	1
4 {A,B,C,D,E,F,G,EF}	544.4	849	8	2
5 {A,B,C,D,E,F,G,AE}	551.9	849	1	2
6 {A,B,C,D,E,F,G,EG}	552.6	850	0	1

Table 6 Results of conditional log likelihood ratio tests of a model of first union disruption, including duration, union status, union cohort, religion and parental divorce and age at union

duration {A}, parental divorce {B}, children {C}, religion {D}, age at union {E}, union status {F} and union cohort {G}

	L2	df	ΔL2	Δdf
1 {A,B,C,D,E,F,G}	476.1	851		
2 {A, C,D,E,F,G}	481.2	852	5	1
3 {A,B,C,D,E,F,G, BG}	472.9	850	3	1
4 {A,B,C,D,E,F,G, AB}	469.8	849	6	2
5 {A,B,C,D,E,F,G, BF}	470.4	849	6	2

* P < 0.01

Table 7 Results of conditional log likelihood ratio tests of a model of first union disruption, including current life course determinants, union status, duration and birth and union cohort

			L2	df	ΔL2	Δdf
0	{ }		1153.4	2592		
1	{A}	duration	1104.1	2589	49	3*
2	{B}	birth cohort	1052.9	2588	100	4*
3	{C}	occupational status	1080.4	2589	73	3*
4	{D}	children	980.1	2588	173	4*
5	{E}	educational level	1136.0	2589	17	3*
6	{F}	union status	671.0	2589	482	3*
7	{G}	union cohort	1102.6	2590	51	2*

controlling for union status

6	{F}	671.0	2589		
8	{A,F}	668.1	2587	3	2
9	{B,F}	661.9	2586	9	3
10	{C,F}	671.0	2587	0	2
11	{D,F}	639.3	2586	32	3*
12	{E,F}	669.6	2587	1	2
13	{G,F}	671.0	2588	0	1

second-order-effect with union status

| 14 | {C,F,CF} | 662.5 | 2583 | 8 | 4 |
| 15 | {E,F,EF} | 664.8 | 2583 | 5 | 4 |

second-order-effect with duration

16	{A,B,F}	657.3	2584		
17	{AB,F}	654.7	2578	3	6
18	{A,C,F}	667.7	2585		
19	{AC,F}	654.0	2581	14	4*
20	{A,D,F}	625.4	2584		
21	{AD,F}	620.1	2578	5	6
22	{A,E,F}	666.7	2585		
23	{AE,F}	663.7	2581	3	4
24	{A,G,F}	667.9	2586		
25	{AG,F}	667.8	2584	0	2

second-order-effect with birth cohort

26	{BC,F}	661.8	2584		
27	{B,C,F}	645.8	2578	16	6*
28	{BD,F}	631.7	2583		
29	{B,D,F}	627.5	2574	4	9
30	{BE,F}	661.5	2584		
31	{B,E,F}	653.8	2578	8	6
32	{BG,F}	658.4	2585		
33	{B,G,F}	657.6	2582	1	3

second-order-effect with union cohort

34	{CG,F}	671.0	2586		
35	{C,G,F}	666.9	2584	4	2
36	{DG,F}	639.1	2585		
37	{D,G,F}	636.4	2582	3	3
38	{EG,F}	669.6	2586		
39	{E,G,F}	668.3	2584	1	2

controlling for the presence of children

41	{A,C,D,F}	624.0	2582		
42	{AC,D,F}	616.1	2578	8	4
43	{B,C,D,F}	630.5	2581		
44	{BC,D,F}	616.9	2575	14	6

* P<0.01

Appendix chapter 7

Table 8 Results of conditional log likelihood ratio tests of a model of first union disruption, including all significant past and current life course determinants, duration and union status: duration (A), children (B), religion (C), age at union (D), union status (E), union cohort (F)

		L2	df	ΔL2	Δdf
1	{A,B,C,D,E,F}	365.9	420		
2	{B,C,D,E,F}	379.1	422	13	2*
3	{A,C,D,E,F}	397.4	423	32	3*
4	{A,B,D,E,F}	376.3	421	10	1*
5	{A,B,C,E,F}	439.0	422	73	2*
6	{A,B,C,D,F}	615.0	422	249	2*
7	{A,B,C,D,E}	370.5	421	5	1
	second-order-effect with union status				
8	{AE}	359.6	416	6	4
9	{BE}	352.2	414	14	6
10	{CE}	347.9	418	18	2*
11	{DE}	352.4	416	13	4*
12	{EF}	346.7	418	19	2*
	second-order-effect with duration				
13	{AB}	360.1	414	6	6
14	{AC}	363.7	418	2	2
15	{AD}	362.2	416	4	4
16	{AF}	365.4	418	0	2
	second-order-effect with union cohort				
17	{BF}	362.7	417	3	3
18	{CF}	365.6	419	0	1
19	{DF}	362.8	418	3	2
	other second-order-effects				
20	{BC}	362.3	417	4	3
21	{BD}	356.1	414	10	6
22	{CD}	362.4	418	4	2
	{A,B,C,D,E,F,CE,DE,FE}	321.4	412		
	third-order-effects				
23	{ABE}	285.0	384	36	28
24	{ACE}	305.1	402	16	10
25	{ADE}	293.6	396	28	16
26	{AFE}	313.9	402	8	10
27	{BEF}	291.5	397	30	15
28	{CEF}	318.5	409	3	3
29	{DEF}	310.5	406	11	6
30	{BCE}	290.9	397	31	15
31	{BDE}	280.5	388	41	24
32	{CDE}	313.4	406	8	6
33	A,B,C,D,E,F,CE,DE	336.7	414		
34	{DE}	347.9	418	11	4
35	{CE}	352.4	416	16	2*
36	A,B,C,D,E,F,CE,EF	329.6	416		
37	{CE}	347.9	418	18	2*
38	{EF}	346.7	418	17	2*
39	A,B,C,D,E,F,DE,EF	336.9	414		
40	{EF}	352.4	416	16	2*
41	{DE}	346.7	418	10	4

Titles in PDOD publications series A (doctoral dissertations):

Mulder, C.H. (1993).
   Migration dynamics: A life course approach, Amsterdam, Thesis Publ.,
   ISBN nr. 90-5170-236-1